What Really Matters for Middle School Readers

From Research to Practice

D1529068

Richard L. Allington

University of Tennessee, Knoxville

PEARSON

Boston Columbus Indianapolis New York San Francisco Upper Saddle River
Amsterdam Cape Town Dubai London Madrid Milan Munich Paris Montréal Toronto
Delhi Mexico City São Paulo Sydney Hong Kong Seoul Singapore Taipei Tokyo

Vice President and Editor in Chief: Jeffery Johnston
Acquisitions Editor: Kathryn Boice
Editorial Assistant: Carolyn Schweitzer
Director of Marketing: Margaret Waples
Marketing Manager: Bridget Hadley
Production Project Manager: Annette Joseph
Operations Specialist: Linda Sager
Cover Designer: Karen Noferi
Cover Art: Digital Vision/Getty Images
Full-Service Project Management: Jouve North America
Composition: Jouve India

PEARSON

ISBN-10: 0-205-39319-5
ISBN-13: 978-0-205-39319-0

Contents

chapter 3

"It's the Words, Man": Limited Meaning Vocabulary and How to Improve It   49

chapter 4

Read More, Read Better: Addressing a Major Source of Reading Difficulties   75

chapter 5

Reading with Comprehension: Understanding "Understanding"   95

chapter 6

Literate Conversation: A Powerful Method for Fostering Understanding of Complex Texts   119

Preface

A long time ago I entered junior high school. I arrived from the one-room country school I had attended since I began school. I was a short, chubby kid getting off the bus at the huge, and old, former high school that was now the junior high school, housing 7th and 8th grade students from both the small town and the surrounding rural areas. I was a small kid for my age and the only member of my five-student sixth-grade class who had placed in the "academic track." So I went to school, for the first time, with strangers and with a teacher who was not Mr. DeGraw, who alone had taught me and all the other kids attending Pioneer Elementary School since second grade. I survived junior high school and later high school and college and then went back to teach elementary school in a neighboring small town (I'm talking about small towns with a total population of fewer than 1,000 folks). Today I am a professor but one who remembers teachers, classes and incidents from those junior high years. Not all these memories are pleasant but many are and every teacher, class, and incident shaped who I am today.

The early adolescent years (roughly ages 11 to 15) can be troubling years for a number of reasons. Some 11-year-olds are close to six feet tall while others are barely taller than four feet. Some have already entered puberty and many have not. Some have excellent reading and writing skills while others have developed few proficiencies in these areas that are central to school success. In many respects early adolescence is the last chance we have to shape these students into young scholars. So let's begin by reviewing just how we are doing.

As a nation, we seem unable to make up our minds about the best way to organize instruction for early adolescents. We have K-8 elementary schools, grades 7 and 8 junior high schools, grade 5, 6, 7, and 8 middle schools, and grades 7, 8, and 9 middle schools. There are other variations but these arrangements capture the organizational scheme for educating most early adolescents. Often, it seems to me, the organizational plan for early adolescents is driven more by enrollment factors than by any other criteria. For instance, in a neighboring community the junior high school (grades 7 and 8) was turned into a middle school (grades 5, 6, 7, and 8) primarily because estimates for adding room onto six elementary schools (for increasing numbers of grade 5 and 6 students) was more expensive than simply doubling the size of the junior high school and relabeling it as a middle school.

In some schools for early adolescents all students have multiple teachers every day and in others students in grades 5 and 6 remain in self-contained classrooms with but a single teacher to provide all aspects of the instruction. In many schools educating early adolescents, the students attend multiple classes taught by multiple teachers every day. I recently had a conversation with a middle school teacher seeking assistance with struggling readers in her classes. When she told me her school had an eight-period day and that each period was 37 minutes long I told her there was little I could offer her for advice.

This unfortunate teacher works in a school where early adolescents make 9 or 10 transitions every day. Where nine 37-minute periods (8 academic classes plus lunch) bounded by 5-minute transition periods create chaos day after day. In another middle school I visited students have two periods each day, basically a morning and afternoon period. Their classes meet every other day on an odd-and-even day schedule. Their curriculum includes English language arts, mathematics, science, and social studies. I am not sure what academic content is covered in the eight periods a day school but one can bet that it is covered less well than in the two-period/four content classes middle school.

I've visited schools for early adolescents that enrolled thousands of children and other schools where barely 100 students comprised grades 5, 6, 7, and 8. I'm not sure what the best size might be for a school educating early adolescents but I am reasonably sure that whenever we put 1,000 or more early adolescents in a single building little good will happen educationally. That "huge" junior high school I attended enrolled just over 200 seventh- and eighth grade students. Nonetheless, it felt big, way big, to me, a country boy from a one-room, 30-student school.

My point is that currently in North America we educate early adolescents in schools of varying sizes, provide curricula sliced up in thin and very thin slices, and expect early adolescents to adjust, adapt, and become productive in organizational schemes that often seem to have been developed by madmen and -women.

Early adolescence is a time of great physical and emotional development. It is a time when students are most likely to need abundant personal support as well as academic support. I hope this book assists you in providing each of these types of support to your students.

I would like to thank the reviewers of this edition: Theresa Barone, Derby Middle School (Lake Orion, Michigan) and Audra Jones, Memphis, Tennessee.

The **What Really Matters** *Series*

The past decade or so has seen a dramatic increase in the interest in what the research says about reading instruction. Much of this interest was stimulated by several recent federal education programs: the Reading Excellence Act of 1998, the No Child Left Behind Act of 2001, and the Individuals with Disabilities Education Act of 2004. The commonality shared by these federal laws is that each law restricts the use of federal funds to instructional services and support that have been found to be effective through "scientific research."

In this new series we bring you the best research-based instructional advice available. In addition, we have cut through the research jargon and at least some of the messiness and provide plain language guides for teaching students to read and write. Our focus is helping you use the research as you plan and deliver instruction to your students. Our goal is that your lessons be as effective as we know how, given the research that has been published.

Our aim is that all children become active and engaged readers and writers and that all develop the proficiencies needed to be strong independent readers and writers. Each of the short books in this series features what we know about one aspect of teaching and learning to read and write independently. Each of these pieces is important to this goal but none is more important than the ultimate goal: active, strong, independent readers and writers who read and write eagerly.

So, enjoy these books and teach your students all to read and write.

Chapter 1

Reading Development in Grades 5 through 9: Problems and Promise

This is a book on reading and the development of reading abilities of early adolescents. We will begin by examining how well early adolescents are performing as readers. The largest evaluation of reading proficiency available for our use is the U.S. National Assessment of Educational Progress (NAEP). The initial NAEP assessments were done in 1971, over 40 years ago, but these national assessments have continued to be administered since that time.

Originally, the NAEP assessment was conducted every 4 years though more recently they have been given every other year. The initial NAEP testing simply reported the national average reading levels of children at ages 9, 13, and 17. More recently they have reported on performances in specified grade levels (grades 4, 8, and 12) that are generally associated with those age levels. The numbers of children assessed have grown larger primarily due to the decision over a decade ago to produce results on a state-by-state basis.

The NAEP reading assessment framework focuses attention on students' abilities to understand texts they have read silently and independently. Below are the three broad areas of literacy that eighth-grade students are assessed on.

- 30 percent of NAEP items ask students to *critique* and *evaluate*.

  Readers are to consider all or part of the text from a critical perspective and to make judgments about the way meaning is conveyed.

- 50 percent of NAEP items ask students to *integrate* and *interpret*.

  Readers are required to make connections across large portions of text or to explain what they think about the text as a whole.

- 20 percent of NAEP items ask students to simply *locate* or *recall* information from texts read.

  Students are asked to focus on specific information contained in relatively small amounts of text and to recognize what they have read.

The NAEP assessments also require some "constructed responses" where students must write their responses to the questions posed. The remainder of the NAEP test uses multiple-choice test items to assess understanding. I mention this because there are so few state tests of reading that have required constructed responses, and so these state tests fail to present a demanding assessment of reading proficiency. Also, most of the NAEP items are complete articles or passages on a topic that is different from that found in state tests, which more often present information in a single paragraph prior to presenting multiple-choice questions. The new assessments that accompany the Common Core State Standards (CCSS) will also require constructed responses, although the responses will be graded using recently developed computer software rather than human evaluators.

The assessments that accompany many of the textbooks used in schools, as well as the assessments created by teachers for use to estimate understanding (or learning) after reading, are far more likely to be focused on *locate* and *recall* tasks, with most focused on recall of information read (Applebee, 2013). However, note that such NAEP items as these comprise only one of every five questions. In other words, too much of what has been tested in schools rarely gets at the *critique, evaluate, integrate,* and *interpret* aspects of the NAEP. The new CCSS also emphasizes what the NAEP emphasizes—higher-order thinking about what has been read. If students are to perform well on the NAEP or on the new CCSS assessments, they will have to have far greater experience with the critique, evaluate, integrate, and interpret tasks than students currently do.

Teaching students to do well at tasks that require them to critique, evaluate, integrate, and interpret what they have been reading will be different from classroom instruction, assignments, and assessments focused on recalling information that has been read. I will argue that CCSS will require many teachers to acquire new ways of teaching. Given American students' lackluster performance on the NAEP (and on the international assessments), such a change should be a good thing.

What the NAEP Tells Us

If we examine recent NAEP testing for reading, we find that many eighth-grade students do not read well enough to accomplish grade-level work. Below I have provided the results of the most recent NAEP reading assessment for eighth-graders with the numbers on the left representing the percentage (rounded) of eighth-graders at each of the four NAEP reading levels (NAEP, 2009).

2	Advanced	Capable of reading texts with a difficulty level above the students current grade placement.
28	Proficient	Capable of reading at grade level and performing well on each of the NAEP tasks.
43	Basic	May be capable of reading grade-level texts but with only the ability to perform the lowest level cognitive tasks (recall). Usually teacher support is needed to accomplish this.
26	Below Basic	Unable to successfully perform any NAEP tasks with grade-level texts.

In this recent NAEP reading assessment more than two-thirds of American eighth-grade students read below the proficient level, the level needed to perform most grade-level tasks. Additionally, a quarter of all eighth-graders read at levels below the sixth-grade level and 10 percent read at levels below the average reading level of fourth-graders! Far too many students enter and leave middle schools with poorly developed reading proficiencies.

If you are lucky you may find a teaching position in Connecticut, Massachusetts, New Jersey, or Vermont where over 40 percent of all eighth-grade students score at or above the proficient level. But teaching eighth grade well will be harder in Louisiana or Mississippi, where fewer than 20 percent of students reach the proficient level and where many more students are performing at the below-basic level.

There are also differences in reading proficiency by race/ethnic group and by family socioeconomic status. In general, students are more likely to have developed strong reading proficiencies if they are white, female, and come from middle-class families. That is what the NAEP data indicate. Children from low-income families, children of ethnic minority backgrounds, and males all are more likely to exhibit difficulties with reading. The achievement gap for boys versus girls was 10 points. The achievement gap between children from low-income and higher-income families was 26 points. There was an achievement gap between white students and black students of 27 points and between white and Hispanic students of 24 points. But while these gaps are substantial, there was also a 23-point gap between the average reading levels of eighth-graders in Massachusetts and Mississippi.

NAEP reading scores for eighth-graders have remained unchanged since 1992. In other words, in the past two decades we saw no improvement in the average reading levels of eighth-grade students even though many of today's eighth-graders have spent their entire school careers under NCLB mandates and accountability schemes. This lack of growth occurred even though fourth-grade NAEP performances have been improving since 1992. However, the average reading levels of American eighth-graders is a tricky thing to compute and even trickier to interpret.

Since 1992 the proportion of Hispanic students in American schools has more than doubled. Table 1.1 shows the racial/ethnic composition of NAEP test takers in 1992 and 2009. The percentage of white test takers has dropped by 14 percent over this nearly two-decade time period from 1992 to 2009, while the

TABLE 1.1 *NAEP Student Demographics in 1992 and 2009*

	1992	2009
White	72	58
Black	16	15
Hispanic	8	20
Asian	3	5
Native American	1	1

Percentage of participants by race/ethnic group in the 1992 and 2009 NAEP assessments at grade 8.

proportion of Hispanic students has more than doubled. Only Texas, California, Arizona, and Florida had substantial populations of Hispanic students 20 years ago while today over 20 states do. When the NAEP began 40 years ago, so few schools enrolled Hispanic learners that the NAEP did not even break out scores for that subgroup. Today Hispanic students account for one of every five students in American schools.

The changing nature of the racial/ethnic composition of school-aged children means that today many more teachers are faced with children from low-income families as well as children who are English language learners. Both of these groups of students have exhibited substantially lower reading levels, historically, than the reading levels attained by children from more affluent families and by white children. I will suggest that maintaining the same average reading proficiency level that American children exhibited in 1992 may represent progress in teaching children to read. While the reading gaps of poor and black children and of English language learners when compared to non-poor, English speaking, and white students remain far too large, the substantial changes in the pool of students being assessed by NAEP might have had the effect of lowering average reading levels had reading instruction not been improving. This addition of many lower scoring students in the NAEP testing pool and the effect that adding these low-scoring students to the sample reflects "Simpson's Paradox" (Bracey, 2003). In other words, while the scores of every group rise, the average score of the sample does not improve because the addition of many low-scoring students hides the improvement.

Reading Proficiency before Grade 8

Over the past twenty years most federal efforts to improve reading proficiency have targeted students in the primary grades, K–3. The reason for this focus is provided by a recent report from the Annie Casey Foundation entitled "Double Jeopardy" (Hernandez, 2011). That report presents a large-scale analysis of the effects of failing to read on grade level by the end of third grade. Students who were struggling with reading in third grade were four times as likely to drop out of school as were their more successful classmates. And if the student who was struggling happened to come from a low-income family, those students were 13 times as likely to drop out as were poor children reading at grade level in third grade.

In fact, being poor substantially contributes to dropping out of school. Roughly one-third of all students from low-income families will not complete high school compared to 6 percent of the non-poor children. Difficulty with early reading acquisition is also a substantial contributor to dropping out. The bottom one-third of readers in third grade account for two-thirds of all dropouts. It is the combination of low reading achievement and family poverty that places these children in "double jeopardy."

The "Double Jeopardy" report tells us that early intervention seems essential if all children are to become literate and productive students and citizens. It also suggests that middle schools have not been successful in turning struggling early adolescent readers into achieving and grade-level readers. When we look at the NAEP data on reading achievement it is clear that the size of the struggling reader population remains largely the same from fourth grade through twelfth grade. So the pertinent question might be: What usually happens when struggling readers arrive at the middle school level?

Reading Instruction for Early Adolescents

Truth be told, we actually know very little about the reading instruction provided to early adolescents. Much of what we do know is focused on struggling early-adolescent readers and not on the typically developing readers. Nonetheless, a brief review of what we do know will be useful as an introduction to this book.

One change in the education of early adolescents that has occurred during my teaching career is the elimination of a separate class devoted to teaching children to read. When I arrived as a beginning teacher, the core reading programs then available were produced as K- through eighth-grade programs. In the junior high I attended we had both a reading class and an English class. So every day I had a 55-minute period devoted to improving my reading proficiency. I had seven classes each day, a day that was 7.5 hours long.

Today, many middle school students attend no reading class. In too many middle schools the academic school day is closer to 5 hours than 8 hours in length. American schools typically fit one of three patterns when it comes to the length of the school day. There are 6-, 6.5-, and 7-hour school days. Unfortunately, it is the urban schools that have the shortest school days, on average, and the suburban schools that have the longest school days. Poor students are more likely to have the shortest school day and middle class students to have the longest school day. Additionally, over 2 hours of each school day is devoted to non-academic time (homeroom, announcements, attendance, meals, lining up, bathroom, transition, cleaning up, getting ready to go home) regardless of the length of the school day (Roth, Brooks-Dunn, Linver & Hofferth, 2002). This typically leaves teachers with between 4 and 5 hours each day to provide instruction. Teachers who work in schools with a 7-hour school day have the equivalent of two additional months of class time each year compared to teachers who work in schools with a 6-hour school day. The gap is even larger for those schools with days shorter than 6 hours.

Perhaps reading class was eliminated from the curriculum because there was too much other content that was deemed to be more critical (e.g., foreign languages, technology, art). Perhaps reading classes were lost as the school day shortened from a day close to 8 hours long to a school day that is more often 6 hours long. Perhaps reading classes were lost because it became clear, as Herber demonstrated in the 1970s, that print content is organized in ways that represent the conceptual hierarchy of the discipline. He noted that the organization of a text is the form of the ideas presented in that text. Because of this, the reading strategies/practices students experience need to provide support, or scaffolding, for engaging those ideas—support and scaffolding from all of their teachers in every content area. Perhaps an additional reading class wouldn't be necessary if middle school teachers were required to teach the disciplinary reading strategies needed to read content area textbooks successfully. However, there is little evidence to suggest that science, social studies, or foreign language teachers are currently mandated, or prepared, to provide beneficial reading lessons.

Whatever the reason, today's core reading programs are more likely to be K through fourth-grade programs than K through eighth-grade programs. Few middle schools have reading classes in which every student is enrolled. Some provide such a reading class to fifth- and sixth-grade students but then drop that class for the seventh and eighth grades. In most middle schools every content teacher does not typically consider herself or himself a reading teacher since they all teach specific subjects (such as science, history, or English). But Herber's original idea—that the best person to teach students to read science texts will be the science teacher (and so too for other content areas)—has never been actualized. And as far as the length of the school day, how can developing the reading proficiencies of early adolescents not be a subject of critical importance? In my "ivory tower" mind, we have made little progress in improving the reading proficiencies of early adolescents simply because we have rarely tried to improve their reading proficiencies.

If reading instruction in the United States largely ends at the fourth or fifth grade, is it any wonder so many of our middle and high school students struggle with the reading demands they face? As Biancarosa and Snow (2006) point out, at least 8 million students between grades 4 and 12 read below grade level and 70 percent of all readers in those grades would benefit from remediation to enhance their reading proficiency.

The general lack of reading instruction beyond grade 5 may account for the fact that only half of the high school juniors who took the American College Testing (ACT) tests read well enough to have a 75 percent chance at earning a grade of C in college history, biology, or literature classes (ACT, 2006). And not everyone takes the ACT exams, just those students intending to go to college. This group is comprised of the more academically motivated 17-year-olds, and of this group, fewer than half will ever complete college because they do not read with sufficient proficiency to do college level reading.

One might think that with statistics such as these there would be a public outcry and federal legislation mandating access to reading instruction above grade 5. However, while there has been some recent attention to developing the reading proficiencies of middle and high school students, I see no clear consensus either politically or professionally that will cause the situation to change much in the near future.

We know providing reading instruction in middle schools and high schools improves students' reading proficiencies. Whether the class offered more self-selected reading (Showers, Joyce, Scanlon & Schnaubelt, 1998), technology-assisted reading (James-Burdumy, Deke, Lugo-Gil, Carey, Hershey, Gersten, et al., 2010), or traditional reading instruction (Biancrosa & Snow, 2006), one can observe that this instruction fostered reading growth. Typically, in these studies only a single period each day was set aside for reading instruction and the resulting growth averaged roughly 1 year's growth per year.

Of course, struggling readers need to advance their reading skills to grow more than 1 year per year if they are ever to bring their reading levels up to grade level. Imagine the difficulties faced across the school day by a sixth-grade boy who reads at a third-grade level. This student will be unable to read any of the grade-level texts he is assigned. Even if this student is lucky enough to attend a middle school that provides remedial reading instruction, he will still have a stack of textbooks he cannot read and a stack of assignments he cannot complete. That is primarily because in too many middle schools no one has paid much attention to the problem grade-level curriculum materials created for struggling readers (Allington, 2002).

It is just this concern that bothers me about the recent CCSS framework. The emphasis on increasing the difficulty, or complexity, of the texts students read seems shortsighted since so many students currently fail to meet the grade-level standards in place at the moment. I can find hope in the CCSS documents that state teachers will be left to decide how to best teach students, but some days this seems like a faint hope if publishers simply increase the difficulty of texts used with early adolescents.

Problem of One-Size-Fits-All Curriculum Plans

Chall (1983) noted that the demands of reading increase dramatically for students in the fourth grade and beyond as their schooling begins to rely more on textbooks. The vocabulary they encounter is less conversational and less familiar, with more specialized, technical terms (e.g., delta, plateau, basin) and abstract ideas (e.g., democracy, freedom, civilization). The syntax of texts becomes more complex and demanding. The reasoning about information in texts also shifts, with a greater emphasis on inferential thinking and prior knowledge. (For example: What stance is the author taking on industrial polluters? Is there another stance that others might take?)

Many students who have been making satisfactory progress in the primary grades now begin to struggle with reading, especially content-area reading. Many never seem to recover. The other children who struggled with learning to read in the primary grades now experience real and sustained failures when it comes to reading the assigned texts. These two groups of students that experience failures in the middle grades have typically been labeled early- and later-developing struggling readers. It doesn't actually matter much which group these struggling readers are in because students in both groups need effective reading instruction and differentiated content area materials and lessons.

Schools have typically exacerbated the problem such students face every day by relying on a single-source curriculum design—purchasing multiple copies of the same science, English, and social studies textbooks for every student. This "one-size-fits-all" approach works well if we want to sort students into academic tracks, but it fails miserably if our goal is high academic achievement for all students. Even worse, research shows that many classrooms use textbooks written 2 or more years above the average grade level of their students (Chall & Conard, 1991; Budiansky, 2001). These students will struggle to keep pace with grade-level reading development.

Even students who read at grade level may have trouble learning from their textbooks. Historically, a 95–97 percent oral reading accuracy level has been considered an appropriate level of difficulty for instructional texts (Harris & Sipay, 1990). But texts of this level of difficulty are simply too hard for independent assigned content-area reading. A student reading a book at this "instructional reading level" will misread or skip as many as 5 words of every 100. In a grade-level high school science or social studies text, then, students will misread 10 to 25 words on every page! They won't misread *if, runs, locate,* or even *misrepresent,* but rather unfamiliar technical vocabulary specific to the content area, such as *metamorphosis, estuary, disenfranchised,* and *unicameral.*

Because of the way textbooks are often used—what I have called "assign and assess" usage—we might profitably consider purchasing content textbooks written at students' independent level of reading proficiency (Budiansky, 2001), where students misread just 1 or 2 words in every 100. In other words, if schools use textbooks as the key curriculum content provider, then students need textbooks that they can read accurately, fluently, and with high levels of understanding.

Unfortunately, the idea of harder textbooks has captured the attention of educators and policymakers interested in raising academic achievement, as is evident from a review of the CCSS. But harder books won't foster the growth of content learning. Think about your own attempts to acquire new content knowledge. Imagine you want to learn about building a website. Do you reject many of the books you might use because they are too easy? People usually prefer to work with the vocabulary they know. Otherwise, they become discouraged and may give up.

Adults won't read hard texts voluntarily—not because they lack character, but because they have had too many frustrating experiences trying to learn from texts that were simply too difficult, had too many unfamiliar words, and had complicated sentences that seemed purposely tangled in an attempt to frustrate. (Consider government tax manuals, any software manual, or even the directions for programming your DVD.) Since adults use the easiest texts they can find when they want to learn about a new topic, why do they think that hard books are good for children and adolescents?

Assuming that we don't want to continue the tradition of using difficult textbooks and allowing large numbers of students to fail content courses, we have two possible solutions. We could search out texts that cover the topics at lower levels of reading difficulty (Beck, McKeown, & Gromoll, 1989), or we can provide more instructional support to help students in grades 4 through 9 develop greater reading proficiency. Observations of exemplary teachers suggest that these teachers use both approaches to produce substantial reading, writing, and thinking growth in their students (Allington, 2002).

How Exemplary Teachers Avoid the Textbook Problem

A number of years ago I served as a member of a research team working out of a federal research center, where we carried out a large-scale research effort to understand how some of our nation's best teachers teach. The research team studied teachers across the United States who had reputations for excellence and who produced superior learning levels in their students as indicated by a variety of measures of student achievement, including standardized test scores. These excellent teachers implemented classroom instruction that combined multiple-level content texts and additional instructional support for struggling readers (Allington, 2002; Allington & Johnston, 2002; Langer, 2001; Nystrand, 1997; Pressley, Yokoi, Rankin, Wharton-McDonald, & Mistretta, 1997).

The exemplary teachers we studied were not typically familiar with the research that supported the sort of teaching that they offered. Research with early adolescents suggests that students will be more successful at new tasks when the tasks they face are closely targeted to their academic skills, developmental stage, and the resources they bring to that task and when families and schools structure tasks in ways that provide appropriate levels of challenge and support (Roderick & Camburn, 1999). But although though none of the exemplary teachers studied were aware of the study, they provided instruction that fit Roderick and Camburn's prescription perfectly.

First and most conspicuously, exemplary teachers created a multi-sourced and multi-leveled curriculum that did not rely on traditional content-area textbooks. They didn't discard such textbooks but saw them as just one component of their total set of materials to be used in social studies, science, and English classes.

In a course on U.S history, for instance, the textbook provided a general organizing framework, but students acquired much of their historical content from trade books of multiple genres. In addition, original source materials, web-based information, and local historians (professional and amateur) all supported students' study of American history.

Second, the exemplary teachers offered students what we labeled "managed choice" as they learned content and demonstrated what they had learned. In a global studies unit, all students didn't study and color the identical map of Europe. Instead, students selected regions or nations to study on the basis of their family history or personal interest. Each student or cluster of students was responsible for learning and then teaching their peers important content about their region.

When they studied insects, each student had to capture an insect and develop field journal data on its habitat and habits. Teachers had each student draw and label diagrams of his or her own insect rather than having all students label the same ditto of an insect. The students chose from several methods of presenting their insect to peers: a two-minute "Be-the-Bug Activity" ("Hi, I'm a dragonfly. Let me tell you a bit about me and where I live . . ."); a HyperStudio presentation; or a written report. Giving students several options helped match assignments to students' abilities and learning styles, and enhanced their motivation (Allington & Johnston, 2002).

The exemplary teachers offered instruction tailored to each student's individual needs. Their classes experienced more personalized teaching and discussion and spent less time on whole-group lecture and recitation activities. Other researchers studying effective teaching at both elementary and secondary levels have reported similar findings (Langer, 2001; Nystrand, 1997; Taylor, Pearson, Clark, & Walpole, 2000).

These teachers provided students with models and demonstrations of the strategies that effective learners use when confronted with unfamiliar words or with difficult text. They demonstrated these strategies in the context of the text that the student was reading or composing. In other words, none of the exemplary teachers used scripted one-size-fits-all instructional materials. These teachers taught students, not programs. They worried less about student performance on state-mandated tests and more about engaging students with reading and writing in the content areas.

While they worried less about state tests, they also produced students with superior achievement; these students had greater achievement gains during the school year when compared to students from typical teacher classrooms in the same building. In other words, teaching well produced higher levels of academic growth. While there is no surprise in that, the surprise was how few middle school and high school teachers actually taught effectively. In fact, as our research team moved from observing exemplary first-grade teachers to exemplary fourth-grade teachers and then to observing exemplary eighth- and tenth-grade teachers, locating effective teachers became more difficult with each increase in grade level. While we could find an elementary school where half of the first-grade teachers were exemplary teachers, at no other grade level did this occur. By eighth grade, we were too often looking for that single teacher in any content area who offered exemplary instruction. Perhaps this explains why while fourth-grade reading achievement has improved over the past 40 years, no such improvement has occurred in eighth- or twelfth-grade students!

Improving learning in content areas of the intermediate grades will require a substantial rethinking of what curriculum and instruction should look like. The exemplary teachers in our studies used practices that fostered improvements in student learning across the curriculum. However, for now, most teachers who want to teach effectively must teach against the organizational grain. Too often, teachers must reject the state and district curriculum frameworks and create their own curriculum packages, often spending their own funds to do so.

Good teaching should not be so difficult. But until more states and school districts dramatically modify their existing one-size-fits-all instructional resources and curriculum frameworks, many students won't receive the support they need to succeed in content-area learning. Think of the sixth-grader reading at the third-grade level.

What Instruction Must Look Like
for Struggling Readers

The current situation in many schools is that struggling readers participate in 30 to 50 minutes of supplemental reading instruction and then spend the remaining 5 hours a day sitting in classrooms with texts they cannot read, cannot learn to read from, and cannot learn science or social studies from (Allington, 2002). If we enter any school and select any struggling reader (remedial reader, a pupil with a learning disability, an English language learner) to observe in a general education classroom, we typically find that student has a desk (or a backpack or a locker) filled with books he or she cannot read. In other words, most struggling readers find themselves spending most of the school day in learning environments that no theory or empirical evidence suggests are likely to lead to any substantial learning.

If struggling readers are provided with appropriate instruction only 10 to 20 percent of the school day, one doesn't need to hire a consultant to determine why these struggling readers fail to exhibit the accelerated reading growth that is necessary for them to catch up with their better-reading peers (Allington, 2013). One doesn't need to hire a consultant to determine why certain students in these subgroups fail to make adequate yearly progress if a school's intervention design results in these students sitting for most of the school day in classrooms with books on their desks that they cannot read.

Worse, in too many schools even the supplemental reading instruction is designed to use classroom curriculum texts—that science book or literature anthology or trade book—that the struggling reader cannot read. The intervention design expects the reading specialists and special education teachers to use the classroom texts in the supplemental intervention lessons (O'Connor, Bell, Harty, Larkin, Sackor & Zigmond, 2002). In other words, the design calls for struggling readers to take their classroom textbooks with them when they travel to the special education resource or remedial reading room, or it expects that the specialist teachers will use these textbooks when working with struggling readers in the general education classroom.

It doesn't seem to matter that those texts are inevitably too difficult. Effective lesson design always begins with selecting texts that are of an appropriate level of difficulty given the skills and development of the learner. This design flaw prevails even though we have compelling research evidence demonstrating that using classroom texts—texts that are too difficult—in interventions produces little or no benefit. In the most recent study (O'Connor et al., 2002) we see yet another demonstration that using grade-level classroom texts with readers who are truly struggling simply doesn't work. On the other hand, O'Connor and her colleagues demonstrated that using appropriately difficult texts—books at the students' reading level—produced substantive reading growth. These findings should not be surprising; but what should be surprising is finding so many middle and high schools that still provide struggling readers with texts that are too difficult, day after day, subject after subject.

We must, as a first and most minimal step, ensure that supplementary interventions for struggling readers are designed in a manner consistent with the scientific evidence. That means—again at minimum—we would not be expecting special education or remedial reading teachers to use the too hard general education texts that many struggling readers are provided. Instead, teachers will provide struggling readers with texts that are appropriately difficult given their level of reading development. Intervention lessons will incorporate these appropriate texts into the core intervention design.

Whenever possible we would select texts that also link to the grade-level curriculum goals and standards (Gelzheiser, 2005). If the social studies focus in the general education classroom is on ancient cultures, we can work to select texts on those topics that are written at a level appropriate for the struggling readers from that classroom. If the language arts curriculum includes the study of biography as a genre, we locate biographies of appropriate difficulty for use with those struggling readers. In many respects this should be largely the responsibility of the general education staff but in too many school districts there seems scant recognition of any responsibility for supplying appropriate texts for struggling readers. Thus, it may fall to specialist teachers to locate such texts, hopefully in collaboration with the general education teachers who teach the struggling readers.

Reading Intervention Programs Are a Necessary But Insufficient Response

Thinking that supplemental reading interventions alone are the solution to the problems exhibited by struggling readers must be reconsidered. It isn't that such interventions are unnecessary but that they are simply insufficient. Struggling readers need books they can read—accurately, fluently, and with strong comprehension—in their hands *all day long* in order to exhibit maximum educational growth.

If accelerating academic development of struggling readers is the goal of districts, they cannot continue to rely on one-size-fits-all curriculum plans with a daily supplemental intervention lasting for a single period. Districts cannot simply purchase grade-level sets of materials—literature anthologies, science books, social studies books—and hope to achieve the goal of accelerating academic development of students who struggle with schooling. There is no scientific evidence that providing all students with this single instructional material results in anything other than many students being left behind.

Likewise, districts should not develop a single intervention design for struggling readers, especially if it is one that relies heavily on a single commercial product. There is no reason to expect that any single intervention focus will be appropriate for all students who struggle with reading. While some older struggling readers have underdeveloped decoding proficiencies, for instance, a greater number can decode accurately but understand little of what they read (Buly & Valencia, 2002; Dennis, 2013; Hock, Brasseur, Deshler, Catts, Marques, Mark & Wu, 2009; Leach, Scarborough & Rescorda, 2003; Pinnell, Pikulski, Wixson, Campbell, Gough, & Beatty, 1995). Some comprehend narrative texts far more easily than informational texts, while some exhibit dramatic limits in the number of word meanings they know. Some seem to be able to locate literal information in a text but cannot summarize the same text or synthesize it with other texts previously read. Struggling early-adolescent readers vary on many dimensions, and those schools that simply view intervention as requiring all struggling readers to spend 50 minutes each day working with a single product or material will see that many students are left behind.

This is likely the reason that only a very small handful of commercial reading intervention programs have any evidence they improve reading achievement. However, three commercial reading interventions designed for use with early adolescents were found to have a moderately positive effect on reading achievement (ES = 0.21 to 0.29). These three programs—Reading Edge, Read 180, and Josten's—have demonstrated modest levels of success across several well-designed studies. At the same time, commercial reading programs with no reliable research supporting their use (e.g., Language!, Wilson, Reading System, Read Naturally) are currently used in far too many schools with little positive effect (Slavin, Cheung, Groff, & Lake, 2008).

The situation is even worse for technology-based programs used to foster reading growth. As Cheung and Slavin (2012) conclude, "The types of supplementary computer-assisted instruction programs that have dominated the classroom use of education technology in the past few decades are not producing educationally meaningful effects in reading for K-12 students." The outcomes of the meta-analysis by Cheung and Slavin reflect the findings of a large-scale federal study of 10 popular software programs used to teach both reading and math. Basically, classrooms using any of the technology-based curricula generated no greater achievement in either reading or math than classrooms without these programs (Trotter, 2007).

Many school districts spend their often-limited money on implementing-or trying to implement-commercial programs that have not demonstrated that they improve either teaching or learning. The desire for something new has attracted many public dollars for tech-based programs whose results have not lived up to their promises. What now seems clear is that more effective teachers who are expert in teaching students are not only the best hope for improving academic achievement, but they remain the only solution for improving achievement that research supports.

Multi-Level Curriculum as the Base of an All-Day-Long Intervention Plan

I know of no evidence to suggest that effective teaching does not always involve selecting and using curriculum materials appropriate to the academic development of the student. We must work to increase the likelihood that struggling readers will have texts of appropriate difficulty in their hands all day long. Our nation's most effective teachers have routinely created "multi-sourced, multi-level" curriculum plans (Allington & Johnston, 2002; Keene, 2002; Langer, 2001) that provided struggling readers in those classrooms with books they could successfully read. That was one of the reasons that struggling readers thrived in their classrooms. I worry that in too many districts struggling readers will continue to struggle because intervention has not been planned as an all-day-long affair. I worry that too many struggling readers spend their days in classrooms using one-size-fits-all curriculum plans.

All-day-long intervention designs begin by focusing on the match between the student and curriculum material throughout the entire school day. The traditional intervention design often allowed the district to adopt a single eighth-grade social studies textbook—a book almost always too difficult for struggling readers to learn social studies from (Chall & Conard, 1991). And with the adoption of a single text, we almost always see whole-class instruction, which is the least effective method of teaching. However, when districts begin to consider an all-day-long intervention design, we see an emphasis on the adoption of multi-level texts as the basic curriculum. Then we more often see small-group instruction becoming more common on a daily basis. When districts emphasize intervention all day long we see an increase in side-by-side teaching as teachers spend more time instructing and monitoring individual students. Using multi-level texts in a multi-sourced curriculum plan literally requires a move away from whole-class lesson designs.

While most teacher education students learn the basics of planning and organizing multi-level instruction during their teacher preparation, most then go to work in schools where effective teaching is not the norm. In too many of these schools, effective instruction is viewed as the "ivory tower" approach, which means, I suppose, an approach to teaching that is largely unlike the way most teachers employed in a particular school actually teach. Beginning teachers are subtly and not so subtly indoctrinated into a career of teaching that is far less effective than they are capable of (Valencia, Place, Martin, & Grossman, 2006). They simply accept the one-size-fits-all approach as "the way we do things here" and no longer plan differentiated lessons, even though they know how to do so. They no longer press for a budget to purchase multi-level materials so they can provide multi-level lessons. In short, they become typical, rather than effective, teachers.

How teachers actually teach is the most important factor in predicting student learning. The more effective classrooms have a distribution of whole-class, small-group, and side-by-side instruction (Langer, 2001; Pressley, 2006; Taylor et al., 2000). The more effective schools simply have more classrooms where whole-class lessons do not dominate. The proportion of the school day allotted to whole-class instruction is a predictor of a school's academic achievement. The more whole-class teaching that is offered, the lower the academic achievement in that school. Unfortunately though, in most early-adolescent classrooms it is far more likely that you will observe what research has demonstrated to be ineffective practice rather than effective teaching. Lack of student learning in these classrooms has more to do with instruction than with the students themselves, their parents, or the community they come from, although they are often blamed for it.

Looking at Your School's Instructional Responses to Struggling Readers

We know a lot about effective instruction for struggling readers. To see how well some of the most basic evidence-based principles have been implemented in your school, I've developed two simple data-gathering tools. The first provides data on whether struggling readers in your school have books in their hands that they are able to read: books that allow struggling readers to learn science and social studies content and that also foster reading growth. The data you can gather using this tool will provide insight on how well your school is responding to the needs of struggling readers.

The second tool provides a snapshot of how lessons are organized in your school. Basically, this tool allows you to examine the distribution of whole-class, small-group, and side-by-side lessons in general education classrooms. The organization of instruction is another important factor in how responsive the general education classroom lessons are to the needs of struggling readers.

These tools are described below.

Reader–Text Match Tool

Begin by gathering the materials listed in the Reader/Text Matching box. Now create a list of all of the struggling readers that attend the school. This list would include those pupils with disabilities, English language learners who exhibit reading difficulties, and any student enrolled in a remedial reading program. Once you have created the list of struggling readers, select a 10 percent random sample from the struggling readers attending your school. The easiest method is simply to print out a list of the struggling readers and then select every tenth student on that list.

Table 2.1 provides an example from a fictional middle school in one small town with approximately 50 struggling sixth-grade readers. I developed the data around a fictional school I've labeled Monroe Middle School. Although fictional, it is a portrait of reality, illustrating the problems we've observed in schools where we have completed the data collection. I made the tally worksheet you see in Table 1.2. This is where the ruler comes in. I simply created five columns of roughly equal width for recording data for each student using the ruler as my

TABLE 1.2 *Text Difficulty for Five Struggling Sixth-Grade Readers at Monroe Middle School*

Student	WCPM	Accuracy %	Fluency	Appropriate
Devon	91, 82, 101, 78	92, 88, 93, 82	P,P,P,P	0
Darnell	96, 121, 88, 101	91, 96, 88, 92	P,F,P,P	25
Ricardo	67, 73, 78, 83	91, 87, 92, 88	P,P,P,P	0
Lakeisha	88, 94, 67, 91	89, 93, 86, 91	P,P,P,P	0
Maria	105,101,97,119	93, 92, 90, 95	P,P,P,F	25

guide. The goal is a representative sample of struggling readers. The sixth-grade students at Monroe Middle School were selected from those who were receiving Title I remedial reading and resource room special education services.

Once the five sixth-grade students had been selected (10 percent of 50), I met with each student and spent 10 to15 minutes with each one collecting words correct per minute (wcpm), accuracy, and fluency data using instructional texts found in each student's backpack and locker. I selected four texts from each student's desk (e.g., a core literature anthology, science book, social studies book, and so on).

Following the general guidelines for collecting wcpm data, I then had the student read aloud for 1 minute from each text. I selected where they began to read and marked that spot with a light slash mark. At the end of the minute I placed a slash mark at that point where the student was when the 1-minute timer sounded. Later, I counted the total words read during the 1-minute period and then subtracted all the words that were mispronounced (creating the wcpm data).

While the student read aloud, I kept track of the number of misreadings on my fingers. What is recorded is how many words are misread or simply skipped. When the reading was finished, I put that number on the sticky note and stuck it on the page the student read. I also indicated the fluency rating on the sticky note. Fluency ratings follow a simple scheme: *Good* means the student read in phrases with expression. *Fair* means the student read mostly in phrases but without much expression. *Poor* means the student read word-by-word, with little phrasing or expression.

I used the total number of words read in each book and the errors recorded for each text to calculate the wcpm and accuracy data and entered them, along with the fluency rating, on the worksheet (see Monroe Middle School example).

Once these data for each student were gathered, calculated, and entered onto the sheet, I was able to complete the final column on the worksheet. The key question this procedure tries to answer is: How many of the struggling readers have classroom texts appropriate to their level of reading development?

On the Monroe Middle School worksheet I derived the percentage data in the final column by looking at how many books could be read at 120 or greater wcpm, the average rate for a typical sixth-grade reader, and with a 97 percent-plus accuracy and with *Fair* to *Good* fluency. This is the traditional independent level of difficulty at which students can typically be expected to read a text and understand, or learn, its content with little teacher support. This accuracy level may seem high but consider that a typical middle school novel, such as *The Ransom of Mercy Carter* (Cooney, 2001), or historical informational texts, such as *When the Plague Strikes: Black Death, Smallpox, AIDS* (Giblin, 1995), will have between 250 and 300 running words on each page. A 3 percent error rate (97 percent accuracy) means that 7 to 9 words will be misread or unreadable on every page! In a 20-page chapter the student would encounter 140 to 180 words he or she cannot read. And typical middle school textbooks have twice as many words per page, creating the possibility that a reader reading at 97 percent accuracy would be unable to correctly read 14 to 20 words per page, or 250 to 400 words per chapter.

As illustrated in Table 1.2, struggling sixth-grade readers at Monroe Middle School are in trouble. Only two of the five students have even one book that would be considered to be at an appropriate level of complexity. In other words, almost all of the texts these students were given are simply too hard for them to learn to read or to learn content from. Few of these struggling readers are likely to exhibit accelerated reading development, regardless of the nature of the supplemental reading intervention programs they participate in. Few of them are likely to acquire much science or social studies knowledge. These struggling readers have books in their hands that no one should ever have ordered for them. These are books they cannot learn to read from and books they cannot learn social studies or science or literature from.

Next we gathered data on general education classroom lesson organization and delivery. To do this I prepared a second data sheet (see Table 1.3) using some

TABLE 1.3 *Classroom Lesson Organization at Monroe Middle School*

Room	Whole Group	Small Group	Side-by-Side	% WG
6a	XXXXXXXX	X		90
6b	XXXXXXXXX			100
6c	XX	XXXX	XXX	20
6d	XXXX	XXXX	XX	40
6e	XXXXX	XXXXX		50
6f		XXXX	XXXXX	0
7a	XXXXXXX	XXX		70
7b	XXXX	XXX	XXX	40
7c	XX	XXXXXXXX		20
7d	X	XXX	XXXXXX	10
7e	XXXXXXXXX			100
7f	XXXXXX	XXX	X	60
8a	XXXXXXX	XXX		70
8b	XXXXXXXXX			100
8c	XXXXXXXXX			100
8d	XXXXXX	XXXX		60
8e	XXXXXXXXX			100
8f	XXXXXXXXX			100

of the same materials used to create the Reader/Text Matching tool. This sheet has five columns. The first column is a listing of each of the general education classrooms at Monroe Middle School. The second column is where we will mark our observations of a whole-class lesson, and the third column is where we will note our observations of a small-group lesson. In the fourth column we will indicate our observations of side-by-side teaching (when the teacher is working alongside an individual student). The final column lists the percentage of observations for whole-class lessons.

The data display in Table 1.3 was developed from twice daily quick classroom observations done over the period of a week. I asked the assistant principal to walk through the building twice each day while varying the time of day the walk-through occurred. On each walk-through she simply entered each classroom and observed the lesson delivery. Then she placed the tally mark in the appropriate column (WG, SG, SxS). At the end of the week it was obvious that too many teachers delivered too many lessons in whole- group formats.

In other words, little balance in lesson organization was observed in many classrooms. However, other classroom teachers did vary the instructional delivery and the research indicates that all students, but especially the struggling readers, benefited greatly from this balanced instructional delivery approach (Allington & Johnston, 2002; Pressley, 2006; Taylor et al, 2000).

The Sad Case of Monroe Middle School

It would be tough to be a struggling reader at Monroe Middle School. It would be tough regardless of how effectively designed the intervention programs might be. And it would be tough because the best most struggling readers can hope for is one period a day of effective instruction offered in the intervention programs (and five periods a day where texts that are too difficult will limit the possibility of learning content or learning to read). Given the focus on whole-class lessons with everyone using the same grade-level text, struggling readers at Monroe spend most of their school day (4 to 5 hours) sitting in instructional environments that neither theory nor empirical evidence suggests will advance their academic development.

Unfortunately, no intervention product or package will much alter the outcomes for the struggling readers at Monroe Middle School. And Monroe Middle School will continue to fail to meet the federal Adequate Yearly Progress goals for both their economically disadvantaged students and their pupils with disabilities. The situation may only get worse as schools move to a CCSS instructional plan and accompanying assessments. In many schools, there will be protests that it is not reasonable to expect all students to achieve. Many instructors and administrators will be reluctant to embrace new research and practices that hold teachers, rather than the students themselves, accountable for struggling readers.

The staff at Monroe Middle wonder why struggling readers, who they feel are lucky to be participating in a daily very-small-group reading intervention class , will never seem to catch up with their achieving peers. No one seems to notice that it is only during that single period each day that the struggling readers are provided with texts and lessons that theory and research support. The other 5 hours each day are largely comprised of texts and lessons that go over their heads, offering lessons that work best for the highest achieving students but don't work at all for those students who struggle.

But at Monroe Middle School the blame for low achievement is placed on the students and not on the ineffective instructional plan. Teachers and administrators at Monroe complain that their students do not pay attention, that parents don't help their children at home, that their community has too many students from homes where English is not the language of the home, and so on. These comments are, unfortunately, not uncommon.

Summary

There has been much concern for a focus on "scientific" reading instruction as the best path to ameliorating the inequities in reading achievement typically observed in American schools. I support that focus. But little of the guidance provided thus far has focused on the critical factors of reader-text matches and the organizational delivery of classroom instruction. We have had evidence for some 60 years about the importance of these aspects of instructional design (Betts, 1946). Yet, as I walk through middle schools, even those with substantial federal funding, I too often see classrooms stocked with textbooks that are simply too difficult for some, if not most, of the students. I too often observe a steady reliance on whole-class interrogation sessions using these one-size-fits-all curriculum materials. I walk through schools where the only appropriate reading instruction struggling readers receive is that single period each day that offers supplemental reading instruction. And in these schools no one seems to have noticed that most struggling readers spend most of their school day in instructional environments where no theory would predict they would learn very much.

We need to reconceptualize interventions for struggling readers as something that must occur all day long. Intervention cannot just be that few minutes working with a specialist teacher. All students need texts of an appropriate level complexity all day long to thrive in school. In too many schools the texts in students' hands are appropriate for the highest achieving half of the students. In too many schools we have a curriculum plan that ensures the rich get richer because it is only the best readers who have books in their hands that they can read accurately, fluently, and with understanding.

When we redesign schools so all students have backpacks (or lockers) full of books they can read accurately, fluently, and with comprehension, we will have schools where fewer students struggle. Only when students have books in their hands all day long that they can read will we be able to expect supplemental interventions to make any difference.

Once we have a more differentiated set of curriculum materials, we might expect a better balance of whole-class, small-group, and side-by-side lessons. While all students benefit from small-group and side-by-side teaching, it is the struggling readers who seem to benefit most. Perhaps this is because these students have the greatest need for explicit teaching and scaffolded instructional support. It is the struggling learners who are the most instructionally needy and thus benefit the most from the more personalized instruction.

Federal legislation (No Child Left Behind Act) has placed new accountability pressures on American schools. The main purpose of these new accountability schemes is an evaluation to see whether the instruction in your school benefits all students relatively equally. Most schools work better for higher achieving students than for lower achieving students. In other words, some students grow more academically each year and others grow less. In most schools struggling readers fall further behind each year. These schools work better for the higher achieving students because the curriculum materials and instructional plans are best suited to the needs of these students. Unless that trend ends many schools will face federal sanctions for failing to create schools that work well for every student.

For too long we have focused our attention primarily on the nature and effects of supplementary intervention programs as one way to address the needs of struggling readers. For too long we have labeled struggling readers and focused on their weaknesses as the root of the problem. Until we recognize that appropriate instruction has to be available to struggling readers all day long, it is unlikely we will meet the challenges of the legislation and the moral obligation to end the struggles of our struggling readers. Until schools are organized in ways that ameliorate the struggles students face, rather than in ways that create those struggles, too many students will be left behind.

Chapter 2

Decoding Is Not the Problem (But That Is What Most Remediation Targets)

Decoding is the ability to use your knowledge of letter-sound relationships to figure out how to pronounce a word you've never seen before. Consider the word *electrotherapies*. I just found this word in the dictionary, and I cannot recall ever having seen this word in print before today. Yet, I didn't need to look at the phonetic respelling in the dictionary to know how to pronounce it. The same is probably also true for you.

So how did you figure out the pronunciation? Did you sound out each letter in isolation, then blend all those sounds into a continuous stream of sounds and say the word? It is doubtful any reader engaged in such a process if only because the word has too many letters. Too many letters means that the initial letter sounds get dumped out of short-term memory before you ever get to the end of the word.

You might have used a single letter sounding strategy in conjunction with a recombining strategy. In this case as you sounded the first three or four letters out, you stopped and combined them into the first syllable or word chunk (*e lec*), then you went on to sound out a few more letters (*tro*) and then recombined them with the first syllable (*electro*), and so on until you reached the end of the word. You then pronounced the whole word and were satisfied with the results.

Or you might have used a strategy where you pronounced the word syllable by syllable without ever having sounded each letter (*e lec tro ther a pies*). The syllables in the word are fairly easy to identify and each syllable appears in many other English words. So while you have never before seen this word, you have seen all of the syllables repeatedly in reading. If you used this strategy, though, it is unlikely you were recalling the syllabication rules you know to identify the syllables.

Alternatively, you might have recognized the root word (*therapy*), pronounced it, then added the prefix (*electro*), pronouncing it again before adding the suffix (*es*), coming, finally, to recognizing the whole word. You might have used some sort of root word strategy but it is unlikely you actually thought about the root word, the prefix, or the suffix as you determined the pronunciation.

Truth is, many readers who never saw the word before simply pronounced it on first sight. Any thinking going on was more likely hypotheses about the word's meaning rather than about its pronunciation.

I've taken you down this road for a reason. My basic point is this: Well-developed decoding abilities, as most readers of this book possess, work most of the time in a manner very different from how those with few decoding abilities work out a word's pronunciation. One reason some folks have well-developed decoding abilities and others do not lies largely in the amount of reading they have done. Beginning readers have no background of reading experiences to draw on when they encounter a word for the first time. Beginning readers would unlikely be able to figure out the word you so easily just decoded.

In part that is because they don't know much about decoding yet. If they are first-grade students they probably haven't yet encountered any word in their reading material as long as *electrotherapies*. They probably are still working on that single letter sounding strategy you didn't use. That strategy works well for short and familiar words like *fan,* but that same strategy does not work so well for a word like *fantastically* because the word is longer and its appearance in written English is much rarer than *fan.*

All words can be placed on a scale of easy-to-difficult to pronounce. One way to think about this is on a scale from "clear" to "opaque." Below are two lists of words, one list where the pronunciation is clear and the other where the pronunciation of the words is opaque.

Clear	*Opaque*
rat	was
save	some
clear	opaque
romantic	equivocal

Pronouncing words correctly from the "Clear" list is relatively straightforward. The words from the "Opaque" list require something beyond simple decoding rules. If we could just apply simple decoding rules to these words, *was* would be pronounced *waz* or as rhyming with *gas* with a short vowel sound for the *a* and the sibilant *s* at the end. But, of course, that word is pronounced *wuz*.

With the second word, *some,* the application of our phonics rules would give us a word that would be pronounced *sohm,* and so on. In the case of each of these opaque words some knowledge other than letter-sound relationships must be applied to deduce the pronunciation. This is part of what makes English a difficult language to read. Nonetheless, all good readers can read the words on both lists and most don't even notice the opaque pronunciation quality of words on the second list.

However, if you don't read well and don't read much you may be stymied by words on the second list. Having a teacher tell you to "sound it out" will simply frustrate *you*. Learning the basics of decoding is essential in becoming a skilled reader. But all the decoding skills in the world will not help you pronounce many English words. Students have to acquire other skills if they are to become able to read many words their textbooks.

Consider what this struggling early adolescent said about her reading experiences:

> *When I went to seventh grade we took a test to see where we were and I was at a third-grade reading level. They put me in class with five other people with the same problem. We were in there one period every day. They taught me how to sound out words better. I still have hard times with some words now. I sound them out and most of them I get but there's a lot of big words that I still don't even know. Sometimes I will just sit there for hours trying to figure out what the word is instead of asking. I don't ask all day. I don't know why, I am embarrassed I think. (Mueller, 2001, p. 21)*

This young woman is still struggling and, perhaps, that is because she has been taught that all words can be sounded out using the phonetic skills that she had been taught. What seems missing here is the fact that every word cannot be sounded out. Words that occur relatively rarely, or words with a low frequency of use, are harder to pronounce, generally, because we have rarely encountered those words in print. One overlooked aspect of decoding success is producing a word that sounds like a word you've heard but never seen. This is called "cross-checking" and it is a skill that readers need.

This ability is one reason few reading researchers have paid much attention to studies of non-word (or pseudo-word) pronunciation. Attempting to pronounce a non-word restricts the ability to cross-check the pronunciation against what you already know. The argument that non-word proponents give is something like this.

> If we want a pure measure of decoding ability we cannot use words because the person we are testing might have already seen that word. With non-words you can be reasonably sure no one has seen the non-word before. Also, you can be sure that the person is relying solely on decoding ability because he cannot cross-check the pronunciation with his listening vocabulary.

Because pronouncing non-words involves a different set of resources, about the only thing you can learn from such tests is how well children can pronounce non-words. This may be the reason that researchers have reported limited correlations between the accuracy and rapidity of pronunciation of non-words and reading achievement (Pressley, Hilden, & Shankland, 2006; Mathson, Solic, & Allington, 2006; Walmsley, 1979).

There is a reason why the most common mispronunciation of the non-word *tox* are *tax* and *fox*. The cross-checking mentioned above is exhibited in such responses. When shown a non-word most readers expect the non-word to be a real word. Thus, *tax* and *fox* are offered because they share the most phonetic features with the non-word *tox* (Walmsley, 1979).

Nonetheless, American elementary schools have gone on a non-word testing binge since the inception of the No Child Left Behind Act. What few educators seem to be aware of, however, is that the federal Inspector General's office found that this reliance on non-word testing was part of the corruption found in the federal office in charge of monitoring the NCLB program (Office of the Inspector General, 2007). That report led to the removal of all federal staff from the federal Reading First program office and the removal of every director of the federal Reading First technical assistance centers. What we seem to know today, after a decade of non-word testing, is that while we can teach children to pronounce non-words, it has no positive effect on their reading achievement. That was the primary finding of the federal evaluation of the Reading First component of NCLB (Gamse, Jacob, Horst, Boulay, & Unlu, 2009).

Investigators found that first-grade students in Reading First schools could pronounce non-words more accurately than students in non-Reading First schools, but they found no differences in reading achievement in the two sets of schools. Personally, I am not surprised by this finding, although the Reading First schools offered a larger daily amount of reading instruction. Some portion of the roughly $1 billion a year that was given to Reading First schools went to support the teaching and testing of non-word pronunciation. It was $1 billion each year squandered on educational activities that wasted the time of both teachers and students, time that could have been spent teaching children to read. And even with the negative results reported by Gamse et al. (2009), non-word testing still continues in schools across the country. The federal evaluation of Reading First, the Inspector General's report, and first-hand experiences of students still failing to read authentic texts any better than they were able to read them a decade ago all point to the need for a different reading intervention program.

The National Reading Panel (2000) reviewed the experimental research on decoding and concluded that spending time in kindergarten and first grade teaching decoding produced both a small positive effect on reading comprehension in later grades and a larger positive effect on the ability to decode real words in isolation. They also found no evidence of positive effects on reading achievement for phonics instruction at grade 2 and above. Their advice was to ensure that kindergarten and first-grade teachers provide a small amount of explicit phonics instruction each day. They suggested only small amounts of phonics because the research suggests that when more than 10 minutes per day is spent on phonics, there is no greater benefit.

It may surprise you that the panel found no positive effects for decoding lessons above first grade. I was not surprised because decoding problems seem rarely to be the primary problem older struggling readers face. Several recent studies explain why.

Hock and Brasseur (2009) assessed the reading development of 436 urban ninth-grade students. They found that the struggling readers performed better on decoding and word reading tasks than they did on vocabulary, comprehension, and fluency tasks. In other words, most older struggling readers exhibited strengths in decoding and reading words in isolation, strengths in relation to the vocabulary and world knowledge. Their primary problems stemmed from the smaller number of words they knew the meanings for, and an inability to read with understanding and fluency.

Likewise, Cutting and Scarborough (2006) found that only 14 percent of students exhibiting poor reading comprehension also had decoding problems. Dennis (2013) found that roughly 10 percent of the urban students who failed the eighth-grade state reading achievement exam exhibited decoding problems as their most serious weakness. Like the Hock and Brasseur study, she found vocabulary and comprehension proficiency were the most common problems these students exhibited.

Finally, Adloff, Perfetti, and Catts (2010) note that specific decoding difficulties declined from second grade to eighth grade while specific comprehension difficulties increased. At second grade, 32.3 percent of struggling readers exhibited specific decoding difficulties while at eighth grade only 13.3 percent of struggling readers exhibited this deficit. Specific comprehension difficulties, on the other hand, were exhibited by 6.3 percent of second-grade struggling readers but by 30.2 percent of the eighth-grade struggling readers.

I cite these studies in explanation of why the NRP found no positive effects of decoding instruction above the first grade. If we create intervention programs for early adolescent struggling readers that focus on fostering their decoding skills, we shouldn't be surprised to see few positive effects on their ability to read. I think the research we have points to the actual sources of most middle school struggling readers and that problem is not a problem with decoding. This is not to say that these struggling readers are strong decoders, since many are not, but their decoding proficiency outstrips the problems they have with vocabulary and comprehension. Yet, too often efforts to strengthen struggling readers, especially in middle school and high school, are focused primarily on developing decoding skills.

Efforts to accelerate the reading development of early adolescent struggling readers requires an intervention very different from what is most commonly found in remedial and special education classes. As Leach, Scarborough, and Rescorda (2003) noted:

> Reading disabilities in children beyond the primary grades appear to be heterogeneous with regard to the nature of their reading skill deficits . . . some children have comprehension problems only, some have just word-level difficulties, and some exhibit across the board weaknesses. . . . Hence both assessment and instruction must be aligned with this reality. Most important, intervention programs need then to be selected on the basis of children's deficit type(s) rather than overall grade level. (p. 222)

The seeming preference in middle and high schools for the use of a one-size-fits-all reading remediation curriculum may explain why so little progress is made in accelerating reading development after grade 4 (Allington & McGill-Franzen, 1989; Vaughn & Linan-Thompson, 2003; Ysseldyke, Thurlow, Mecklenburg & Graden, 1984).

What the research suggests is that if you have 10 struggling sixth-grade readers, you will need ten different interventions to address the needs of those 10 students. I'm reasonably sure that if the research studies emphasizing decoding instruction had limited that instruction to the 10 to 15 percent of early-adolescent struggling readers who exhibit substantial decoding difficulties, the outcomes would have been more positive. Schools need to attend to the specific problems that struggling readers present if only because the time in the school day available for reading intervention is short for early adolescents and we cannot waste any time on misguided instruction.

What We Know about Fostering Improved Decoding in Early Adolescents

It seems that around grade 4 and onward, children who are developing reading proficiency will normally exhibit decoding proficiencies that begin to operate in what we could call the skilled reader model. By grade 4 children who have been developing their reading proficiency so that they are considered good readers have had much experience with reading, writing, and spelling and have encountered most of the words in print that they will most commonly be reading for the rest of their lives. By the end of fourth grade, good readers have developed a large "sight vocabulary," a large number of printed words they recognize immediately with no sounding out stage. This occurs primarily because by now they have read these words so many times that word recognition is automatic.

Struggling readers by the end of fourth grade are millions of words behind good readers in reading practice. Unless we do something about it, this "practice gap" will simply continue to grow larger and larger with every additional year. When we begin to worry about how best to assist early adolescents who are struggling readers, we must consider how best to expand the volume of reading that they engage in every day. Torgeson and Hudson (2006) argue:

> The most important factor appears to involve difficulties in making up for the huge deficits in accurate reading practice the older children have accumulated by the time they reach later elementary school. . . . One of the major results of this lack of reading practice is a severe limitation in the number of words the children with reading disabilities can recognize automatically, or at a single glance. . . . Such "catching up" would seem to require an extensive period of time in which the reading practice of the previously disabled children was actually greater than that of their peers. (p. 147)

Note that they do not mention work in developing decoding proficiencies here, but instead focus on dramatically expanding what I have called "high-success" reading activity (Allington, 2013). It is the research that is available that has led them to draw this conclusion. In general, decoding interventions improve children's ability to decode words correctly but they have little effect on reading comprehension performances.

As an example, in a large-scale study comparing the effects of four different commercial reading intervention programs, each of which incorporated explicit and systematic decoding instruction, Torgeson and his colleagues (2007) found little to cheer about. The fifth-grade students they worked with (in some 50 schools) were poor readers with reading scores below the thirtieth percentile and vocabulary scores above the fifth percentile. They found that none of the four programs they tested (Corrective Reading, Wilson Reading, Failure Free Reading, and Spell Read P.A.T.) had any positive effects on student reading comprehension. In fact, they report that instruction provided by "the four interventions combined lowered the reading and mathematics scores" (p. xiv). In other words, using any of these commercial reading interventions led students to learn less than did the control group students who were not provided the instruction! Nor did using any of these programs improve student scores on the state reading assessment.

In considering the common word decoding focus of intervention efforts, perhaps these limited outcomes on reading comprehension is not surprising. I say this because the research evidence demonstrates that word reading accuracy decreases as a factor in defining struggling readers. In other words, as students age, how well they pronounce words (or non-words) becomes a far less significant influence in defining reading proficiency. Adlof et al. (2010), in summarizing their work on the relationship between word reading accuracy and reading comprehension, note the substantial change that takes place over time. "Word reading by itself accounted for 94% of the variance in reading comprehension in second grade, whereas it accounted for only 38% of the variance in eighth grade, and all of that was shared with language comprehension" (p. 189).

The findings of these large-scale randomized field experiments largely reflect what other studies have shown. Developing early adolescent decoding abilities alone does not foster better reading or better reading achievement test scores. As Torgeson and Hudson (2006) noted, while the typical decoding intervention did raise decoding performance (from the third percentile to the thirty-ninth percentile) that same intervention had virtually no effect on reading comprehension performance (from the third percentile to the fifth percentile).

Many schools have decided to use one of these commercial reading intervention programs, which are not supported by research. Although commercial programs are often accompanied by appealing advertising campaigns, they are not as often developed by using research and practices that have proved successful in real classrooms. "Buyer beware" is the best advice for all commercial educational products but especially for commercial products advertised for reading interventions.

Pitcher, Martinez, Dicembre, Fewster, and McCormick (2010) take a different approach to the study of struggling readers. They describe the cases of Tamika, a sixth-grade student with on-level word reading proficiencies and a second-grade level of reading comprehension, and Kathy, an eighth-grade student again with on-level word reading proficiencies and first-grade reading comprehension. Tamika is enrolled in an intervention class where the curriculum material being used is the Language! program that focuses on decoding, grammar, and spelling development but has no focused work on vocabulary development or comprehension strategy development. They note, "Comparing her needs with the school's instruction, there seems to be a disconnect between the two. The school's reading program focuses on decoding strategies, grammar, and spelling, whereas she needs vocabulary development and comprehension" (p. 638).

In Kathy's case, she is enrolled in an intervention program again focused on decoding proficiencies, primarily SRA Corrective Reading, when her needs are in vocabulary development and comprehension strategies development. In both cases, and in too many similar cases across the nation, early-adolescent struggling readers are participating in interventions that are largely a waste of their time—interventions focused on all of the wrong aspects of the reading process.

Pitcher and her colleagues (2010) also present the cases of several students with reading problems who were receiving no assistance from their schools but were participating in a curriculum that required them to read with understanding. What they found was what may be the most common deficiency found in middle schools—ignoring the reading problems students present.

So why then are so many reading intervention programs for early adolescents focused primarily on developing decoding skills? Perhaps many of the administrators in charge of deciding what sort of intervention design should be offered do not know the current research or are attracted by the advertisements that accompany every commercial intervention program. Perhaps they do not realize that improving word decoding abilities has little positive influence on improving reading achievement. In other words, they are impressed by the data showing improved decoding and mistakenly think that working on improved decoding represents something worth doing. In truth though, we want the early-adolescent struggling readers to be better able to read their school texts with understanding, and decoding interventions have a research record that indicates they provide no help toward this goal of improving reading with understanding.

There is one other possibility to explain the fascination with these commercial intervention programs: Most middle schools and high schools have few, if any, reading specialists on their faculties. Thus, someone who is not an expert in teaching struggling readers is teaching the reading intervention classes. In such a case it might make sense to purchase a "teacher proof" commercial product, if there were such a product—but there are no such products. All commercial programs work as well as the teacher can make them work and when the teacher is inexpert and the program is narrowly focused we get intervention efforts that rarely succeed in improving reading achievement.

In middle schools, the most commonly used commercial reading intervention programs are typically narrowly focused on something other than improving students' abilities to read with understanding. This is true whether the struggling readers have been labeled as learning disabled, whether English is their second language, or whether they are just "garden variety" struggling readers, often children from low-income families. In fact, there are literally no commercial reading intervention programs with a focus on improving reading comprehension. Again, I have no idea why this is so but it may simply be that it is easier to create a scripted curriculum focused on decoding development than it is to create a program focused on improving reading with understanding.

Finally, the focus on decoding development may be related to the most obvious signs of reading difficulty, the inability to accurately read all of the words. That is, when early adolescent struggling readers read aloud, especially when someone asks them to read aloud from a grade-level text, they sound terrible. Their reading is often expressed in a herky-jerky manner with many segments read literally word-by-word and often with many misreadings of words, especially long and relatively rare words of academic content vocabulary. Without even assessing reading comprehension we can tell that this reader is struggling. Perhaps, someone thinks, if I improve her ability to pronounce those words correctly, her reading will improve. Unfortunately, research suggests something very different. It is not so much that *decoding* is the problem; it is that *reading* is the problem. If we never get past the explicit initial feature of trouble pronouncing *some* of the words correctly, we may never develop an intervention that actually addresses the problem in front of us.

It is the narrow focus on decoding that is the larger problem with many, if not most, commercial reading intervention programs. Consider for a moment that not a single state reading proficiency test asks students to pronounce either non-words or real words in isolation. State tests of reading achievement generally assess how well the student understands the test material he or she has read. Much of what is tested on too many state tests is low-level literal recall of what the text said, the lowest form of comprehension. But state tests will be changing as almost all states (45 so far) have adopted the Core Curriculum Standards and accepted the challenge of developing new tests that measure "deeper" learning. My point is, skill in the rapid and automatic decoding of words and non-words will become even less important in the future.

What Might Help Struggling Early Adolescent Readers?

Struggling early-adolescent readers need to engage in a lot of high-success reading to improve both their decoding proficiencies and their ability to read with understanding (Allington, 2013; Ivey & Johnston, 2013; Miller, 2009). What has been largely overlooked in considering the development of decoding abilities is the role of "self-teaching." Self-teaching, though, seems central to accurate decoding. One key proficiency largely self-taught is self-monitoring. Self-monitoring is being aware that what you are reading makes sense—makes sense semantically, syntactically, and in terms of content knowledge. Look at the example below:

Original sentence: "The Third Cavalry Division was attached to the Army of the Potomac prior to the great battle at Gettysburg."

Student's misreading: "The Third Calvary Division was attacked by the Army of the Pot-o-mack prior to the great battle at Gettysburg."

Consider the different nature of these misreadings:

1. *Cavalry* and *Calvary* are visually similar words and for many Christian church-attending students the word *Calvary* is far more familiar than the word *cavalry* (semantic/word frequency).
2. *Attacked* makes some sense because this piece is about the Civil War. *Attached* makes less sense unless you know what *attached* means here (semantic/content knowledge).
3. Reading *by* for *to* indicates attention to making sense since *attacked to the army of* . . . just doesn't sound right (syntactic).
4. *Pot-o-mack* is a reasonable phonetic pronunciation of the word *Potomac*—reasonable but wrong (content knowledge).

The sort of knowledge the student would need to correctly pronounce the misread words or to self-correct an initial mispronunciation is shown parenthetically. The point here is a simple one: Almost none of the mispronunciations were solely initiated by a lack of decoding abilities. Prior knowledge, familiarity, and background content knowledge all contributed to these misreadings. Closer attention to the letter sequence in the word *cavalry* might have helped but if *Calvary* is a known word, that fact alone will likely interfere with pronunciation. The same goes for *attached*. But again if the reader knows she is reading about the Civil War era, then that will also interfere with

Elementary Level Historical Texts on the Civil War Era

Thunder at Gettysburg, by Patricia Lee Gauch published by Random House.

A Ballad of the Civil War by Mary Stolz published by HarperCollins.

Pink and Say by Patricia Pollaco published by Penguin.

The Boys' War by Jim Murphy published by Houghton Mifflin Harcourt.

Across Five Aprils by Irene Hunt published by Penguin.

How I Found the Strong by Margaret McMullan published by Houghton Mifflin Harcourt.

Soldier's Heart by Gary Paulsen published by Random House.

Turn Homeward, Hannalee by Patricia Beatty published by HarperCollins.

Bull Run by Paul Fleishman published by HarperCollins.

the correct pronunciation of the word. And for *Potomac,* she did sound it out, incorrectly but legally. The only way one can figure out the correct pronunciation is to already know the word.

The solution for this reader is, first, developing her background knowledge about the Civil War era, including developing knowledge of the meanings of key academic content vocabulary. No student can self-monitor without the relevant and necessary content knowledge. In order to self-monitor, the student must not only know this content but also must accept the responsibility for self-monitoring.

In too many cases, hundreds of hours of oral reading of texts that are too difficult and accompanied by frequent teacher interruptions has created a struggling reader who expects others to monitor his or her reading. To foster self-monitoring and eventually self-teaching, you will need to begin providing this reader with texts he can actually read with a high level of accuracy. In this case I would begin with one of the many historical fiction novels set in the Civil War era. These texts range in difficulty down to primary-grade reader levels with literally hundreds of Civil War era texts written at the third- and fourth-grade levels. (See the feature box.)

Remember that getting early-adolescent struggling readers actually reading has to be a central goal if they are ever to become achieving readers. It is through engagement in reading, particularly reading something that the readers finds interesting, that self-teaching occurs. As Clay (2005) wrote: "It is most helpful to think of the learner (who is successfully solving reading problems) as building a neural network for working on written text and that network learns to extend itself. It is the successful strategic activity called up by the learner that creates the self-extending system" (p. 103).

That neural network Clay refers to includes white matter observable in human brains. It is the white matter that transfers signals from one area of the brain to another. The stronger the white matter, the better the transfer and the learning. Keller and Just (2009) recently reported on an intensive reading intervention with early-adolescent struggling readers. The intervention improved the quality of the white matter and the amount of white matter improvement predicted reading proficiency growth. Perhaps if more interventions for struggling early adolescent readers emphasized dramatic increases in high-success reading volume as Keller and Just did, a greater number of those struggling readers would become achieving readers.

Readers are only likely to self-monitor if they are reading something that is both interesting and important to them. They must also be able to accurately read the text. All of these factors, plus a long history of failure in reading, works against self-monitoring in early-adolescent struggling readers. There are useful routines teachers can use to promote better self-regulation. Next we will discuss some potentially powerful routines you should be using to support struggling readers and to foster the development of their self-monitoring abilities and attitudes.

Model the Word Structure of Important Academic Words in Each Unit

There are instructional routines that all teachers can add to their repertoire that will foster better word recognition and better word analysis by struggling readers in the middle school and high school, if only by improving readers' abilities to self-monitor. Each of these routines can be adapted to fit any classroom instructional plan, each will require only a few minutes each day, and each will improve word reading accuracy in content area materials.

Model the Word Structure and Pronunciation

On the chalkboard (or white board or smart board) present a listing of the key academic vocabulary in any readings being assigned that seems likely to give struggling readers difficulty. (Limit the list to four or five words that appear in the reading the students will be doing on that day.) Now,

1. Read the first word on the list to your students.
2. After you have pronounced the word aloud, write the word in syllables right next to it. Now pronounce each syllable separately, then blend the syllables and pronounce the whole word again.

3. If there is a root word, write that next to syllable breakdown of the words. Pronounce the root word.

4. Now add any prefix or suffix that is part of the word and pronounce it one more time. (Below is a daily sample academic word list with these steps illustrated.)

Write/Pronounce	Write/Pronounce	Root	Pronounce with students
Fort Donelson	Don el son		Donelson
Confederate	Con fed er ate		Confederate
ammunition	am mu ni tion		ammunition
preparation	prep a ra tion	prepare	preparation
insurrection	in sur rec tion		insurrection

These five words are from a middle school social studies unit on the first Union victories in the Civil War. There may be other words in the assigned reading that are also likely to be problematic but the goal isn't to introduce every such word. Instead, the goal is to introduce the academic content words that are central to understanding the text.

The premise here is that by showing the syllable structure you will aid students later in either recalling the pronunciation or aiding in later sounding out the word themselves. Early-adolescent struggling readers need all the help they can get in reading and learning the content knowledge so central to schooling. Taking 3 minutes or so every day to assist them in their pronunciation of key content vocabulary is an important first step.

Using Words They Know

Using words they know to teach the pronunciation of unknown words is another useful strategy and another one that takes but a few minutes to teach. In Cunningham's (2011) discussion of this strategy, she points out that all readers have some words they already know but often fail to use when attempting to pronounce new words. Early-adolescent struggling readers typically can read many—hundreds or more—small, frequent words but struggle with word pronunciation of infrequent and longer words.

Infrequent words often share a word structure with higher frequency words. Consider the words listed below. The first word in the list is a frequent and short word that struggling readers are likely to be able to pronounce. Beneath that frequent word is a list of infrequent and often longer words that share word structure with the frequent words.

ice	cool	say	bug
lice	tool	pray	smug
splice	drool	slay	shrug
device	stool	payable	struggled
sacrifice	whirlpool	betrayal	juggernaut

As outlined by Cunningham, the usual routine for using known words as you introduce new words should follow this general plan:

1. Model the activity with an example or two. Say, "If *ice* is spelled *i-c-e* then the second word on the first list must be *lice* because it is spelled *l-i-c-e*. So the second word on the first list is *lice*.

2. Model again with the second word on the list, in this case, *splice*. So if *i-c-e* spells *ice* and *l-i-c-e* spells *lice,* then *s-p-l-i-c-e* must be *splice*. The third word on the first list is *splice*.

3. Model with the fourth word on list one last time. "Look at the fourth word on the first list. Underline the word *ice*. What other letters begin the word? Right, *d-e* followed then by *v-i-c-e*. If we pronounce the *d-e* as *dee* and then add the *v* to *ice* we get *device*.

4. Now turn their attention to the second list, under *cool*. You don't need to go through every word on the list as we did with the first list. You might have students pair up as teams to pronounce to each other the remaining words on the lists.

(For a far more detailed discussion of a similar strategy, along with fully developed lessons you can use, see Cunningham and Hall [2009].)

This routine helps students develop their ability to use what they already know to figure out what they do not yet know. Too many early-adolescent struggling readers are too ready just to skip over words they don't know at first glance. One way to change this into a more positive behavior is by working with them to develop alternatives that work for them. Using what you know is just such a strategy!

Glass Analysis

One commercial decoding program that might be considered is Glass Analysis (Glassanalysis.com). I mention this older program for several reasons. First, like the other routine mentioned here it is designed to help student see the similarities in spelling (and pronunciation) patterns in English words. It uses a sequence of real words to help students begin to acquire larger-unit decoding strategies. As designed, it is also a quickly paced routine that should occupy perhaps 3 to 7 minutes per lesson. The design is largely failure proof for students and requires a fast-paced set of decoding activities. Many teachers use this as an opening activity for each class period. It is basically an every-pupil-response activity, and it literally elicits whole-class involvement.

Conclusion

These various instructional routines all work to teach decoding using the patterns one can see in the words and by using analogy. In each routine you guided struggling readers through a process that focused their attention on units of each word that are larger than the single letter as well as helpful in decoding. Too often struggling readers, even older struggling readers, have only a single decoding strategy, letter-by-letter sounding. It isn't that letter-by-letter sounding is a bad strategy but it works far better in first and second grades when few words students encounter are either rare or long. By sixth grade most of the words that present difficulty for many readers are both rare and long. By rare I mean words the child most likely has never heard or perhaps heard once in a trade book read-a-loud, words such as *scurvy* or *delta*.

Using In-Text Aids

A final activity you need to consider is the use of in-text pronunciation tools. Content area textbooks differ in the sorts of tools they offer students as aids for correct word pronunciation. Some textbooks contain glossaries, usually at the end of the text. The glossaries provide a list of words the authors have decided are important for readers to know. In addition to the pronunciation guide, a glossary usually also provides a specific definition of the word (the definition being the one central to the text). Other textbooks provide sidenotes with pronunciation and meaning information. These sidenotes appear in the side margins of the page and are typically printed in a different font or color to set them off as different from the primary text. Other textbooks provide pronunciation information in the running text, often in parenthetical form.

All of these different forms of pronunciation support indicate that textbook authors understand that many of the words they have used are unfamiliar to the students, many are long, and many are difficult to know how to pronounce. However, these pronunciation tools are only helpful if students know how to use them. And too many early-adolescent readers have neither noticed the glossary in their textbook nor used the sidenotes to assist in pronunciation.

Another reason these pronunciation tools are not used is because students have no idea how to use them. Different textbooks use different techniques to assist in pronunciation. Some use a phonetic respelling of the word, much like a standard dictionary. (Example of a phonetic respelling, *es pˉe enahz*. Can you tell me what the original printed word was? It was *espionage*.) Unfortunately, students who cannot read the original word often cannot do any better at reading the phonetic respelling of the word. Phonetic respellings involve specialized markings for long versus short vowels, accent marks, special symbols for special vowel sounds (such as the *schwa*), and so on. Learning all these specialized symbols is more than a bit much to ask struggling readers to master. Other textbooks use a simplified respelling to show a word's correct pronunciation (e.g., *Treaty of Versailles—Treaty of Ver-sigh*). No matter what technique you may find in your textbook, take the time to ensure students at least are familiar with the tool and familiar with how to use it.

Teachers, too, should use these tools, especially if some of the academic content vocabulary is unfamiliar to them. As I wrote the preceding section, the Versailles example popped into my mind. This word was pronounced, or should I say mispronounced, as *ver-say -lees* by my eighth-grade basketball coach and European history teacher. Worse yet, the textbook had a glossary with the correct pronunciation indicated. Someone who was more confident in their basketball playing abilities than I was pointed out that the glossary indicated the correct pronunciation was *Ver-sigh*. "Yes," said the teacher, "that's how they pronounce it in France, but here we call it the *Treaty of Ver-say-lees*. " Enough said.

Anxiety and Word Reading

Years ago, back when I was a new assistant professor, Florence Roswell and Gladys Natchez (1977) published a revision of their book on reading disabilities. They noted that older struggling readers, whom they identified as students in grades 4 and above, suffer from a form of performance anxiety situated in their longstanding problems with reading. A decade later Peter Johnston (1985) published similar findings about adult struggling readers. These authors noted that after years of failure and years of frustration every marker of anxiety went off the scale when these older struggling readers were asked to read aloud.

These anxious readers also often exhibited word reading difficulties when called upon to read aloud in class. However, the words they stumbled on when asked to read aloud were words they could pronounce correctly when assessed in isolation and in a less anxious one-on-one testing situation. In other words, being asked to read aloud in front of peers created anxiety and that anxiety triggered a sort of panic that led these students to be unable to read words that they were able to read in a less-anxious setting. When reading aloud, these anxious students often slurred over words they didn't know at first glance. They often simply uttered some words, often a word with some visual similarities, and went on reading. Whether it was the anxiety, or the fact that slowing down to sound out a word made their reading sound less capable, we don't know. But what we do know is that asking struggling early-adolescent readers to read aloud in class is a bad idea because it undermines their ability to read as well as they can.

This decrease in reading performance when reading aloud may be the reason that early attempts to establish optimum levels of text difficulty for learning (Betts, 1946) allowed readers the opportunity to read the text silently before reading it aloud. Somewhere in educational history we seem to have lost the silent prereading aspect of assessing reading ability with oral readings of texts. The potential of engaging in a prior silent reading of a text before reading it aloud seems understood by students today. That is the reason many of my graduate students can recall times in earlier schooling when a class was being asked to read aloud from a text and they along with everyone else seemed to be reading some part of the text they hadn't yet reached. My students, like me, could remember practicing the upcoming text so that if we were the next ones to be called upon to read aloud, we would be ready.

Of course that meant we were paying no attention to the classmate who was now reading the text aloud. Learning what the text said was less important to me than sounding good when I was asked to read. So much for the efficacy of having students read textbooks aloud in class!

One of the mysteries of schooling is that struggling readers are the ones called upon to read aloud most often (Allington, 1984). Even in first grade, good readers are asked more often to read silently than to read aloud. But in sixth grade, poor readers are still assigned more oral than silent reading. Reading aloud, often from a grade-level text, simply requires struggling readers to make public their reading difficulties. The result is performance anxiety (and too often misbehavior).

As anxiety builds, the students not only are no longer able to demonstrate the same competencies they had when unstressed, but also are paying little attention to what is being read. The other students are being exposed to a flawed and incompetent oral reading of assigned material, and in the worst-case scenarios these other students begin to interrupt the reader with corrections or comments. (Interruptions are most likely to come from those students who have already completed their turn to read aloud since the others are too busy to interrupt because they are reading ahead silently, preparing for their turn to read aloud.) The interruptions, when they come, add to the stress the struggling reader faces.

In addition, faced with a steady supply of interruptions from other students, or from the teacher, struggling readers now often adopt a self-survival strategy. This strategy involves slowing the reading pace down, often to a word-by-word pace (Allington, 1980). This slow pace makes it easier to know which word the interruption concerns. At the same time struggling readers begin to demonstrate an intonation pattern I've called the "query" pattern. This pattern is exhibited when the reader produces a rising intonation when reading words. This intonation pattern almost invites interruption because when used it suggests an "I'm not really sure about this word" to listeners. This then fosters "help" from other students and often from teachers.

Far too many early-adolescent struggling readers now always read aloud in a word-by-word mode that demonstrates the query intonation pattern. This is true even when they can read the material accurately—accurately but not fluently.

Reading Fluency

Fluent oral reading has exhibited rising popularity during the NCLB era largely as a result of having reading fluency named as one of the five "scientific pillars" of reading by the National Reading Panel (2000). Reading fluency should rightly be of concern with beginning readers. As children learn to read they move from a word-by-word stage to the phrase reading stage, which occurs almost naturally for most readers. However, some readers never develop the ability to read fluently, which is the ability to read accurately, in phrases, with appropriate intonation and understanding.

Why some readers never develop fluent reading behaviors is the dilemma. Much current thinking suggests that the problem is with substandard decoding proficiencies. In fact, most routines and programs available target fostering faster and more accurate decoding as the keys to fostering fluent reading behaviors. Personally, I think that the weak decoding hypothesis is only part of the story. (I've written about my alternative hypothesis fairly extensively in another book in the What Really Matters series: *What Really Matters in Fluency*.)

My hunch is that many struggling readers never developed fluent reading abilities because they have often been fed a steady diet of texts that are simply too hard. These are texts they cannot read accurately, and they have little understanding of what they do read. Couple these factors with an interruptive reading environment and you create readers who read word by word with little appropriate intonation or expression. Now provide this sort of instruction for 5 or 6 years and you get struggling word-by-word readers in the middle school.

The most powerful instructional framework for fostering fluent reading in early-adolescent struggling readers seems to be primarily an engagement of struggling readers in large amounts of high-success reading

(Kuhn, 2006; Kuhn, Schwanenflugel, Morris, Morrow, Woo, Meisinger, Sevcik, Bradley & Stahl, 2006; 2010). In these studies extensive independent reading activity was contrasted with comparable amounts of repeated readings of texts. While repeated readings had been shown to foster fluency growth, the independent reading condition worked to foster more fluency growth faster.

The independent reading was high-success silent reading. In other words, it seems that the additional reading practice involved in the independent reading condition was the factor that led to the fluency improvement. It wasn't just fluency that improved. The students who were engaged in the independent reading lessons also acquired a greater number of new vocabulary words and increased their reading comprehension more than the students in the repeated reading condition.

The research now available suggests several things about the development of fluency:

1. Most struggling readers do not read aloud fluently.
2. Many early-adolescent struggling readers have a long history as struggling readers and a long history of being assigned to reading texts that were simply too difficult for them.
3. In too many cases early-adolescent struggling readers have experienced primarily oral reading of these too-hard texts.
4. During these oral reading events other students and the teacher were likely to make the oral reading an interruptive reading experience.
5. In response to the anxiety produced by both too-hard texts and constant interruptions, struggling readers then began to adapt their oral reading performance to better fit the interruptive reading environment, primarily by slowing their rate of reading and by providing a query intonation pattern as they read.
6. Word-by-word reading then became habituated and "normal" reading practice.

The longer the reader has struggled with school reading, the more firmly entrenched the word-by-word reading becomes. We can foster fluent reading behaviors, though not typically through lessons designed to foster decoding proficiencies (Torgeson & Hudson, 2006). Instead, what seems most powerful is expanding the volume of high-success reading for struggling readers. This means primarily working to locate high-success texts for them to read in every class, all day long.

I'll argue, based on our experience, that if you have worked on fostering fluency with a struggling reader for more than 3 weeks and have not yet had success, then the plan in place is simply somehow flawed. Fluent reading is not a difficult ability to foster, but to be successful four aspects of reading lessons must be present:

1. There must be easy access to texts that can be read accurately and texts that the student is interested in reading.
2. There should be substantial opportunities for the student to engage in reading the high-success texts silently.
3. The reading environment must be non-interruptive. Neither other students nor the teacher should interrupt (or help) the struggling reader.
4. Each reading lesson involves some literate conversation about what was read.

We can help early-adolescent struggling readers become fluent readers but to accomplish this will require substantial shifts in the way that texts for early adolescents are selected and used.

Summary

Too often schools have assumed that decoding was the problem experienced by struggling early-adolescent readers. While some struggling early-adolescent readers do have deficiencies in their decoding skills, many more have decoding skills that far outstrip their levels of vocabulary development, inferential comprehension abilities, and world knowledge. We also have substantial research showing that improving decoding abilities of early adolescents has little if any effect on their understanding of what they read or on their reading abilities as generally measured.

Virtually every learning theory begins by noting that after deciding what is to be taught, the next step is selecting appropriate instructional materials. That means selecting texts that students can read, accurately, fluently, and with understanding. There seems to be neither a theory nor any research evidence supporting the practice that is all too common of assigning struggling readers texts that are too difficult. Yet, that is precisely what most schools have done. Such a plan may make planning lessons easier but the same text makes it unlikely that the lesson will be equally effective for students who present different levels of reading proficiency. Struggling readers often fail in their courses simply because no one has planned a lesson based on either theory or evidence. They fail in science class because they cannot read the text assigned. Such a failure is more a system failure than a student failure but, nonetheless, it is the student who receives the failing grade and pays the cost of being assigned an inappropriate text.

You may be surprised to learn that the reading level of the average sixth-grade student is somewhere between the middle fourth- and eighth-grade reading levels. The bottom quarter of the sixth-grade class reads below the fourth-grade level and the top quarter reads at the high school level. You can observe the range of reading achievement found in many classrooms by examining Table 2.1. That table presents the range of reading levels for a national sample of early adolescent readers.

You read Table 2.1 this way. The section on the far left and up until the first bracket represents the reading grade levels of the bottom quarter of all students at that grade level. The area of the line between the brackets represents the reading level range of the middle half of the students and the area of the line to the right of the second bracket represents the reading levels of the top quarter of readers at that grade level. In other words, at seventh-grade level a quarter of the students read somewhere between the second-grade and mid-fifth-grade levels. Half of the seventh-grade students, the middle group, have reading levels between the mid-fifth-grade and the mid-ninth-grade reading levels. A quarter of the seventh graders read between the mid-ninth-grade level and the twelfth-grade level. The range of reading levels at every grade level represents one challenge for teachers of early adolescents. Planning lessons so that students of very different reading levels can succeed is not easy, but it is doable.

Teachers can do many things to facilitate struggling readers' ability to correctly read key academic words. But teaching decoding skills in isolation is unlikely to be the effective choice a teacher might make. Helping students see the syllable structure, fostering their use of words they know so they can decode longer and rarer words, and using the various text tools that are typically available are all necessary routines that teachers of early adolescents must consider.

In the end, though, all teachers need to return to that "ivory tower" lesson planning model they learned in college. In that traditional lesson planning

TABLE 2.1 *Reading Levels of Early Adolescents*

Grade	Range of reading levels
9	....(....)
8	....(....) ....
7	....................................(....) ....
6	..........................(....) ....
5	..............(...................) ....
RL	2 3 4 5 6 7 8 9 10 11 12

Source: From Hargis, 2006, Table 1, p. 394. Reprinted with permission of Phi Delta Kappan International, www.pdkintl.org. All rights reserved.

event, the second step, the one that follows choosing what you are going to teach, requires you to locate "appropriate" instructional texts. *Appropriate* means texts that meet students where they are developmentally in content learning and developmentally in terms of how well they have developed their reading proficiencies.

Always remember that no research and no theory supports one-size-fits-all instruction. Children differ and because of that much of what makes teaching effectively lies in the ability of the teacher to provide a multi-level and multi-sourced lesson that achieves the learning goal. Effective teaching is always both difficult and rewarding. When teaching becomes "easy," too many pupils fail to learn much because not enough effort went into designing effective instruction.

Chapter 3

"It's the Words, Man": Limited Meaning Vocabulary and How to Improve It

Words are important. The number of words one knows the meaning of has been used as a measure of intelligence. We say someone is "well spoken" when they impress us with the words they use when making an argument to support an assertion. And the number of words we know in a particular domain stands largely as evidence of our expertise in that domain.

For instance, reading specialists all know the meaning of the term "basal reader." That term is also familiar to most elementary education teachers. But the term is less familiar, or entirely unfamiliar, to many middle school and high school teachers. A basal reader is that thick anthology of reading selections often used in grades K through 4. It is also what we mean when we speak of a "core reading program," though it is not precisely identical because not all core reading programs have that thick book with all those excerpted stories and most core reading programs have more pieces than just that thick anthology.

I mention basal reader programs because if you do not know what they are, you also probably are unsure about how to pronounce the word *basal* (*bay sul*). In English knowledge of a word's meaning typically goes hand in hand with knowing the correct pronunciation of the word when it is encountered in print. Even in graduate school I can tell which of my students are secondary teachers based on their responses to the word *basal*. Sometimes when they ask a question they will pronounce the word *bass ul,* or *buh sal*. When writing the word they will spell it *basil* or *basel*. All the mispronunciations and misspellings, however, are good phonetic attempts to pronounce or write the word, though they are often incorrect. And even when I have clarified for these students the pronunciation and meaning of this word, my secondary teacher students still know a lot less about the meaning of the word than do my elementary grade teachers, many of whom have used a basal reader program as part of their reading instruction.

Like my middle and secondary school teachers and basal readers, early adolescents will encounter many new academic words in their content-area classes (e.g., science, social studies, mathematics, etc.). Like my middle and secondary school teachers they may never have heard the words they must read before and they have no experience with the words or with what those words mean.

As Stahl (1999) noted, "A richer vocabulary does not just mean that we know more words, but that we have more complex and exact ways of talking about the world, and of understanding the ways more complex thinkers see the world" (p. 1).

In the most general terms students from low-income families arrive at school knowing many fewer words, exhibiting knowledge of perhaps one-third of the words that young middle-class students know (Hart & Risley, 1995). Too often poor children never make up this initial deficit, especially if they struggle with learning to read. Additionally, students from low-income families read less outside of school than do their peers who are financially better off. Some of this deficit results from their schooling where there is a focus on skills development while reducing the volume of reading that students are expected to do (Valli, Croninger, Chambliss, Graeber, & Bluese, 2008). Some of the deficit is derived from the smaller school and classroom libraries found in schools serving many students from low-income families (Guice, Allington, Johnston, Baker, & Michaelson,

1996). And some of the deficit in vocabulary stems from the failure to read much outside the school day and school year (Allington & McGill-Franzen, 2013).

We found, for instance, that simply providing low-income students with 12 self-selected books to read over the summer improved their reading achievement as much as did attending summer school (Allington et al., 2010)! That these students also developed a larger vocabulary is not surprising since most words we know are words we acquired while reading independently. The best estimates we have are that children add about 3,000 new words every year they are in school, although explicit instruction accounts for only about 300 of those words in most classrooms. In other words, most of the unknown words students learn the meanings for are words they encounter while reading voluntarily (Stahl, 1999). However, neither students from low-income families nor students who struggle with reading engage in much voluntary reading, in or out of school. This means that every year they are in school their level of vocabulary knowledge falls further and further behind their better-off and better-reading peers!

Students with better reading achievement read more than students who are struggling with learning to read. By the end of third grade the better readers have already engaged in reading roughly two to three million more words in texts than the struggling readers. These differences in volume of reading practice represent one critical deficiency of older struggling readers. As Stanovich, West, Cunningham, Cipielewski, and Siddiqui (1996) reported on their study of reading growth between third and sixth grades:

> In short, exposure to print is efficacious regardless of the level of the child's cognitive and comprehension abilities. Even children with limited comprehension skills will build vocabulary and cognitive structures through immersion in literacy activities. . . . Inadequate exposure to print prevents children from building important knowledge structures such as vocabulary, meta-linguistic knowledge, and general world knowledge. These knowledge sources are necessary for efficient reading comprehension at the more advanced levels. (p. 29)

In other words, even struggling readers who read more benefited from this additional practice, benefited as much, in terms of growth, as did normally achieving readers. One strategy for improving both the vocabulary and comprehension of early-adolescent struggling readers, then, is to increase the amount of reading they actually do. Ideally, this increase in reading activity would focus mostly on reading self-selected books and magazines. We have recently finished a study of providing low-achieving and low-income middle school students with two free magazine subscriptions over several years. The students were in sixth grade in two rural Tennessee county-wide school districts. We simply provided some of the sixth-graders with 2 magazines that they selected from a pool of about 30 magazines. We did not provide magazines for the remaining students; they became our control, or comparison, group. The magazines were generally not available in their school libraries and focused on topics of interest to middle school students. The magazines were generally not available in their school libraries and focused on topics of interest to middle school students (Gabriel, Allington & Billen, 2012).

The boys in this study selected a number of different magazines but *GamePro* and *North American Whitetail* were the magazines they most commonly selected. Simply providing these magazines improved reading achievement for the students, but it was almost impossible to generate a single reading difficulty level for the magazines. Using traditional readability procedures (Flesch, Dale-Chall, Lexile, etc.), the difficulty, or readability, of the magazines often selected was almost always above the reading achievement levels these students had earned on standardized achievement tests. On top of that, we found that the kids could accurately read these magazines rated to too difficult for them by the readability procedures.

Our results simply reminded us that all readability procedures only provide *estimates* of the text's level of difficulty. It also made us even more aware of the fact that both interest in a topic (computer games, deer hunting) and background knowledge on that topic are important considerations when attempting to match

Chall's *Qualitative Analysis of Text Difficulty* (1996)

We were initially drawn to this instrument because it had specific scales for different genres (Literature, Popular Fiction, Physical Science, Life Science, Narrative Social Studies, Informational Social Studies). We found that the popular fiction scale was the best fit for all of the magazines. Magazines with a focus on hunting or electronic gaming did not fit into the physical or life science scales because they did not typically assume scientific background knowledge or scientific vocabulary.

Unlike the readability formulas, the QATD considers the following categories that contribute to text difficulty in popular fiction: familiarity and range of vocabulary; familiarity and length of sentence structures; depth and breadth of required background knowledge; and required cultural or literary knowledge. The QATD is therefore designed with a focus on reading with understanding rather than word recognition and sentence reading fluency as measured by traditional readability formulas.

In addition, the QATD involves human judgments about text difficulty. Sample texts of each type at various grade levels are offered in the QATD and you must rate the text you are examining by deciding which level of the sample texts best approximates the text you are examining.

students with texts they can actually read. In the end we found that the Chall, Bissex, Conard, and Harris-Sharples' text, *Qualitative Analysis of Text Difficulty* (1996), was the most useful for estimating text difficulty and I suggest you consider using it if examining text difficulty, or readability, is of interest to you.

A central factor in expanding the vocabulary of early adolescents is expanding the volume of reading they do. However, it seems that even modest amounts of daily reading (e.g., 10 minutes) can have an enormously positive effect. Struggling early-adolescent readers arrive at middle school with huge deficits in reading practice. While it may be unlikely that we will expand their reading activity to the point where they catch up with their better reader classmates (which might require 3 or 4 hours of daily reading throughout the middle school years), working to bring the level of reading activity these students engage in to the level of their better reading classmates is not difficult but it does require a plan. You will find more information to support such planning in Chapter 8.

Textbooks May Be the Problem, Not the Answer

Given all the criticisms that have been made of the standard school textbook, it surprises me that many middle and high schools still accept the single textbook model, or the one-size-fits-all model, as typical practice. Here are some of the criticisms of standard textbooks used in science, social studies, English, and mathematics classes.

Too-Hard Text

Many students in grades 5 through 9 struggle to learn from content-area textbooks that don't match their reading levels (as do many students in grades 10 through 12). As one ninth-grader told me, "You can't learn much from a book you can't read." I'm not sure his teacher understood that he couldn't read the textbook she had assigned him. I say this because in my later discussion with his earth science teacher there was no indication that she knew this young man had a reading problem. But he did have a reading problem! His tested reading level at the end of eighth grade was fifth grade, fifth month. Roughly a quarter of all ninth-graders have reading levels at the sixth-grade level or below, so this student was not an exception (Hargis, 2006). However, no one had ever provided his teacher with any indication his reading was so far below grade level. Of with student record files increasingly available online, it is easier today for teachers to look up students' reading levels. Unfortunately, they often don't.

Worse—for this student and other struggling readers in her classes—this teacher used a single commercial earth science textbook for all of her earth science classes. This was a textbook with a difficulty level equivalent to the eleventh-grade reading level! From a national perspective, only about 25 percent of ninth-graders could be expected to read that text with understanding. In others words, three of four students in these earth science classes cannot be expected to learn much earth science from this textbook.

Perhaps someone else selected the earth science textbook this teacher was using. Basically though, it doesn't matter who selected that textbook: It was simply too difficult for the ninth-grade students this teacher taught (and too difficult for the majority of ninth-graders in the United States). My hunch is that the person or team that selected this textbook never actually estimated its readability level. Instead, they assumed that if the textbook company marketed the book as a ninth-grade textbook, then the readability level must be appropriate. Always keep in mind that for textbook publishers, and for their sale representatives, the best textbook is the one that sells the most copies. Also always remember that the typical science and social studies textbooks used in American middle and high schools have readability levels one to three grade levels above the grade level it is assigned to (Budiansky, 2001; Chall & Conard, 1991).

One of my concerns with the CCSS is that much of the focus is on providing students with more complex texts. The last thing struggling early adolescents need is texts even harder than the ones they have today. What we do know is that older struggling readers (in this case fifth-grade students reading at the third-grade level) benefit most when they are given texts that match their reading levels, not texts that match, much less exceed, their current grade level (O'Connor et al., 2002). Struggling readers who were tutored using classroom texts (grade-level materials) made virtually no progress in advancing their reading development while students who were tutored using texts matched to reading level (in this case third-grade reading level) made accelerated reading growth. In addition, students tutored with grade-level texts learned less science and social studies content than students tutored in texts matching their reading levels. Thus, if we continue to distribute grade-level textbooks to all students, many students will learn little and will improve little.

Chall (1983) noted that the demands of reading increase dramatically for students beginning in the fifth grade as their learning begins to rely more on textbooks. The vocabulary they encounter is less conversational and less familiar, with more specialized, technical terms (delta, plateau, basin) and abstract ideas (democracy, freedom, civilization). The syntax of texts becomes more complex and demanding. The reasoning about information in texts also shifts, with a greater emphasis on inferential thinking and prior knowledge. (For example, "What were the causes of the Boston Tea Party?")

Many students who have been making satisfactory progress up to this point now begin to struggle with reading, especially content-area reading. Many never seem to recover.

Schools have typically exacerbated these problems by relying on a single-source curriculum design—purchasing multiple copies of the same science and social studies textbooks (as well as the same mathematics textbook, the same literature anthology, and so on) for every student. This "one-size-fits-all" approach works well if we want to sort students into academic tracks, but it fails miserably if our goal is high academic achievement for all students (Baumann & Duffy, 1997).

As noted earlier, even your students who read on grade level may have difficulty reading their textbooks. Basically, the problem is that the scores given on group administered reading tests have a large standard error of measurement. That means that a score earned by any given student is likely inaccurate – too low or too high. Group standardized tests typically include warnings not to use the individual scores for placing students in texts. Group tests can provide useful information about the average reading level of different groups of students because that is what they were designed to do. In other words, you could get reliable information that tells you your first period class has a higher reading level than your second period class. But that is about all any group test can be expected to provide.

The level of accuracy of oral reading of independent level texts, texts used as assigned reading that will be read independently (as opposed to read in small teacher-led group, is 99 to 100 percent accurate reading of all words in the text. When accuracy falls below this level understanding what you are reading becomes problematic. Problematic because you recognize too few words for context facilitation to occur. Not being able to pronounce almost all of the words means that when you encounter a new word you probably cannot deduce it's meaning. It isn't the high-frequency words that on-level readers won't be able to pronounce. Instead, it is the key content or academic vocabulary that will remain unrecognized. Words such as *commensalism* or *phloem* cells. It is precisely the meaning of words such as these words that is the central aspect of learning in the content areas. Such academic vocabulary must be introduced before students are assigned content area reading.

If you plan to use textbooks in the common "assign then assess" approach, then selecting texts that students can read with 99 percent accuracy is a reasonable idea. Even when students cannot recognize one of every one hundred words (99% accuracy) they will still then encounter three to five words on every page of their textbooks that they do not recognize. Imagine the frustration you might feel if I had written this text such that every page had that many words you couldn't pronounce and didn't know the meaning of!

While engaging students in the reading of more texts of greater complexity is a central theme of the Common Core State Standards the potential downside of increasing text difficulty is that our current students with reading proficiencies that are below grade level will only be more likely to have an even greater number of assigned texts that they cannot read. Nonetheless, harder textbooks have captured the fancy of politicians and state agency officials but neither group actually has to teach using these harder texts.

I wish we had some evidence that using more complex texts actually improved reading development. Unfortunately, we don't. Texts currently used in middle school are already complex texts for some students. Doing a better job of introducing those texts or selecting alternative texts are about the only things middle school teachers can do (Beck, McKeown, & Gromoll, 1989: Herber, 1978). if they want their students to learn the subject matter. Observations of exemplary content- area teachers suggest that these teachers use both approaches to produce substantial reading, writing, and thinking growth in their students.

How Exemplary Teachers Avoid the Textbook Problem

As noted earlier, I was a member of a research team working out of the National Research Center for English Learning and Achievement at the University at Albany, conducting a large-scale research study to understand how some of America's most effective teachers teach. The research team studied teachers in six states with reputations for excellent teaching and who produced superior learning levels in their students as indicated by a variety of measures of student achievement, including standardized test scores. These effective teachers designed and implemented classroom instruction that combined multiple-level content texts as well as instructional support for struggling readers (Allington, 2002; Allington & Johnston, 2002; Langer, 2001; 2004; Nystrand, 2006; Presssley, Wharton-McDonald, Mistretta-Hampton, & Echevarria, 1998; Pressley et al., 2001).

The exemplary teachers we studied were not typically familiar with the research that supported the sort of teaching that they offered. None had seen the findings of a recent study of success and failure in high school:

> *Research in adolescence suggests that students will be more successful at new tasks when the tasks they face are closely targeted to their academic skills, developmental stage, and the resources they bring to that task and when families and schools structure tasks in ways that provide appropriate levels of challenge and support. (Roderick & Camburn, 1999, p. 336)*

Nonetheless, these exemplary teachers provided instruction that fit Roderick and Camburn's prescription almost perfectly.

Multiple Levels of Instructional Resources

First, exemplary teachers created a multi-sourced and multi-leveled curriculum that did not rely on traditional content-area textbooks. The single textbook that all students had was used but it was used only one or two days per week, and it was used as only one part of the printed curriculum materials from which the students read and learned their academic content.

Second, the exemplary teachers offered students "managed choice" as they learned content and demonstrated what they had learned. Managed choice is different from free choice. In the former the teacher selects multiple texts that students might read to acquire what they need to know. In the latter, free choice, students might attempt to find such texts but the texts selected are less likely a good fit with content as lesson goals.

The exemplary teachers offered instruction tailored to each student's individual needs. Their classes experienced more personalized teaching spent less time on whole-group lecture and recitation activities. Other researchers studying effective teaching at the fifth- through ninth-grade levels have reported similar findings (Keene, 2002; Knapp, 1995; Langer, 2001, 2004; Nystrand, 2006; Taylor, Pearson, Clark, & Walpole, 2000).

These teachers provided models and demonstrations of the strategies that learners use when confronted with unfamiliar words or with difficult text. They demonstrated these strategies in the context of the material that the student was reading or composing. In other words, none of the exemplary teachers used scripted one-size-fits-all instructional materials.

Good teaching is what struggling early-adolescent readers need—good teaching all day long. But until more states and school districts dramatically modify their existing mandates concerning one-size-fits-all instructional resources and curriculum frameworks, many students won't receive the support they need to succeed in content-area learning. Too many students will continue to be handed textbooks that they cannot read with understanding. Many of these students will fail to learn much because their problem is a problem with one-size-fits-all lessons.

Textbooks that are too difficult for struggling readers have been termed "inconsiderate" textbooks. Even when students are given textbooks they can read accurately and with understanding, those textbooks can still be inconsiderate. There was a spike in the interest of researchers in the quality of textbooks about 30 years ago. Anderson and Armbruster (1984) conducted a series of studies and from these derived a list of features of "considerate" textbooks. Considerate

> ### *Features of Considerate Textbooks*
>
> Considers age of audience
>
> Does not make assumptions about readers' prior knowledge
>
> Uses everyday and scientific language
>
> Defines and explains new concepts and vocabulary
>
> Uses concise, but not dense, sentences
>
> Follows logical organization within and across sections
>
> Aims to engage students as they begin reading new assignment
>
> Provides scaffolds and supports for students and teachers
>
> *Source:* Anderson and Armbruster (1984).

textbooks are the opposite of inconsiderate textbooks. Their list of considerate text features (see the accompanying feature box) should be central to any evaluation of textbooks you or others in your school might be considering.

I would expand the final item to include resources in the text for the correct pronunciation of longer and less frequent but important words, the academic vocabulary. Vocabulary is one of two central features of all procedures for estimating text difficulty. The other feature used in all estimations of text difficulty is sentence length, which is the fifth item in Anderson and Armbruster's (1984) list of features of considerate texts. A few readability procedures also use a measure of word frequency in their estimations of text difficulty (e.g., Dale-Chall, Lexile), which is the third item on Anderson and Armbruster's list. Words matter when it comes to thinking about text difficulty and when it comes to learning content-area subjects. That is why the fourth item in the list indicates that considerate textbooks provide students with definitions when new academic vocabulary is introduced. All students benefit from good vocabulary instruction but struggling readers benefit more than anyone else.

Fostering Vocabulary Growth

I hope you are now convinced that focusing some of your instruction on fostering vocabulary development is an essential idea. In the following section I sketch several evidence-based routines for fostering students' understanding of words they have never seen (and often never heard) before.

The first questions you will need to answer are provided by Allen (1999). She lists a series of questions to ask before preparing to select the words for vocabulary instruction:

1. Which new words are important to understanding the text?
2. How much prior knowledge will students have about this word and its related concepts?

3. Is the word encountered frequently in the text?
4. Does the word have multiple meanings?
5. Can the word meaning be derived from the context?

Selecting the right words to focus instruction on is the critical first step in effective vocabulary lesson design. Pat Cunningham (2009) notes that you need to select the words carefully, or, as she wrote, select words "as if you were paying for each word and needed to keep them forever" (p. 71). Once you have used these questions to guide your selection of which words to teach, thinking about how to develop word meanings comes next.

Reed and Vaughn (2010) note: "Studies have found that vocabulary instruction employing semantic maps and semantic feature analysis is more effective in improving students' vocabulary and comprehension performance than traditional methods relying on dictionary definitions . . . " (p. 156).

Relying on dictionary definitions seems the most common procedure for fostering vocabulary development. While knowing how to use a dictionary is both powerful and useful, in truth few adults ever use a dictionary, especially to identify the meaning of an unknown word. Few students ever acquire an understanding of a word from the traditional instruction to "Look the word up in the dictionary, write down the definition, and use the word in a sentence." But such assignments seem too common in schools, especially given the evidence of the fruitlessness of this approach.

Instead of sending students to the dictionary to look up words and copy out the definition, there are several other options to consider. First, engage students in the activities described in Chapter 2. Simply aiding students in acquiring the correct pronunciations of new and unknown words is an important

Dictionary Usage

Take a survey of your classmates or friends by asking them these questions:

Have you looked a word up in the dictionary this week?
If so, were you trying to locate the correct spelling or locate the word's meaning?
Or did you look up the word for another reason?

Based on my experience, I expect you will find that fewer than 1 of every 20 adults of whom you ask these questions will indicate they were searching for a word's meaning. Although some will have checked on the word's spelling, that reason for dictionary usage has been dropping steadily since spell checking capability was introduced in word processing software.

step. But learning each word's meaning is the ultimate goal if we want students to be able to understand their textbooks and acquire content knowledge.

Semantic Webs

As noted above by Reed and Vaughn (2010), semantic maps, or semantic webs, are one useful tool for fostering vocabulary knowledge. A semantic web is illustrated in Figure 3.1. The steps in developing a predictive semantic web are:

1. Write the targeted academic vocabulary word in the space at the center of the web.
2. Encourage students to think of as many words as they can that relate to the target word.
3. As students offer words, write those words in the circles.
4. At least initially you should help students categorize each of the words they've offered and have the students list the features under the appropriate category.
5. Now explain, as necessary, how the categories and words are related to the text(s) they will be reading.

FIGURE 3.1 *Semantic Web*

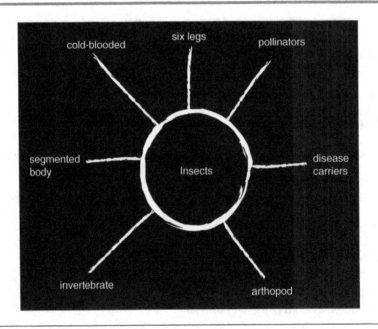

6. After the students have the read the assigned text(s), have students return to their semantic webs and see if the categorizations should be changed. You might also ask them to offer additional words they read that would fit on the web.

7. Over time, as students become more familiar with the semantic web activity, you can pair them up to create their own webs they will share both before and after reading the text(s).

The initial responses—the words offered—will help you estimate how much background knowledge students have on the word featured and how much scaffolding you can be expected to provide. One reason semantic webs seem to work to foster vocabulary growth is that they focus student attention on only a few key academic words central to understanding the topic under study. A second reason is that it helps students understand the word in a sense much greater than is found using the dictionary.

Semantic Feature Analysis (SFA)

Pittelman (1991) offered a description of the SFA procedure:

1. Select a category related to topic/unit of study. For example, African nations, the American Revolution, transportation, water, life forms, free markets, and so on.

2. Then list words in the category on the left side of chart or on a transparency. Begin with words likely to be familiar to students.

3. Now list features across the top of the chart. Typically, these features represent characteristics, traits, or properties of words/concepts listed on the left side of the chart.

4. Determine which features the first two words possess with students. Use a plus sign to indicate the presence of a feature and a minus sign to indicate that feature is absent for each word. When students are unsure about a feature, use a question mark to indicate this.

5. Have students work together to complete the feature analysis of the words on the grid. Students may need to read to collect the information needed for this. You might have students note where they located the information needed to complete each item. This is especially useful if students disagree about whether a feature is present or absent.

6. Once the students have completed their grids discuss the completed grid with them. This discussion is a central component and is most effective when students do most of the discussion of common features of the items the words represent as well as distinguishing features.

Semantic Gradients

Cunningham (2009) suggests the use of semantic gradients to foster vocabulary growth. She presents the opposites, *wealthy* and *destitute,* as one example. One semantic gradient for these two words would look like this:

wealthy   prosperous   affluent   rich   well-off   poor   broke   penniless   destitute

She notes there are several ways to construct and use semantic gradients. You might create the semantic gradient and write the words on the blackboard (or white board or smart board). Then you would read each of the words aloud to the students. Virtually all students will be familiar with the terms *rich* and *poor* in the gradient above but you will have to explain what the other words mean and why they are located where they are on the gradient.

Greenwood and Flanigan (2007) provide other examples. For instance, two words of opposite meaning were drawn from a story assigned for an American literature course. The two words were *despondent* and *euphoric*. The semantic gradient they created is shown below.

despondent   glum   sad   unhappy   happy   elated   euphoric

Again, middle school students will likely know the meanings of the words in the center (*sad, unhappy, happy*) but will likely be unfamiliar with the remaining words (*despondent, glum, elated, euphoric*). The same is true in the following example.

prehistoric   ancient   old   new   modern   futuristic

The use of semantic gradients does not work for every new vocabulary word, but it works often enough to be a useful routine for fostering vocabulary growth. This is true, in part, because the use of synonym-like lists help students understand the small meaning shifts that occur from word to word across the semantic gradient.

Conclusion

Semantic webs, semantic feature analysis, and semantic gradients have all been shown experimentally to foster substantial vocabulary development. While either activity takes but a few minutes to complete, and all readers will benefit from taking the time to complete such activities, struggling readers will benefit the most.

Extensive Reading

As noted earlier, most of the words you know are words that no one ever taught you. They are words you learned as you read on your own. Since it is around grade 5 when voluntary reading activity begins to decline, it is in the early-adolescent years when schools can accomplish much just by creating an environment in which all readers, but especially struggling readers, read both in and out of school. Fielding, Wilson, and Anderson (1986) noted that,

> We found that among all the ways children can spend their leisure time, average minutes per day reading was the most consistent predictor of standardized comprehension test performance, size of vocabulary, and gains in reading achievement between second and fifth grade. . . . There is a particular form to the relationship between amount of book reading and reading achievement. Specifically, the first few minutes a day of reading are associated with sharp increases in achievement. After that, for each additional minute of reading there are smaller and smaller increments in achievement. The data suggest that if children could be induced to spend as few as 10 minutes a day, on average, voluntarily reading books their reading proficiency would improve considerably. (p. 151)

They studied the out-of-school behaviors of fifth-grade students. What was striking to me, as a reader, was the large number of fifth-graders who read nothing outside of school. Also striking was the finding that indicated that only 10 minutes of daily reading outside of school was the most powerful amount of time in terms of enhancing reading achievement.

Few teachers of early adolescents create inviting environments for reading out of school. This, I believe, is one reason why there are out-of-school reading declines beginning in the fifth grade. In addition, fewer teachers of early adolescents, when compared to teachers in grades K through 4, read aloud to their students, fewer middle school teachers offer "book bites" (reading aloud a sample of the text but not reading the complete text aloud to students), and fewer middle school teachers provide large classroom libraries with hundreds of books their students cannot wait to read.

Worthy, Moorman, and Turner (1999) studied the reading done by sixth-grade students. They found that what these students read was rarely available in schools. What sixth-grade readers read outside of school rarely came from the school; school libraries and classroom libraries were the two least used sources for what sixth-grade students read! Worthy and her colleagues comment:

> The results showed that the majority of students obtained their preferred reading materials from home and stores rather than from schools and libraries. Classrooms ranked a distant last for availability of interesting books or magazines, even among low-income students. (p. 24)

The sorts of books these sixth-graders wanted to read covered topics such as:

scary books

comics and cartoons

books and magazines about popular culture

books and magazines about sports

Interestingly, these are the same topics chosen by the students who selected books and magazines in our studies (Allington et al., 2010; Gabriel, Allington, & Billen, 2009). Given the popularity among adults of Stephen King's novels, the daily comics in the newspaper, and *People* and *Sports Illustrated* magazines, it may be that early-adolescent readers simply prefer to read the same sort of material that most adults read! In any event, the study by Worthy and her colleagues (1999) suggests that middle schools typically do little to foster an interest in out-of-school reading.

Reading Aloud to Students

Here is another short survey you could do. Ask a number of middle or high school teachers how often they read books aloud to their students.

Reading aloud to students—even to middle and high school students—is an easy way to develop both content and vocabulary knowledge, and to foster an interest in reading outside of school (Worthy, Broaddus, & Ivey, 2001).

Such read-aloud activities do not need to consume much class time. The most efficient use of the read-aloud option occurs when teachers begin class by reading aloud to students. This activity settles students into class. Time typically spent getting the class settled in is replaced by a short read-aloud period. For this to be an effective routine, what is being read aloud must be of interest to the majority of the students. Again, teachers can develop this interest simply by preparing the students before reading aloud to them. By this I mean describing just why this book is interesting at this point in time and perhaps setting students up for discovery. For instance, if I were a sixth-grade social studies teacher and my students were going to be studying the American Civil War, selecting a book such as Beatty's *Turn Homeward, Hannalee* might be my choice.

This historical novel presents a true incident of a 12-year-old girl and her younger brother who are both working in a southern factory that makes Confederate uniforms. Hannalee and her brother are captured by the Union army when the Union forces take the town. Both are convicted of treason and Hannalee is to be shipped north to Indiana to work as an indentured servant for Union families that have lost a son in the war. Her brother is to be sent to a northern prisoner of war camp. Hannalee manages to disguise her brother as a girl and gets him on the train taking her north. After a short while working on an unfriendly farm she and her brother escape and flee south, hoping to return to their mother who was left, pregnant, at their burned-down farm house. I'll stop there but it isn't hard to get sixth-graders interested in this book because few have ever considered what life was like for 12-year-olds during the Civil War era.

But there are also many other books I could choose from—some easier, some harder, some shorter, some longer. For instance, Murphy's *The Boys' War* is written by a historian and uses the diaries and letters written by drummer boys, North and South, about their lives in combat during the Civil War. Again, virtually all of the boys featured in the book are early-adolescent boys. A central feature that makes this book so appealing is Murphy's use of photographs of the boys featured and of boys in the Civil War armies. This book does not present war as an attractive venture. At the same time, the most horrific events are not exceptionalized either. Being a drummer boy is depicted as dangerous and more often boring than anything else.

Both of these books present a multitude of vocabulary linked to the Civil War era and present key aspects of that war that are too often ignored by history textbooks. Reading either, or both, aloud will foster vocabulary and relevant concept development and enhance the opportunity to learn more about the Civil War.

One thing we have learned about students' reading outside of school is that the teachers of the students are far more influential than the parents of the students. When classroom teachers read aloud from powerful and appropriate books, students of those teachers are far more likely to read voluntarily outside of school. But the typical middle school has few teachers who read aloud every day or who bless books their students might read. These are books that will foster interest in the topic the class is studying and build academic vocabulary and world knowledge, both essential to reading with understanding.

If we intend to reverse the current pattern of decreasing amounts of voluntary reading outside of school that begins around grade 5, then we need to help our students locate books that they can read accurately and with understanding. Teachers reading aloud is one proven routine for fostering increased voluntary reading in middle and high schools (Ivey, 2010).

Discussion and Vocabulary Development

While there is less research on the effects of classroom discussions on student learning, Nystrand (2006) reviews what we know about the effects of discussion on adolescent learning. He notes that the studies that have been done all indicate that discussion is a rare phenomenon in middle and high school classrooms. It is even rarer in classrooms where most of the students are poor readers. When struggling readers are tracked into classrooms together, we can expect discussions of 3 minutes in length. It is shocking, actually, when contrasted with the 12- to 13-minute discussions in classrooms serving higher achieving students. If, as Nystrand (2006) and others (Almasi & Garas-York, 2009; Applebee, Langer, Nystrand, & Gamoran, 2003; Anderson, 2009; Elleman, Lindo, Morphy, & Compton, 2009; Mueller, 2001; Schmoker, 2011; Wiske, 1998) argue, discussion fosters vocabulary and concept development and improves reading comprehension at least as much as any other instructional activity, we might ask why our struggling students rarely get involved in discussions in class and even why discussions are relatively rare for high-achieving students.

Professional Books on Developing Students' Vocabulary

Allen, J. (1999). *Words, words, words; Teaching vocabulary in grades 4-12.* York, ME: Stenhouse.

Beck, I. L., McKeown, M. G., & Kucan, L. (2002). *Bringing words to life: Robust vocabulary instruction.* New York: Guilford.

Cunningham, P. M. (2009). *What really matters in vocabulary: Research-based practices across the curriculum.* Boston: Pearson Allyn & Bacon.

Graves, M. F. (2006). *The vocabulary book: Learning and instruction.* New York: Teachers College Press.

Stahl, S. A., & Nagy, W. (2009). *Teaching word meanings.* Mahwah, NJ: Erlbaum.

Technology and Learning to Read

Rather than building expansive classroom or school library collections that will serve to foster such student growth, too many schools, in my view, have invested heavily in computers and software in hopes of improving reading proficiency. Take the scenario Ivey and Fisher (2006) describe in which a student is sitting at a computer reading a passage about the rainforest. The software includes music in the background. The student can click on any word he or she doesn't know and the computer will provide the pronunciation and a definition. After reading the passage the computer produces a multiple-choice test about passage content that provides immediate feedback about the correctness of each response the student makes. Here is what Ivey and Fisher (2006) conclude:

> Now take away the music and the clickable features and what do you have? It's a textbook passage. It's easy to find a program like this one but difficult to ascertain what students learn about reading or writing from such a program. Having students read and answer questions to check their understanding is certainly not a new idea even if it is packaged in an attractive software program. Such routines have never been useful in helping improve students' reading. (p. 79)

Indeed, as mentioned earlier, the large-scale federal research study on such programs found no evidence of improved reading achievement. In fact, James-Burdumy and her colleagues (2010) report that some of these computer-based commercial programs actually produced a negative effect on reading achievement. Finally, after reviewing almost 100 experimental studies Slavin, Lake, Davis, and Madden (2009) concluded: "Traditional computer-assisted instruction programs have little impact on reading" (p. 113–114).

So why do we see so many schools using computer-based "solutions" to the problems struggling readers face? Perhaps as Cuban (2001) noted a decade ago,

> To educators, dependent on voters and taxpayers for funds and political legitimacy, it often matters little whether the new technology is costly and fully tested to do what vendors and promoters say it can do. Pressed by parents, business leaders, public officials, and computer vendors, few school boards and school administrators can resist the tidal wave of opinion in favor of electronic solutions to education's age old problems" (p. 192).

Additionally, providing computer-based reading instruction makes it look like the school is doing something even if that something isn't working to solve the problems struggling readers present.

A quarter century ago I wrote an article describing the case of a middle school struggling reader named Jeremy (Allington, Boxer, & Broikou, 1987).

Jeremy attended a remedial reading period every day, and every day he worked on a computer trying to develop his vocabulary. But while attempting to read his assigned textbooks, Jeremy encountered word after word he couldn't read and didn't know the meanings of, though none of those words ever appeared on the computer screen. Instead, he was exposed to 20 new words every day but not words that had any short-term utility. Jeremy benefited little from his remedial reading class and he flunked seventh grade. It would be more accurate to say that it was his middle school that flunked because Jeremy did everything they asked him to do.

Similar to the situation Ivey and Fisher described above, Jeremy basically was completing electronic worksheets that presented a word in isolation along with four options as to its meaning. He had to keep clicking until he located the correct response. Every day he worked on these words that he typically could not pronounce. Jeremy did not become a reader but it wasn't because of any lack of effort on his part. I wrote the article because Jeremy was a special education student and I knew that the poverty of effective resources could not be due to a lack of funding. The federal government spends about $10,000 annually for every pupil with a disability. some of which I hope goes to teaching students like Jeremy how to read.

I wish I could say that Jeremy was the only case I've ever seen like that, but I can't because, in my experience, Jeremy's case is more often typical of what schools provide older struggling readers. They too often provide these students not with the opportunity to engage in large amounts of self-selected reading but, rather, time to complete low-level computerized worksheets, traditional worksheets, or some other activity that no research has ever supported as fostering reading growth.

Enticing Early Adolescents to Read

There are any number of strategies that teachers of early adolescents and their schools might use to stimulate more extensive independent reading. Perhaps the first question that needs to be asked is, "How many books that each student *can read* and *wants to read* are easily accessible in your classroom?" Access is, simply, the most important factor if we want to entice students to expand their reading activity—especially when the students are struggling readers.

Imagine you are in a back room at a major university library. The room has heat, light, furniture, and a supply of books, but the books are all old and all are on the topic of Crohn's disease. In addition, these books are all medical reference texts, meant to be read by researchers studying Crohn's disease and related topics. So what you have is a ready supply of difficult-to-read books on an arcane topic that you may have no familiarity with and no interest in. You have easy access to a supply of books of little interest to you. How many of these books do you think you will read?

This is a situation similar, in many respects, to that in which early-adolescent struggling readers find themselves. They are surrounded by books they are neither interested in reading nor able to read with understanding. Now you may see why struggling readers are typically not readers. Worse for early adolescents is that often they feel as if they are mingling every day with the researchers who might visit the room in the university library. These researchers can read the books and are interested in the books' topic, and they know quite a bit about Crohn's disease. You listen to their discussions but understand almost nothing. It is enough to drive you mad. If we hope to entice all early adolescents to read more extensively, then you will have to create classrooms that are wholly unlike that room in the library.

Access and Choice

Guthrie and Humenick (2004) conducted a meta-analysis on a number of studies designed to improve both reading comprehension and reading engagement. Most of these studies were done with early-adolescent populations. They report that two factors had huge effects on both reading comprehension and engagement. Increasing students' access to books they found interesting produced an effect 10 times as large as the effect explicit phonics instruction had in the NRP meta-analysis! The two factors that had the most powerful influence on improving reading comprehension were access to interesting reading materials and student choice of reading materials. Too few middle schools score well on either factor. Middle school classrooms need large and multi-level collections of books that students cannot wait to read as well as lessons constructed around student self-selection from a list of books related to the topic at hand.

Research provides no clear information on the number of titles reflecting a particular range of reading difficulty as precisely adequate. But we do know that far too many classrooms attended by early adolescents have few books titles and even fewer books that struggling readers can read accurately and with understanding (Ivey & Fisher, 2006; Worthy, Moorman, & Turner, 1999). Far too many classrooms have multiple copies of older trade books that students rarely find interesting. As one sixth-grader told me about the book, *The Outsiders* by Hinton, "It's a book about how teenagers used to be, like when my grandma was a teenager." When I asked this young woman if she liked the book, she replied, "Not really, but my teacher likes it." *The Outsiders* was a popular adolescent novel back when I was a fifth-grade teacher. Of course, that was before schools had copy machines, much less computers. I don't mean to pick on this book because I liked it 40 years ago and I liked again last summer when I read it. But I doubt that it speaks to my granddaughters now in middle school.

Today, given their choice, middle school readers would be more likely to choose *The Hunger Games* by Suzanne Collins. This is a novel about a post-apocalyptic America where young adults are randomly chosen each year to represent their regions in a live telecast battle where only one is left alive. A movie is currently available based upon this best-selling book, which makes it an even more attractive selection for early-adolescent readers.

The larger problem is the too widespread use of the "class novel," the use of a single book that all students are expected to read. As Fisher and Ivey (2007) point out, "You have students with a text they do not like, which they are directed to read for purposes other than own, with little time in school to do so" (p. 496). If one wanted to create an unmotivating reading experience, such a plan would be a good start. Selecting a book that is difficult for most students to read is perfect for fostering reading avoidance. Many students will not read the book, will not complete the assigned worksheets, and will not improve their reading proficiency.

Again, Fisher and Ivey (2007) argue that, "Students are not reading more or better as a result of the whole-class novel. Instead, students are reading less and are less motivated, less engaged, and less likely to read in the future" (p. 495). This is the result of plans focusing on teaching books rather than on teaching students that too many schools have created. The end result of such plans is, as Kelly Gallagher (2009) has noted, *readicide*: the killing of any desire to ever read anything voluntarily. Readicide seems the most common outcome of the programs we create for early adolescents.

Over the years when I asked teachers about the use of one-size-fits-all curricula (either a single textbook or a whole-class novel), I've been told they are required to teach such material. Such requirements, though, are not found in state curriculum documents.

As I noted earlier, the first step in planning effective instruction is ensuring that students have texts they can actually read accurately, fluently, and with comprehension. When lesson plans ignore this essential step we can expect lessons to be ineffective for all students. Some have books that are too hard for them while others who can read the book accurately could care less.

Extensive reading, both in reading development classes and in content-area classes, is the most powerful activity teachers can assign. As Miller (2009) argues,

Any activity that substantially replaces extensive reading, writing, and discourse in the classroom needs to be better than the activity it replaces, and nothing, not even test prep, is better for students' reading ability than just plain reading, day after day. (p. 134)

One-size-fits-all curriculum plans are neither scientific nor effective. They make life easier for teachers if they comply and teach the texts available, but they make learning to read and learning science (or social studies, mathematics, or literature) content far more difficult, especially for struggling readers.

Fisher and Ivey (2007) offer the following guidelines for teachers when selecting the texts they will use:

- Identify universal themes and concepts rather than individual titles.
- Select texts that present these themes and concepts.
- Select texts that span a wide range of difficulty levels.
- Select texts that are engaging.
- Orchestrate instruction that builds students' competence.
- Teach reading comprehension strategies using texts that are readable and meaningful.

This then is the planning model for all teachers, not just those teachers who teach struggling readers. Lesson planning, even when using differentiated texts, always requires you to ask, "What background knowledge and what vocabulary do I need to develop before the students are assigned to read this text?" (Brunn, 2010). Vocabulary and background knowledge go together because much of what we call background knowledge is represented by a few critical vocabulary words.

Let's take an example from a book titled, *Herbaceous Perennial Plants* by Alan Armitage. First, read the selection below:

Plants multiply by rhizomes and have alternate leaves, usually grouped in whorls at the end of stems. Although grown mainly for the foliage, the flowers provide interest as well. They are monoecious (male and female flowers on the same inflorescence), and the long stamens of the male flowers give rise to the generic name. . . . The spurges are easily propagated by divisions, or by rooting softwood terminal cuttings in the summer. (p. 436)

Now that you've read this excerpt could you sketch a picture of what this plant is like? Would you disagree with any "fact" the author provides? Are you largely stumped as to how to grow new plants so as to expand your collection? What if I had included the sentence I omitted, where currently there are ellipsis points?

Pachysandra comes from *pachys,* thick, and *andros,* man, in reference to the thick stamens.

Does knowing this is a description of the common groundcover we call pachysandra make the excerpt more understandable? However, even knowing that this excerpt is about pachysandra, you may still be in the dark about the words *rhizomes, whorls, monoecious, stamen, propagated,* and *inflorescence* unless you have some expertise about plants in general. You would also be helped by knowing that a whorl is three or more leaves or flowers in a circle and that the stamen is essential for plant reproduction, and so on. However, not knowing that this bit of text is about pachysandra plants basically creates a real mystery for a reader. This excerpt is from a book for gardeners, not scientists. It would be a good bet that it is a better book for experienced gardeners who are also good readers.

My point here is that one can locate text that is difficult to understand in any field. What makes any of these texts "difficult" for a reader is the lack of familiarity with the vocabulary and basic ideas that would seem "common" to the reader with the appropriate background experience. It is these experiences that build familiarity with the vocabulary and concepts that are central to understanding the writing. Likewise, once we have a general idea of the text's topic, in this case pachysandra, we can make better sense of the writing. That is simply drawing upon what we already know to expand our knowledge of the topic.

Always keep in mind that you are usually teaching a subject you know really well. Your students may be studying that same topic for the first time and will likely be naïve about much of what you take as "common" knowledge—much as I have done with you by assuming everyone has enough lawn care experience to recognize "pachysandra." Assisting students in the development of their expertise in your subject area is precisely what effective teachers do, every day they are teaching.

Summary

Words are not just words. Words are the aural representation of the concepts and the information seen as essential to your subject area. Developing students' vocabulary is central to teaching any topic or subject. Early adolescents vary enormously in the number of words they know and can use effectively. Those early adolescents who have long struggled in developing reading proficiency are the same students who exhibit the smallest vocabularies. These students, in particular, need the strongest vocabulary instruction you can provide.

Fostering growth of vocabulary that is central to the topic or subject of study is an initial aspect of all lesson planning. Helping students understand the pronunciation of these words is the initial phase of vocabulary development. Focusing on syllable structure is, perhaps, the most useful strategy.

Once you have pronounced the new vocabulary words for your students, the next step is focusing on developing students' understanding of their meaning. The most efficient routine in this regard is to simply and directly teach the word meanings. This is different from asking students, "Does anyone know the meaning of this word?" It is different because student responses may further confuse the meaning of the word and because it takes substantially less time to provide word meanings than to engage students in a form of a "20 Questions" game. Whenever possible, link the new word with a word you are sure the students already know.

You might also engage students in more structured word meaning activities such as word webs or semantic gradients. While these routines have been proven effective at fostering student's understanding of word meanings, they also take more time than directly teaching the meanings of new and important words.

Finally, remember that extensive reading is the way your students who possess large vocabularies were able to grow those vocabularies. At the middle school level, expanding the reading of your students on the topics they are studying, as well as independent and self-selected voluntarily reading, is an absolute essential. You will find more information on developing a schoolwide plan for wide reading in the final chapter.

Chapter 4

Read More, Read Better: Addressing a Major Source of Reading Difficulties

As noted in Chapter 3, early adolescence is the point where the amount, or volume, of reading that students do begins to decline. This is true of both reading in and out of school. I'm always puzzled by this because it is at early adolescence when students have begun to develop the ability to read far more texts of far greater variety than in earlier years when their reading proficiency was just developing.

The National Endowment for the Arts released a study in 2007 entitled, *To Read or Not to Read,* which focused on the reading activities of young Americans. They noted that almost half of our young adults report never having read a book for pleasure. Never! Only 20 percent of our nation's 17-year-olds reported having read a book for pleasure in the past year—only one of every five American adolescents. The report also notes that adolescent reading activity has been declining since at least 1984 when these data began to be collected. Today adolescents report spending less time reading than readers in any other age group, and both younger and older people are more likely to read voluntarily than are adolescents. Early adolescents need school experiences that foster their love of reading.

Being able to read but electing not to read is called *aliteracy.* Aliteracy is different from illiteracy, or the inability to read, but perhaps just as damaging to learning. And widespread aliteracy seems to begin in fifth grade or thereabouts. I am unsure why fifth grade is such a marker for the decline of voluntary reading. The time I've spent in schools over the years suggest that far too few fifth-grade classrooms, like classrooms for sixth, seventh, eighth, and ninth grades, have an adequate classroom library. Few teachers of early adolescents read aloud to their students and few allocate much class time to sustained silent reading. As Trelease (2001) notes, "The evidence for reading aloud to children and sustained silent reading is overwhelming—yet most children are neither read to nor experience sustained silent reading in the course of a school day" (p. 107). Consider also that Terenzini, Springer, Pascarella, and Nora (1995) found that students who reported reading more books voluntarily were the college students who earned the highest grades. To put it another way, wide reading is not just the single activity most related to higher reading achievement, it is also a predictor of the grades students will earn in their college careers. Perhaps this will make the recent push to dramatically expand the volume of reading that adolescents do easier to understand. Students who read voluntarily and frequently are the students who achieve the greatest academic success while the aliterate students continue to move along life's pathways always less informed regardless of their interests or their careers.

It is when students reach early adolescence that schools begin to focus almost exclusively on assigned readings in one-size-fits-all lessons. In other

"Unfortunately, putting good books in front of our students has not been the focus in many of our nation's schools."

(*Source:* Kelly Gallagher, 2009.)

words, what we have described as multi-sourced and multi-leveled curriculum materials (Allington, 2002) are generally rare in middle and high school classrooms. I am unsure why curricula are often composed of a single textbook instead of differentiated lessons because, as Ivey (2002, p. 21) notes, "I know of no one textbook that contains enough information to help a student become even mildly expert on any topic." In other words, textbooks are typically corporately written compendiums that attempt to touch on every item noted in 50 separate state subject matter standards. No one has ever become excited reading a textbook. Worse, there exists almost no research demonstrating that using commercial curriculum materials is an effective practice. As Chingos and Whitehurst (2012) have recently noted,

> *The first limitation is that many instructional materials have not been evaluated at all, much less with studies that produce information of use to policymakers and practitioners. (p. 6)*

Given that American middle and high schools spend about 50 percent more per pupil than do American elementary schools, it does not seem that the expense of multi-sourced and multi-level curriculum materials is the source of the problem. Today most middle and high school teachers, unlike elementary school teachers, are required to have majored or minored in the subject areas they are teaching. Because of this, it doesn't seem that a lack of expertise in the subject matter being taught is the rationale for use of one-size-fits-all curricula. The only reason I can imagine that explains this phenomenon is that most middle and high school teachers have always used a one-size-fits-all curriculum, and so the old pattern continues even though not a single model of high quality instruction suggests the use of such a plan.

Even common lesson planning models don't support the use of a single text. The second step, after deciding what you are planning to teach, is always "selecting appropriate curriculum materials." Note the plural -s at the end of materials, indicating the selection of several different curriculum materials or several different texts for students to use when planning adequate instruction. This is true even in English language arts classes, the classes most think are primarily responsible for fostering reading development in middle and high schools.

Trelease (2001) comments on this English class phenomenon: "An interesting thing happened to the classics: About the only people in this country who read them are teenagers—and only because they have to" (p. 140). Suddenly, beginning around fifth-grade English language arts, teachers begin using the whole-class novel as a primary unit planning routine. So reading in and for school largely involves reading either inconsiderate content-area textbooks or novels written by dead white males (Allington, 2002; Wolk, 2010). Is it any wonder, given this reading agenda, that students begin to turn off to voluntary reading?

Brozo, Shiels, and Topping (2008) report on the findings of the international PISA study of reading in three English-speaking nations. They note that American 15-year-old students ranked fifteenth out of the sample of students drawn from 32 nations. This was the lowest performance by students in any English-speaking nation. This report found the highest reading achievement in students who read the most pages each day, and children who had daily school-based sustained silent reading experiences scored much better than students who had sustained silent reading opportunities less frequently. The NAEP analyses on U.S. students report the same pattern from data from hundreds of thousands of students. In both the PISA and the NAEP data, volume of daily reading predicted reading achievement regardless of the socioeconomic status of the students' families.

Adolescent males exhibited greater declines in reading activity than females, which may explain why colleges now admit and graduate far more women than men (National Endowment for the Arts, 2007). Zambo and Brozo (2009) report that boys are more likely to drop out of school and also more likely to be labeled learning disabled (LD), emotionally disturbed, and language impaired. They are also more often placed in remediation, retained in grade, and identified as attention deficit hyperactivity disorder (ADHD), and they are more likely to receive Ds and Fs on school report cards and have smaller vocabularies than is the case for girls. What is the relationship of these outcomes with reading proficiency? In general, all of these factors can be linked to the lower reading proficiency exhibited by boys.

Nonetheless, while schools now seem to work better for girls than for boys, there remains the fact that students of both genders are struggling and too often failing in their school careers. Both engagement in learning and classroom behavior are influenced by a student's reading proficiency, regardless of gender. It isn't only how well students read that is important; it's how well the reading demands of their school texts match the reading proficiencies that students have developed.

Textbooks as a Curriculum

Chall (1983) noted that the difficulties with reading increase dramatically for students in fifth grade and beyond as their instruction begins to rely more on one-size-fits-all textbooks. The vocabulary they encounter in their textbooks is less conversational and less familiar, with more specialized, technical terms

With the adoption of the Common Core State Standards (CCSS), the problems students face may be expanded. The CCSS emphasizes increasing the amount of informational text reading that students will do across the K-12 grade spectrum so that in eighth grade only 45 percent of the texts students study will be literary texts and 55 percent will be informational texts. In addition, the CCSS focus is on substantially increasing the amount of reading of complex texts that students do. So, students will potentially be faced with greater amounts of reading of complex informational texts. This does not bode well for those seventh-graders whose reading development is at the fourth-grade level.

(cell, cytoplasm, nucleus) and abstract ideas (capitalism, free market, labor). The syntax of textbooks becomes more complex and demanding than the literary texts students have typically read in lower grades. The reasoning about information in texts also shifts, with a greater emphasis on inferential thinking.

Many students who have been making satisfactory progress up to this point now begin to struggle with reading, especially with their assigned reading content-area classes.

Schools have typically exacerbated the problem for struggling readers by relying on a single-source curriculum design—purchasing multiple copies of the same science and social studies textbooks for every student. But there are alternatives that schools must consider.

Better Readers, Better Students

It is our better readers in middle and high schools who are most likely to earn high grades, complete more difficult coursework, and ultimately enroll in college. Basically, the top quarter of any class also largely represents the top quarter of the readers. These are the sixth-grade students already reading at the tenth-grade level. Every text they are assigned to read in middle school will be an easy text for them, and they can read them with 99 percent accuracy and with 90 percent comprehension. These are the students who will survive the implementation of more rigorous reading standards as called for by the CCSS.

The better readers in our schools are not the students we need to be worrying much about. We need to worry about the majority (75 percent) of the students who read at or below grade level and who have difficulties in our present-day schools. These students will have greater difficulties in the schools implementing the CCSS framework. Our better readers are also the students who are most likely to read voluntarily. Anderson, Wilson, and Fielding (1988) reported that millions of words of reading activity was the obvious difference between the top quarter of readers and the bottom quarter, which represented millions of words of additional voluntary reading practice every year. They argue that even as little as 10 minutes of daily voluntary reading would substantially improve the reading proficiencies of our lowest performing students. If we are asking why some kids read better than other kids, we must look at the amounts of voluntary practice our best readers engage in.

Access and Choice as Keys to Reading Activity

If we are to get serious about fostering expanded reading activity among our early adolescents, then we have to pay attention to what we already know. Guthrie and Humenick (2004) completed a meta-analysis of studies and report that improving the ease of access students have to books they find interesting had a huge impact on reading comprehension development. In other words, creating large and multi-level classroom collections of trade books was a powerful strategy for improving the abilities of students to read with understanding. Improving access to allow students to self-select what books they would read was also a powerful factor for improving comprehension.

We also know from the study of almost 2,000 early adolescents (Ivey & Broaddus, 2001) that access to books, self-selection, and time to read in school were the most common factors these students listed as motivating them to increase their voluntary reading. However, as a number of researchers have noted, none of these three powerful factors are present in most middle schools (Gallagher, 2009; Ivey, 2011).

Research suggests that the three most powerful factors in fostering voluntary reading are unlikely to be found in the middle schools we have created. These factors are powerfully related to reading motivation and reading engagement, both of which decline during middle school. How many more studies must be published before American middle schools begin to make the shift to more powerful forms of instruction? It isn't a lack of funding that keeps most classrooms devoid of large, multi-level classroom libraries. We know that it isn't a lack of funding that keeps most classrooms devoid of large, multi-level libraries and rich and interesting sets of curriculum materials. We know it isn't a funding issue if only because middle schools currently purchase large quantities of materials that have never been shown to be effective (workbooks, test prep, computerized reading programs, class sets of novels by dead white males, etc.).

It would be beneficial for literacy leadership at middle schools to become more familiar with what the current research tells us about effectively teaching early adolescents how to read. It is not that the middle schools need harder texts; what middle schools need is an abundant supply of interesting texts, interesting and readable by the students. With the current fascination with providing harder texts to students, it seems the folks in charge have never read a research study on the appropriate level of difficulty of texts to be used if learning is to occur.

Are Harder Books Better?

Alfie Kohn (1999) wrote this in a section entitled "Confusing harder with better":

> John Dewey reminded us that the value of what students do resides in its connection with a stimulation of greater thoughtfulness, not in the greater strain it imposes. If you were making a list of what counts in education—that is, the criteria to use in judging whether students would benefit from what they were doing—the task's difficulty level would be only one factor among many, and almost certainly not the most important. To judge schools by how demanding they are is rather like judging an opera on the basis of how many notes it contains that are hard for singers to hit. In other words, it leaves out most of what matters. (http://www.alfiekohn.org/teaching/edweek/chwb.htm)

Assuming that we don't want to continue the tradition of using too-difficult textbooks and allowing large numbers of students to fail content courses, we have two possible solutions. We could search out texts that cover the topics at lower levels of reading difficulty (Beck, McKeown, & Gromoll, 1989). Or we can provide more instructional support to help students in grades 5 through 12 develop greater reading proficiency. In a model school both options would be followed. In most American middle and high schools neither option is even considered, much less followed.

Teachers who want to know whether students are having difficulty with the textual materials they have assigned can note which behaviors Brozo (1990) describes that struggling adolescent readers exhibited in their classes:

1. Avoiding eye contact with the teacher. There was little evidence of teachers reaching out to students who did this.
2. Engaging in disruptive behavior. This included leaving seats, making inappropriate comments to the teacher, and snatching items from other students. When teacher-student interactions occurred they were typically irrelevant to the academic work.

Interviews with students suggested other coping strategies:

3. Relying on a "with it" classmate/good reader to get help with directions, reading assignments, and doing homework.

4. Forgetting to bring books and other materials needed for oral reading.

5. Using manipulative techniques in and out class to gain teacher's favor.

An eleventh-grader, Scott, says,

> *I'm always scared the teacher is going to call on me. I'll fool around . . . and she tells me to shut up . . . you can do that or act sick or something. (Brozo, 1990, p. 324)*

Notice how many of the above behaviors can upset the balance of classroom lessons. All are created by struggling readers typically trying to avoid being embarrassed in front of their peers.

Consider the too-common phenomenon of having students read aloud from their textbooks. This is called round-robin oral reading. As Mueller (2001) notes in her book, *Lifers:*

> *In the context of generic instruction, round robin reading can probably be considered one of the most harmful components of group learning. By providing students with a misguided sense of reading as a word-perfect activity, by causing unnecessary sub-vocalization, by hampering listening comprehension, and by instigating inattentive behavior that can lead to discipline problems, it poses many problems for students caught up in the circle of stop-and-go recitation. . . . The damage to struggling readers is more far reaching. . . . Asking these struggling adolescents to read sections of a text "cold" in front of an entire class serves only to underline their deficiencies. (p. 21)*

My hunch is that round-robin reading of textbooks contributes to the negative views so many struggling readers have about reading, any reading. Nonetheless, it is still common to walk into a middle or high school content-area classroom and observe students engaged in round-robin oral reading of a textbook. When I have questioned content-area teachers as to why they have students reading aloud, the most common responses I receive typically fall along the lines of, "If I don't have them read it aloud they will never read it." This response suggests that from the students' point of view the textbook is boring, difficult, and/or considered irrelevant to life. The second most common comments fall in the "They can't read the book" category. If they can't read the book, though, why should they read aloud to their classmates? It won't help either the struggling readers or their classmates. Some of the comments also suggest the primacy of the textbook as the place where necessary information is found. But this view suggests that teachers do not have much faith in their own knowledge of the content.

More Effective Classroom Models

Wade and Moje (2000) contrast the role of texts in "transmission" versus "participatory" classrooms. In transmission classrooms, where teachers with less content expertise seem to rely more heavily on textbooks, few expect students to actually learn much from textbooks; thus, lecture-recitation becomes the dominant theme of such classrooms as students work through texts with the teacher. In participatory classrooms texts are seen as tools for learning rather than as repositories for needed information. Participatory classrooms have more student discussion, including peer-led discussions, than has also been found in transmission classes. In most of the participatory classrooms we have studied there was no single textbook that students were expected to use.

I remember sitting in on a parent night at a middle school. After discussing the science class and course demands one parent noted, "You haven't mentioned the science textbook yet." The science teacher responded, "I don't use a textbook. I don't want kids just reading about science; instead, I want them doing science. But if you would like a science textbook for you or your child, see me after the session because I have a number of them you can choose from." As a parent and a professor of literacy I was cheered by what he said. I'm not sure though that every parent felt the same way.

However, if Wade and Moje are correct—and I suspect they are—then often the reliance middle and high school teachers have on a single textbook seems to be linked to their lack of expertise in the subjects covered in the textbooks. Content-area teachers who are experts in the content areas they teach do not need a textbook to prop them up. Instead, they get students busy doing science, local or American history, geography, and such.

These participatory teachers are also more likely to have their students read, though typically not from a textbook. Instead, they induce kids to read journal and newspaper articles, to read real science or history books, to read biographies and memoirs written by scientists, historians, and historical figures. In addition they also have students write. They write everything from transcriptions of interviews with local people recounting historic events or describing historic structures to descriptions of planting a garden to pruning fruit trees. They have students write field reports of scientific observations and explanations of how an experiment was conducted. There are content-area teachers in our middle and high schools who expect their students to be engaged readers and writers. There are not enough of them, however, and they seem particularly absent in schools serving students from low-income families. As the Alliance for Excellent Education (2011) noted recently,

> For years, U.S. schools have tended to offer a two-tiered curriculum, in which some students, primarily white and relatively affluent, have had opportunities for deeper learning, while others, primarily low-income and students of color, have focused almost exclusively on basic skills and knowledge. More-affluent and white students get to analyze works of literature and write extensively, while low-income and minority students tend to complete worksheets that focus on memorization. (p. 3)

So how do some content-area teachers nudge kids into reading and writing activities? One common theme is that they routinely comment on books, or articles, or websites that the students might want to read. In many such classrooms teachers "bless" at least one book every day. By blessing a book (Gambrell, 1996), I mean that the teacher simply showed the book to students while providing a 30-second commentary on the book, or, perhaps, the teacher just read a short segment from the book to give the students the flavor of it. The effective teachers we studied typically blessed several books every school day. Then they set those books out for display for students to select and read. This was not an activity typically observed in the neighboring classrooms of less effective teachers. Blessing books was yet another characteristic that defined the nation's most effective teachers.

How can a content-area teacher know that many books? If they bless even one book a day, that means 180 books are blessed every year. What science teacher knows 180 books? We found that the most effective science (or social studies, or math, or music) teachers were the ones who knew 180 (or 360 or 720) books they might recommend to students. Less effective teachers simply did not know many books that they could recommend to students. Perhaps they are not avid readers in the content area they teach or perhaps they are avid readers but it has never occurred to them how much they learned about their subject matter from sources other than textbooks.

When I've presented these data to audiences I am routinely asked, "Where do they find all these books?" When I tell the questioner that books typically come from the teacher's classroom library I am often, too often, met with blank stares. "Who bought the books for the classroom library?" is the usual follow-up question. I tell my audiences that usually the books had been purchased by the school district, but purchased only after the teacher had made a request (or made a fuss, in some cases). In some cases, these books had been purchased by the PTA or another group linked to the school. And, yes, some of the books had been purchased by the teachers themselves.

However, in most schools it isn't a lack of funding that is the reason few middle and high school teachers have classroom libraries where they can find books to bless each and every day. As Donalyn Miller (2009), the Texas sixth-grade teacher who writes the *Book Whisperer* blog, notes, schools spend enormous sums of money on materials that have never mattered when it comes to developing early adolescents' reading or writing proficiencies (or their math, science, or social studies proficiencies).

> *I believe this corporate machinery of scripted programs, comprehension worksheets (reproducibles, handouts, printables, whatever you want to call them), computer-based incentive packages, and test-practice curricula facilitate a solid bottom line for the companies that sell them. These programs may deceive schools into believing that they are using every available resource to teach reading, but ultimately, they are doomed to fail because they overlook what is most important. When you take a forklift and shovel off the programs, underneath it all is a child reading a book. (p. 3)*

Content-area classes must begin to reflect what we've learned about effective literacy instruction. Four aspects of improved classroom instruction will involve you in four distinct activities.

1. *Collect real books and other content-rich materials.* Teachers at Thomas Harrison Middle School in Harrisonburg, Virginia, pulled together a variety of content-related trade books and arranged them by subject themes in a teacher planning area. Teachers could then select from novels, biographies, poetry, photo-essays, picture books, and original source materials. When teachers began using multi-sourced curriculum the key concepts became the focus rather than textbook details.

2. *Read aloud to students.* Read-alouds can inspire students to want to read a book or article (or reread it). Read-alouds can make harder texts accessible for students who struggle with reading. They provide the opportunity for teachers to model the sorts of strategic thinking skilled readers use as they read.

3. *Provide time for independent reading.* Almost two-thirds of kids reported that more time to just read in content classes was their preferred change in classes (Ivey & Fisher, 2006). This works especially well within the multi-source framework where kids select the texts on the topic. While readers with more skills are reading independently, the teacher can provide more up close and personal support for the kids who are struggling.

4. *Make reading support manageable.* Translate professional development agendas into a focus on the three areas discussed above rather than one-shot sessions. Provide teachers with time and resources to build the multi-source

collections and to become familiar with alternative texts that develop core content concepts. Focus on teacher-to-teacher development plans rather than one-size-fits-all workshops.

If you can get your school involved in each of these four activities, you will be on your way to creating a more effective learning environment for your students.

Reading Volume and Reading Development

The data we have accumulated over the past three decades suggests that reading volume is related to reading development. I am not surprised this might be the case if only because we know a lot about the effects of voluntary practice in the development of expert performances. As Ericcson and his colleagues (1993) noted, "deliberate practice," meaning voluntary practice, seemed to be the critical factor in expert levels of performance in athletics, chess, and music. Even more powerful than "natural abilities," it was deliberate practice that determined who became a star and who became a talented but unrecognized performer.

When it comes to reading development we have much correlational and developmental research that suggests the same role for deliberate practice in reading development. As the National Reading Panel (2001) noted, there are too few large-scale studies that manipulated the volume of reading experimentally for anyone to argue that research proves that reading volume drives reading development. Nonetheless, as Jim Cunningham (2001) noted in his review of the NRP report in *Reading Research Quarterly,* the federal government has implemented a number of rules regarding cigarettes based also on correlational data similar to that available for reading volume and reading development. The same holds true for federal rules for alcohol use during pregnancy. In other words, no one has ever experimentally assigned some folks to smoke cigarettes or pregnant women to drink alcohol.

Even without the "gold standard" evidence that is derived from experimental studies where subjects are randomly assigned to one group or the other, federal officials (and medical professionals as well) have seen fit to use the available correlational data to put in place rules regarding both tobacco and alcohol usage. The various data available on the relationship between volume of reading and reading proficiency is likewise consistent in indicating a powerful relationship between the two.

For instance, in a study conducted at the Center for the Study of Reading, a federally funded research center, Anderson, Wilson, and Fielding (1988) reported a strong relationship between the reading achievement of fifth-grade students and voluntary out-of-school reading. As they reported, "There is a strong, direct correlation between the amount of independent reading students do and their percentile rank on standardized tests. For example, students scoring in the 98th percentile read independently an average of 67 minutes per day while students who score in the 10th percentile read independently for an average of only 1 minute per day" (p. 301). Again, this relationship was observed between daily reading logs the middle school students kept and their end-of-year reading achievement.

Other large-scale studies have reached similar conclusions. Lewis and Samuels (2004) conducted a meta-analysis on 49 studies of reading volume. They reported a moderate effect size of 0.42 across all of the studies. Reading practice, in this study, was related to reading development. In addition, Stanovich (2000) argues that the research evidence available indicates that volume of reading is related to reading development based on the experimental work he and his colleagues have conducted as well as the research completed by others. He closes his argument by noting simply that researchers need to pay more attention to reading volume and its relationship to reading development.

Complimenting Lewis and Samuels's meta-analysis is the report by Ivey and Johnston (2013) who describe how a group of middle school English teachers dramatically altered their curriculum and their classes so that self-selected reading became the central focus of the course.

Each of these four teachers taught three sections of this 90-minute class. Roughly half of the students were from low-income families and about one-third were members of an ethnic minority group. However, this shift in the class focus dramatically altered the volume of reading that students were engaged

Independent Reading during the School Day

Krashen (2011) notes that the average effect size on reading achievement of eight longer-term studies of Sustained Silent Reading was ES = .70. Compare this effect size, a large positive effect, to the ES = .11 effect size the National Reading Panel reported for effect size of phonics instruction on reading comprehension! So why do so many struggling adolescents get decoding emphasis interventions? Particularly poignant is that the NRP found *no* positive effects for phonics emphasis intervention beyond first grade! These data point to the need for teachers and school administrators to invest time and effort into becoming familiar with and implementing research-based strategies that adolescent struggling readers need to become better readers.

This review provides more evidence that in-school self-selected reading works. It must be emphasized that effect sizes were uniformly positive and typically quite impressive. In-school self-selected reading is effective and its effects are robust. (p. 40)

in. It also substantially improved the numbers of students who achieved the rating of "proficient" on the state reading and language arts assessment.

The new course design featured "edgy" novels of the sort that were attractive to middle school students. The students became more skilled readers in large part because they needed to develop more effective strategy use to understand and extend the novels they had selected. As Ivey and Johnston (2013) write,

> *Strategic behavior for these students, though, appeared to be less the result of strategy instruction than a response to their own need to make sense. Their reading processes suggest that although it is possible to teach particular strategies, instructional time might be better spent supporting engaged reading, a context in which students are more likely to actually become strategic. (p. 48)*

In other words, use of reading strategies was driven by individual motivation to better understand the novels they had selected.

Ivey and Johnson also report that the new curriculum and instructional framework generated a greater sense of personal agency as well as greater motivation to read with understanding. The changes also generated enhanced social interactions with their peers and led to new friendships based on the reading of common texts. Thus, beyond improved test performances the project resulted in a number of outcomes that seem important in developing an engaged citizenry.

Finally, Donalyn Miller's sixth-grade classroom of engaged middle school readers provides yet another example of the power of redesigning English language arts classes with a focus on extensive self-selected reading. Like the middle school students in the Ivey and Johnston (2013) study, Miller's student dramatically increased their volume of reading during their year in her class. The extensive self-selected reading that she demands not only produces improved test scores but also creates actual readers! She expects her students to read 40 books each during the school year or one book every week. As she notes you can only know whether your students are actually reading if you can watch them reading. Thus, her 90-minute class period involves assisting students in locating books they can and want to read, with time available for peer-to-peer discussion of the reading students have done.

Ladson-Billings (2009) presents case studies of eight successful teachers of early adolescents (grades 4, 5, and 6). Five of these teachers are African American and three are Caucasian. There is no single type of teacher presented here, except that all are successfully developing the academic proficiencies of African-American students. These teachers see teaching as an art; they see themselves as part of the community; they believe all children can succeed; they help students make connections between community, national, and global identities; and they view teaching as "pulling knowledge out" versus putting it in. These teachers work to develop a community of learners while encouraging students to learn collaboratively, to teach each other and be responsible for each other. The challenge is to create many more teachers just like these few Ladson-Billings reports on.

Ladson-Billings (2009) also notes that of the teachers she has studied, the most effective teachers accepted personal responsibility for the success or failures of their students while less effective teachers attempted to shift that responsibility to special education teachers or to reading specialists or to anyone else, including the parents of the children who were failing. The effective teachers of early adolescents sought to develop the academic potential of every student through powerful forms of personalized and differentiated instruction. The less effective offered one-size-fits-all lessons and then blamed the victims—their students—for their failure to develop the academic proficiencies the school targeted for them.

Students cannot learn much from textbooks they cannot read accurately and understand. Blaming students for their lack of learning from textbooks that are simply too difficult for their current level of reading development is not a characteristic of effective teachers. As Fisher and Ivey (2006) note,

> Without . . . access to high-quality, readable texts and instruction in strategies to read and write across the school day—it is doubtful that a specific, limited intervention will make much of a difference. (p.181)

In other words, struggling readers cannot be helped much by a single period intervention coupled with another 5 hours of instruction every day from grade level textbooks they simply cannot read! Schools must begin to consider what I have dubbed "the full day plan" of high-quality instruction for all struggling readers. This plan requires an effective intervention class along with content-area instruction matched to student reading levels in every class, every day. While some folks consider this plan too ambitious, for me such a plan provides effective teaching for every student every day. Remember that too many students begin to fail in early adolescence because too many rarely experience high-quality lessons as they attend school day after day. We can do better for these students than we have been doing.

Reading Lessons in Schools Today

In too many school systems early adolescents are engaged in little, if any, voluntary reading. This seems to stem from teachers' insistence that they are required to teach certain novels. Often teachers of early adolescents argue that effective teaching using self-selected books is impossible because they are required by state standards to teach *Silas Marner* or *To Kill a Mockingbird* or Shakespeare. However, Fisher and Ivey (2007) again note,

> Even a cursory review of content standards from several state departments of education reveals that specific texts and authors are not actually named. Rather, students are expected to learn how to read, write, and speak about a variety of texts, and the standards typically emphasize literary devices, reading comprehension skills, and writing strategies. . . . The bottom line is that, when teachers require all students to read the same book at the same time, English classes are neither standard-centered nor student-centered. . . . Students are not reading more or better as a result of the whole-class novel. Instead, students are reading less and are less motivated, less engaged, and less likely to read in the future. (p. 495)

The CCSS and One-Size-Fits-All Lessons

Even the adoption of the new CCSS by states provides no mandate to teach particular texts, much less use a "class novel" framework for fostering reading growth. Quoting from the CCSS document approved by the various states,

> The Standards leave room for teachers, curriculum developers, and states to determine how those goals should be reached and what additional topics should be addressed. . . . Teachers are thus free to provide students with whatever tools and knowledge their professional judgment and experience identify as most helpful for meeting the goals set out in the Standards. (2010, p. 4)

If anything, the CCSS is designed to move schools away from a heavy reliance on a single textbook for all content-area subjects, not just for English classes. It is through the reading of multiple texts that the designers of the CCSS expect our students to develop the sorts of college- and career-ready reading proficiencies that are now the intended outcomes in the education of all adolescents.

Returning once again to Fisher and Ivey (2007), because of the nature of far too many courses adolescents are required to take far too many students never have the opportunity to self-select the books they will read. Instead, adults, teachers, tell them which book to read. Often the assigned book is neither a book that the student would choose nor a book they can actually read.

Instead of this now archaic model of lessons for adolescents Fisher and Ivey suggest that schools:

- Identify universal themes rather than individual titles that students will study.
- Select texts that span a wide range of difficulty levels within these themes.
- Select texts that address contemporary issues and that are engaging with adolescents.
- Orchestrate instruction that builds students' reading and writing competence, through.
- Teach literary devices and reading comprehension strategies using texts that are readable and meaningful to the students.

Accomplishing these new, effective lessons across all content areas will be the major challenge for teachers of adolescents for the next few years. We can expect, I assume, an uneven development in schools and in grade levels. But unless something drastic occurs, this development will occur and our students will become better readers and writers than the students we teach today.

It is important to understand that the CCSS sets expectations for reading and writing in all content areas that are the responsibility of the teachers of earth science, American history, and world cultures to develop. It also sets expectations for English teachers to develop the literary reading and writing proficiencies of their students. Under the new CCSS all teachers of adolescents have responsibilities to foster the specific disciplinary reading and writing strategies central to their content area. Under CCSS, American students will be expected to read and write in every class and will do far more reading and writing than schools expect of adolescents today.

Read the CCSS goal for third-grade students below and consider how many of today's ninth-graders could achieve this standard. In fact, ask how many high school seniors could demonstrate mastery of the goal. I use this third-grade goal simply to suggest that the CCSS expects far more of students well before they reach adolescence.

> Describe the relationship between a series of historical events, scientific ideas or concepts, or steps in technical procedures in a text, using language that pertains to time, sequence, and cause/effect. (Informational Text, Grade 3, Objective 3)

Designing a lesson to address this objective would require two main steps. First, the teacher must decipher the objective—identify the key outcomes in terms of specific skills or knowledge. Then, the teacher must find or design an appropriate lesson to enable students to meet the expected outcomes. Finally, the teacher must select an array of texts that students might read in meeting the standard. This is quite different than teaching the next lesson from a commercial curriculum material (or textbook).

Think about the first step. What is the intended outcome of this objective? After the lesson is offered, students should be able to *describe the relationship*; that is, use language to compare things. The relationship to be described is *between a series of historical events, scientific ideas or concepts, or steps in technical procedures in a text,* indicating that the student is to read a text containing one or more of these features. Finally, students are required to do this by *using language that pertains to time, sequence, and cause/effect,* meaning that students are to be describing the order (chronological, sequential, and causal) in their description of the relationships. That is a bundle of accomplishments that need to be met for this single CCSS goal. It is a bundle far more complex than simply handing out a worksheet from a commercial core program that is today's most common lesson component.

Sixth-graders in a CCSS-aligned classroom won't be simply reading a textbook summary of the American Revolution but, instead, will read speeches made by Patriots, look at propaganda from both Loyalists and Patriots, weigh the reasons people took sides in that war, and imagine themselves in the shoes of people who hold different views on this topic. Again, this sort of student activity is quite different from the typical American history class offered in middle schools today. The lessons expect more of both teachers and students.

The CCSS expects students to sort and categorize, compare and contrast, evaluate, analyze, and reason about texts they have read. This is quite different from answering multiple-choice or fill-in-the-blank questions that dominate most worksheets now in use. Students will not find the demands of the CCSS easy to meet nor will teachers find the goals easy to achieve—but that is the point, I assume. If we are going to expect all students to achieve more powerful reading and writing proficiencies, much will have to change in American schools, especially in American middle and high schools.

Summary

It is as students enter early adolescence that their reading activity begins to decline. In other words, beginning at around fifth or sixth grade, students begin to read less than they read at earlier ages. As they pass through middle and high school, their reading activity continues to decline until by twelfth grade

Locating Quality Informational Books

Each of the following websites provides a collection of award-winning titles of informational books that teachers will need to use to meet the CCSS standards in all content areas.

Orbis Pictus Award

www.ncte.org/awards/orbispictus

Notable Books

www.ala.org/ala/mgrps/divs/alsc/awardsgrants/notalists/ncb/index.cfm

Good Reads

http://www.goodreads.com/shelf/show/childrens-informational-books

Robert Sibert Award

www.ala.org/ala/mgrps/divs/alsc/awardsgrants/bookmedia/sibertmedal/index.cfm

Amazon

www.amazon.com/Middle-High-School-Nonfiction/lm/R2282VN15N850K

Lexile

www.lexile.com

Google

www.google.com

Search for "informational books" and note all the school URLs with their lists of top books.

No book, library, or learning environment in human history has had the capacity to make available to students the volume of information, the variety of forms of information, and the connections within and across information sources that we now have in digital environments. The digital-global age is making knowledge available in ways not experienced by previous generations. To be ready for college, the workforce, and life in this digital-global world, students need the ability to gather, comprehend, evaluate, synthesize, and report on information and ideas from an extensive volume and range of print and non-print media.

only one in every five high school seniors reports reading a book voluntarily! Gallagher (2009), a high school English teacher, writes that the situation is even worse:

> *Let's see whether we have this straight: We immerse students in a curriculum that drives the love of reading out of them, prevents them from developing into deeper thinkers,*

ensures the achievement gap will remain, reduces their college readiness, and guarantees that the result will be that our schools fail. (p. 23)

As Gallagher (2009) argues in his book, *Readicide,* we often approach struggling readers with a plan that fails to actually foster reading development, much less foster a love of reading:

Readers who are undernourished need good books. Lots of them. Instead, what do many undernourished readers get? They are often placed in remedial classes where the pace is slowed and where the reading focus moves away from books to a steady diet of small chunks of reading. In an effort to "help" prepare them for reading tests, we starve readers. Rather than lift up struggling readers, this approach contributes to widening the achievement gap" (pp. 32–33).

Is it any wonder that few students who enter middle or high school a couple of years, or more, behind in their reading ever become readers or scholars? All adolescents need to engage in daily reading and writing activities that will foster further growth in both arenas. What all adolescents need is a far better selection of texts to read, especially texts they read accurately and with understanding. They also need the opportunity to write within a supportive classroom environment. Instead, we fill up their days, especially the days of low-achieving students, with texts that are too difficult and fill-in-the-blank worksheets that simply require copying out of low-level factual information from the assigned text. We can do better.

The newly adopted CCSS sets out expansive instructional goals for our students in grades K through 12. Central to the CCSS is an increased focus on engaging students in reading and writing across the school day. In addition, the CCSS expects that students will read a variety of texts, and many of these texts will be more difficult than the texts in use today. But it is the CCSS focus on reading multiple texts on topics and then analyzing those texts seriously that is the substantial change that will be required. It is difficult, if not impossible, to imagine CCSS classrooms where a single textbook dominates the instruction provided. That will be a major shift in the lessons provided to adolescents as the CCSS is implemented into every classroom across the nation.

In the end, schools will have to substantially expand the supply of texts that are available for students to read. Teachers will have to become more familiar with many more texts than most are familiar with today. Lessons will necessarily be designed around multi-level and multi-sourced curriculum materials, in every content-area class. Content-area teachers are now responsible, under the CCSS, for developing the specific disciplinary reading proficiencies needed in their discipline. Big changes are afoot! How states, districts, schools, and teachers adapt to these new instructional expectations will be linked to whether our students develop the intended reading and writing proficiencies. The next decade will be an exciting time in American schools!

Chapter 5

Reading with Comprehension: Understanding "Understanding"

Understanding what we have just read is the whole point of virtually any reading activity in which we engage. Reading without understanding is not actually reading; I would call it "barking at print." When it comes to school reading assignments, understanding what was read is assumed to be the ultimate outcome.

But when our students fail a quiz or a test or when they are unable to join a discussion about what they were supposed to read, too often the diagnosis is that such students are lazy, which usually means that we assumed they didn't read the assigned text. That is always a possibility, of course, but it is not always the reason students fail the quiz or fail to join in the discussion. In far too many cases they did read the text but failed to understand what they had just read.

Sometimes this is the result of giving an assignment from a text that was simply a mismatch between the students' reading level and the complexity of the text. Sometimes it is more directly related to the lack of relevant background knowledge that the author of the text assumed the reader possessed. In some cases it seems that a lack of interest in and motivation for understanding the text or even the topic of the text is the source of the lack of understanding (Wigfield & Guthrie, 1997). Interest, task motivation and comprehension are highly related and some students have little of any of these when it comes to reading for school.

In addition to the lack of prior knowledge and lack of motivation, Duke, Pressley, and Hilden (2004) note that each of the following may be contributors to the reading comprehension problems students exhibit: limited short-term or working memory; limited oral language development; inadequate knowledge of the particulars of written language, including differences in genres; lack of strategic thinking before, during, or after reading; difficulties with word reading or decoding or both; fluency problems; and insufficient vocabulary, or conceptual knowledge pertaining to the text. In other words, problems with understanding what has been read can stem from a number of different sources. In addition, some students experience multiple sources of problems when they try to read the texts they are assigned.

Textbooks as a Problem

Then again, it could be the text that is the primary source of the problem, not because it is a complex text but because it is a poorly written text. This seems especially likely when the text assigned is the typical school textbook. Textbooks are a unique type of text. No one takes a chemistry textbook to the beach to read, and no one is likely to take their American history textbook on vacation with them as a source of really engaging material.

Simply put, textbooks are often poorly written and often poorly designed to support learning. Textbooks cover an enormous amount of material, often with just minimal information on the topic. Take the Civil War battle at Shiloh, Tennessee, the first major confrontation between the Union and Confederate armies, as an example. Most American history textbooks provide less than half a page of information on the battle and many fail to mention the battle at all. This brevity of information is one issue because the best we can hope is that students learn just a "little bit" about the Battle of Shiloh or any other historical event or person. (This brevity problem is also true when you examine science, U.S. government, or language texts, or textbooks for any other subject.)

After brevity, we could examine the quality of writing found in textbooks, which is often hackneyed and poorly organized. One problem here is that textbooks are typically written at a "grade level" determined by a readability formula. These readability formulas typically use sentence length, and sometimes the number of polysyllabic words, to estimate a text's difficulty. Generally there is nothing wrong with this process when it is a simple attempt to estimate text difficulty. However, when during development of the text it is noticed that readability estimates on the textbook are too high (say at the twelfth-grade level on an eighth-grade textbook), and as a solution the readability estimate is lowered by chopping longer sentences up into shorter ones, then textbooks come to reflect not good writing but chopped up writing.

Read these two renditions of the same ideas:

> *The colonial farmer also often served as a soldier in the local militia and when needed left his fields to join others in protecting the settlements.*

> *The farmer/militia member sometimes left his fields. This happened when the settlements needed protection.*

The first of these extracts might have come from an American history textbook. But then, so could the second, two sentences that are a rewrite of the first sentence that lowers the readability level of the original. However, while the rewritten sentences lower the estimated difficulty of the original sentence, the rewrite actually does nothing to make the concepts presented any clearer. In fact, I will suggest that the rewritten sentences make understanding more difficult, and not easier as intended.

There are other possible attributes of textbooks that you will read about later in this chapter. For now, though, assume that the textbook you will use was probably chosen from among three to five others by someone other than you. None of these people, including the textbook authors, have ever met your students, so they do not know what interests or topics might be unique to them. If you had been able to select course materials yourselves, you might not have selected the textbook you are using, but since you are required to use a particular textbook, it means that you will have to work harder to make it a useful aspect of the instruction your students will receive with your direction.

You might be asking yourself, "Why are textbooks so shallow, yet so thick? Why are textbooks often not very interesting although often filled with illustrations?" There are several reasons why American textbooks suffer from a variety of weaknesses.

First, textbooks have these weaknesses because they represent a whole series of potential authors and whole sets of concessions made in an attempt to gain the largest market. While textbooks list "authors" of the textbook, many of the folks who actually "wrote" the text go unlisted. Different publishers have different procedures when developing a new textbook and in many cases different procedures for developing textbooks for different subjects or content areas. Nonetheless, the best that educators can hope for is that the folks who are listed as authors have actually read the textbook before it was on the market.

Two or three states largely control textbook content because they are the states with the largest markets for textbooks. Thus, the state textbook adoption committees in Texas, California, and Florida largely control what is in a textbook and what is omitted. Some readers may recall having read about the Texas state committee objecting to American history texts that provided too much emphasis on the contributions of women and minorities to our nation's development with too little emphasis on the contributions of white males. Or perhaps readers have heard about California objecting, and refusing, mathematics textbooks that followed the guidelines developed by the professional associations because those guidelines reduced the amount of memorization and low-level computational activities that students were given while expanding the focus on mathematical conceptualizing and problem solving. Or you may have read about the adoption by Virginia of an American history textbook that indicated vast numbers of African Americans fought for the Confederacy during the Civil War, something that stirred up a hornet's nest of opposition. The author of the textbook ultimately conceded that the source of this information was a website linked to the Ku Klux Klan! To solve this problem of misinformation, the offending section was blacked out. My point is this: Never trust that the textbook provides either accurate or full information on any topic.

However, those rumblings are just the tip of the textbook iceberg. Long before a textbook is developed, editors for every textbook publisher are surveying the textbook adoption committees in each of the 19 states that continue to exercise state control over which textbooks can be purchased with state funds in their states. What Texas, California, or Florida textbook committees will find acceptable then shape the content of the all textbooks used, not only in the 19 textbook adoption states but the textbooks used in every state!

The actual development of an American history or introductory biology textbook is a burdensome task even once the decisions have been made on the content that will be included and excluded. Someone has to purchase the rights to use any artwork , maps, and photos, and someone must locate and hire someone to draw the illustrations, maps, charts, and graphs. Typically, several teams employed by the publisher actually write the textbook simultaneously while other teams who create the teachers' guide that supplies the summaries, the purpose setting statements, the questions that students will be asked, and the worksheets or assignments that are suggested for students to complete. Another team develops the quizzes or tests that accompany many textbooks used in American schools. Literally, hundreds of folks have their fingerprints on the development of a textbook available on the national textbook market.

I mention all this because textbooks so often play such a dominant role in the instructional environment of so many middle schools and high schools. While there are public schools where students learn American history, as I did, without the use of those large and heavy history textbooks, such schools are few and far between. I'm not sure why that is the case but I assume that purchasing and assigning a single thick, heavy American history textbook is the cheapest and easiest solution for both the school district and for individual teachers.

Least expensive solutions rarely are the best solutions when quality is the major concern. You will have to trust me when I tell you that I have observed not just American history but also biology and chemistry—including AP chemistry—being taught superbly without the use of a textbook. As one of those chemistry teachers told me, "You cannot learn chemistry from a textbook. You learn chemistry by doing chemistry. So we do chemistry every day in my classroom."

I will not continue this rant about textbooks because it seems largely futile. But I will assert that virtually any subject taught in American middle and high schools would likely be improved if schools simply stopped ordering the textbooks they buy today. You will notice that throughout these chapters on learning in the content areas, I will frequently refer to alternative texts when I could be simply focusing on textbooks usage.

Understanding "Understanding"

Like the RAND study group on reading comprehension, I define reading comprehension as the process of simultaneously *"extracting* and *constructing* meaning" (Sweet & Snow, 2003). The new Common Core State Standards seem to focus more on the "extracting" aspect of comprehension, but even extraction sometimes involves construction of meaning.

Comprehension is comprised of three elements:

1. The reader who is understanding.
2. The text to be read and understood.
3. The task or activity in which understanding is part. (Sweet & Snow, 2003, p. 2)

These three elements are embedded in the socio-cultural context of the classroom (for school related comprehension). Whether or not the student values reading (or school tasks) is part of the socio-cultural context that educators must worry about. Likewise, how the reading is done—orally or silently, individually, with a partner, in a small group, or in a large group (say as part of a whole-class activity)—and the nature of the reading task—reading to remember, reading to challenge the text, or reading for pleasure—are all socio-cultural variables that influence the act of reading. Finally, whether the text can be highlighted or annotated are also socio-cultural factors that may influence how the reading is done and whether the text is understood.

In addition to these socio-cultural facts, it is also true that readers change over time. Thus, as Sweet and Snow argue, "The process of comprehension . . . changes over time as the reader matures and develops cognitively, as the reader gains increasing experience with more challenging texts, and as the reader benefits from instruction" (p. 4). In other words, if you are lucky, your students will be well practiced in discussing the veracity of multiple accounts of a historical event and they will arrive in your classroom having been well taught how to estimate the veracity of historical (or even contemporary) documents. If you are unlucky—and many of you will be—your students will have had no experience examining multiple original sources and no instruction on how to judge the veracity of each. As Pressley and his colleagues (1998) noted after their observation of fourth- and fifth-grade teachers nominated by their principals as effective: Most teachers seemed to assume that their students already knew how to analyze texts

Round-Robin Oral Reading

Round-robin reading (RRR) occurs when a teacher has students read aloud from a text. One student after another reads aloud, usually a paragraph, and then another student picks up and continues reading aloud from the text. Over 80 percent of middle school teachers report using RRR, even though we've known since 1920 that RRR is more often destructive than constructive (Ash, Kuhn, & Walpole, 2009). If you wanted to identify any single activity that marks classroom instruction as ineffective, I would choose RRR when it is observed in a classroom.

What seems most damaging is that RRR is used most frequently in classrooms where the text assigned is too difficult for the students. That means that we now have classrooms where students are being asked to publicly display their lack of reading proficiency! If you wanted to create an environment that fostered inattention, low comprehension, and off-task behavior, you would create a classroom where RRR was regularly scheduled.

so they rarely, if ever, engaged in the sort of instruction designed to improve their understanding of them. Instead, they filled the days with lots of low-level questions during and after the reading of assigned instructional materials and with lots of low-level worksheets that, like the questioning, simply assessed what students had recalled from their reading.

Confusing Assessment with Instruction

Confusing assessment with instruction looms large in most American middle and high school classrooms. Over 85 percent of all school lessons followed the "recall of textbook information in recitation format." The recitation format will be familiar to most readers based upon their own school experiences. It goes something like this:

- Teacher assigns a text, or a portion of a text, to be read by students.
- Then follows the reading with a series of recall questions.
- Teachers assign worksheets that require locating or recalling information from the assigned text.

These low-level question and worksheet tasks seem the commonly preferred sort of work for students, perhaps because they require little student cognitive effort or engagement and usually just a single word or phrase is considered the correct response. Because adolescents have had years of practice with such tasks, they are familiar tasks. Moving up the cognitive complexity scale to tasks that require problem solving, analysis of the quality of the material in the assigned text, summarizing the material read, identifying an author's stance or point of view, and so on are less familiar tasks, and tasks that require greater cognitive effort from the reader (as well as from the teacher if teaching comprehension strategies is a goal).

The lack of familiarity with the higher order tasks means that teachers will have to model and demonstrate the sorts of thinking that will need to be done in order to complete such new tasks. The evidence developed on classroom instruction that improves comprehension accumulated over the past 40 years suggests that this rarely happens. This suggests that helping teachers develop the ability to deliver lessons that promote comprehension is an important area for teacher development.

Useful demonstration lessons, however, can provide readers with the cognitive strategies they need to successfully do this higher order work. The new CCSS provides a listing of which of these tasks are most appropriate as students move through school. But the CCSS provides only statements of standards that students are to achieve. There is nothing in the CCSS documents that now guide most state education agencies about how to assist students in achieving the standards that have been adopted. The CCSS documents note that developing such lessons and instructional activities is what teachers (or the district or state education agencies) are to do. What I worry about is that while defining the tasks students are to be able to complete provides schools and teachers with a basis for designing the sorts of tasks that students are given, there is little information in the CCSS documents on designing the sorts of instruction that will benefit students. Thus, we may find that fewer students are successfully completing their schoolwork. The CCSS framework won't be very useful if classroom teachers don't quickly develop the expertise needed for fostering comprehension development.

Consider the CCSS standard below. The first aspect that differs from much of the instruction offered in classrooms today is that students are to have read "*two or more texts*" on a topic and those texts are to contain "*conflicting information.*" Very few of your students will likely have ever been assigned to read two or more texts containing conflicting information on a topic, though in real life we often read texts with conflicting information. Just think of almost any election cycle!

In fact, for the first time my daily newspaper carries a regular feature where the "truthiness" of a campaign advertisement or a political flyer is assessed and rated on a scale of "outright lie" to "basically true," with variations in between. I'm not sure how many others bother to read these features but I find them interesting and useful. What the CCSS standard below suggests is that our students learn how to do this sort of evaluation. I agree, but developing this propensity will require classroom lessons quite different from the locate and recall lessons that dominate today.

In the case of these two CCSS standards, the first one (RI.8.8) indicates that students will be able to evaluate arguments and claims in a text for their sufficiency and recognize when irrelevant evidence is introduced. The first issue for me is determining what proportion of the students in my eighth-grade classroom have any idea of what "sound," "sufficient," and "relevant/irrelevant," might mean in this context. This focuses on the use of academic language that is common to classrooms and textbooks. However, language that is common to classrooms and textbooks does not mean that it is readily understood, which is especially true of students from low-income neighborhoods and English language learners (Townsend, Filipinni, Collins, & Biancarosa, 2012).

Often, middle and high school teachers with expertise in a particular content area do

Grade 8: CCSS

- Delineate and evaluate the argument and specific claims in a text, assessing whether the reasoning is sound and the evidence is relevant and sufficient; recognize when irrelevant evidence is introduced. (RI.8.8)

- Analyze a case in which two or more texts provide conflicting information on the same topic and identify where the texts disagree on matters of fact or interpretation. (RI.8.9) not realize that their lessons contain too much unfamiliar academic vocabulary. A content specialist in, say, American history or biology will often assume too much when it comes to students' understanding of the academic vocabulary common in a particular content area. Worse, few textbooks spend much, if any, time on developing the meanings of such words. While the textbook may provide a listing of vocabulary words to develop, the general academic vocabulary words are rarely on those lists. The CCSS standards above could be, and should be, applied to all content areas. We can locate two texts, for instance, in biology or in American or European history that have statements that are at odds with one another. In fact, how one demonstrates "sufficient" or "relevant/irrelevant" will differ from one content area to another. Thus, students need support in developing the sorts of disciplinary thinking that satisfies that CCSS standard.

Students Differ

It should be obvious that students in your classroom differ from one another when it comes to reading the assigned texts with understanding. Students differ from each other on the level of prior knowledge they hold about the topic they will be reading about in the texts you assign. This difference is also typically observed in the level of both the general and academic vocabularies they are familiar with and in the level of interest they have about the topic they have been assigned to read about. Students also differ in their word reading abilities, their level of fluency demonstrated when they read from the text, and in their knowledge of and automatic use of various strategies they might use to understand a complex text. In other words, just as students differ in their physical appearances, so do they differ in the proficiencies and motivations they bring to any school reading activity.

It is these differences in students that make one-size-fits-all teaching both ineffective and inappropriate. Let's examine just one of these areas of difference—background knowledge. We might begin with a commonly studied topic such as the American Civil War or photosynthesis. With either topic you can find adolescents who come to your class already knowing much about them, but even these students who possess high background knowledge are not identical. Some may know much about the Battle of Shiloh, while others who may know a great deal about the Civil War don't know much about that particular battle and may not even recognize that Shiloh is located in the state of Tennessee. Another high background knowledge student may know more about the USS *Monitor* than you or any other student in the class, but that student may be largely uniformed about the Battle of Shiloh. This variation in how much prior knowledge students have about a topic or task is, in large part, what makes teaching so interesting and so frustrating.

Schema Theory

A classic point of view on the role of prior knowledge is to think of developing understanding by filling the gaps in your prior knowledge. This is how schema theory predicts understanding occurs—it is built piece by piece as you read and gain bits of information that are inserted in your knowledge base and enriches your understanding of a topic (Anderson, 1984). With schema theory every topic has a script, and this script is our prior knowledge and experiences with the topic. Perhaps the most famous script is the restaurant script. Think about restaurants. Virtually every reader of this text has multiple restaurant scripts. In other words, you can imagine eating at a fine restaurant where waiters attend to your needs and you are given a printed menu after being seated, and it is not uncommon to be given a wine list before the meal and a dessert menu after you have finished your meal. You also have a script for a fast food restaurant. Here there are no waiters, the menu is above and behind the counter, you find your own seating, if available, and there are sodas for drinks but not much else is offered in the way of beverages. And you probably have a script for a self-serve buffet style restaurant that is different from both the fast food and fine restaurant scripts. However, there are students in your classes with fast food scripts but no fine restaurant script.

Imagine that you have always eaten in fine restaurants and have just entered a fast food restaurant. You wait by the entrance doorway for a few minutes but no one comes to seat you or to deliver a menu, so you decide that since this must restaurant where you seat yourself you locate an available table or booth. Now although you continue to wait for service, no waiter appears and it seems that, as you scan the fast food restaurant, there is no wait staff on call. A few minutes more of observation suggests to you that people enter and go right up to the counter and order the food they want. Then you notice the gaudy looking menu behind the counter that has photos of the food products for sale along with a price of each. So, still hungry, you approach the counter and tell the counter attendant you want a double cheeseburger, medium rare, and with no mustard. The counter attendant tells all the burgers served here are served well done and without mustard. She also asks, "Do you want the number 4 or just the sandwich?" Confused, you mumble, "Just the hamburger." She responds, "Do you want something to drink with that burger?" And you say, "Of course." After waiting a few seconds the counter attendant says, "Well, what do you want to drink?" You reply, "A ginger ale, please." She points to the section of the brightly colored menu behind her and says, "We don't serve ginger ale, what else would you like?" She prompts you again in about 10 seconds and you blurt out, "A root beer, please." Now she wants to know whether you want to supersize your drink. Having no idea what she is talking about you say, "No." She then says, "That will be $5.87." You pay her and return to your table awaiting delivery of your order.

The point to consider here is that students with only fast food script will likely by confused by a scene in a novel where the characters eat at a fine restaurant. They will likely have no way to understand waiters, menus, wine, or tips, and have no idea why not being attended to by waiter in a reasonable period of time might lead a patron to protest or depart. They will have no idea why poor service or poor food, or both, might lead to leaving no tip (or leaving a quarter as the tip on a $75 dinner bill). If there were students in your class with fine restaurant experiences, and who had no fast food experiences, they might be just as puzzled when reading a scene set in a fast food restaurant as in the example above.

The restaurant script demonstration is but a simple strategy for helping you think about what your students bring to class in terms of prior knowledge. Now substitute a Battle of Shiloh script for the restaurant script. Or substitute a rich photosynthesis script for the restaurant script.

My point here is a simple one. Some students know more about the topics you are intending to teach than do other students; while prior knowledge differs it also varies from student to student. Attempting to plan a unit on the Civil War or on photosynthesis with little or no information on just what levels and types of prior knowledge your students possess is a recipe for disaster. So a good first step in planning instruction is one of data gathering.

You can gather such data quickly with techniques such as simply telling your students that you want them to provide you with one important fact about the Battle of Shiloh (or about photosynthesis or any other topic). Tell them to simply take out a piece of paper and write a few sentences about the topic. With this "quick write" you don't even need to have them put their names on the paper, although having their names can be useful if prior knowledge of a topic is widely different from student to student. There are also techniques such as matching key dates or the names of generals or the location where the Battle of Shiloh occurred (and maybe even which war it took place in). Likewise, a simple listing of key words related to the topic where students rate their own prior knowledge on a "much knowledge" to "little or no knowledge" scale also provides useful information.

This assessment of prior, or background, knowledge should be a brief activity taking no more than 3 to 5 minutes or so of class time. The goal with pre-assessments is for you to gather general information about what students already know about the topics they will be studying. Once it becomes clear that your students, for instance, know little about either the U.S. Civil War or the Battle of Shiloh, then lesson planning is made easier and your lessons stand a chance of becoming more effective at developing the knowledge you hope students will acquire.

One eighth-grade social studies teacher I observed used pencil drawings in his assessment of background knowledge. He asked students to sketch a scene from the Battle of Shiloh for him. When he saw that students had drawn tanks, flamethrowers, and aircraft, he learned how limited their knowledge was of the battle or even the nature of war in the mid-1800s. Thus, he began the unit by providing the students with a myriad of scenes sketched by artists during the Civil War. Discussion around the illustrations helped build a knowledge of foot soldiers, camping tents, wood fires for cooking, and horse-drawn cannons and such. In a single class period he both gathered information about what the students knew and then provided materials that actually illustrated the conditions of life and war in the 1860s.

Developing your students' background knowledge before they read an assigned text will improve their understanding as they read that text. However, as with all aspects of teaching, efficiency is the rule. The most efficient method of developing background knowledge is not asking, "Who knows something about the Battle of Shiloh?" This is especially true if you have already established that most students know almost nothing about that battle with a quick write assessment. Instead of asking that question, you should offer a short video clip of a Civil War battle scene; photographs of Civil War re-enactors; photos of the National Cemetery at Shiloh where the thousands of soldiers, both Union and Confederate, are buried; or pictorial materials relevant to the battle or the era. Again, the basic goal is developing student background knowledge before they read the text.

Web Resources for the Battle of Shiloh and Photosynthesis

When I type the words "The Battle of Shiloh" into my search engine, literally hundreds of websites appear that have photos, illustrations, and original source materials (such as diaries of soldiers from the 16th Iowa Volunteer Infantry one of the 11 Iowa regiments that fought at Shiloh), along with video clips of the historic battlefield and collections of artifacts from the battle. In other words, the Web provides a treasure trove of materials that you could use to build background knowledge (or to extend what is learned beyond the usually minimal material found in a textbook).

A similar situation occurs when I type the word "photosynthesis" into my search engine. Literally dozens of websites, some with animation and others with photos and illustrations, are listed, and again you can locate much material that could be used to develop greater background about the process of photosynthesis.

A Short History of Learning and Thinking

Back in the 1950s, Benjamin Bloom and his colleagues developed a classification of levels of intellectual behavior that are important in learning (Bloom, Engelhart, Furst, Hill, & Krathwohl, 1956). Bloom's taxonomy has long been used by educators and psychologists to define what we commonly call *thinking*. In the late 1990s, a group of cognitive psychologists led by Lorin Anderson (a former student of Bloom's) updated the levels of the taxonomy to creating, evaluating, analyzing, applying, understanding, and remembering (Anderson et al., 2001).

The point of introducing Bloom's taxonomy is to clarify that the locate/recall emphasis found in too many classrooms reflects little of what we know about learning or about thinking. "Remembering" is but one of the six categories of thinking that define learning, and remembering may be the least important aspect of learning, especially today. I say this because only in the past decade have portable computing devices become so small and so popular that virtually every American adolescent owns at least one. With "smart phones" or electronic tablets, almost all students can locate almost instantaneously answers to many questions as well as resources that will enable them to understand topics they know little about. It is the widespread availability of these portable devices that seems at the root of the recent responses from university freshmen indicating that they felt that looking up the answer to test questions on their cell phones was not cheating! Or as a twenty-year-old asked me, "Why should I have to memorize this information? I can find the answer with my cell phone in about 10 seconds and with my cell phone I don't have to worry about forgetting something."

It may be that within another decade education will be more about identifying reliable sources of information on the Web than about remembering the names of the state capitols or the dates of the Battles of Saratoga and Shiloh. The problem our students now face is, perhaps, unlike the problem students have always faced. Instead of worrying about remembering information, they now need to worry about the reliability of the information they have located. Instead of having a "truthful" textbook with information to be remembered, our students now have textbooks and a myriad of sources addressing the same topics and providing the same or similar information.

Instead of reading about World War II they can now explore hundreds of websites providing information on that war. They can view Hollywood productions such as *Saving Private Ryan* or any number of other movies made about WWII. However, again they will have to decide on the reliability of the information presented in print, in video, or in photos or diaries of soldiers. While we are all overwhelmed with information, both reliable and unreliable, this especially true for students.

Helping students develop their abilities to analyze and evaluate will become a more central task of teaching adolescents. If the new assessments being developed to evaluate student acquisition of the CCSS standards mimic the items on the National Assessment of Educational Progress (NAEP), students will be given four original source materials describing the Battle of Lexington. Two sources are from civilians and two are from military personnel and both groups contain Loyalist and Patriot statements about the Battle of Lexington. This NAEP task for students asks them simply to select the one account they feel is the most reliable and then write an essay detailing why they selected that account. On a recent NAEP, fewer than 10 percent of twelfth-grade students successfully answered that item. Most had no idea how to judge differing original source materials. I worry that too many of our students graduate from high school never having had to respond to an item such as the NAEP item. They leave K–12 schooling largely believing everything they read, especially when the reading they have done is from a single textbook.

Disciplinary Thinking

One potentially positive effect of having the CCSS standards guide instruction is that students will be asked much earlier than high school to evaluate multiple and conflicting sources of information. However, learning environments, texts assigned for reading, and lesson planning will have to change if this is to occur. Today far too many of the lessons offered in schools require only that students remember what they have read from a single and unchallenged text. In many respects the

Research on Reading Comprehension

Research designed to improve student understanding of what they have read is a relatively recent phenomenon. As Martin and Duke (2011) note, virtually every study on this topic has been published since 1975 with most published since 1990. It may be because this research is so recent that there are few classrooms providing any useful lessons on improving reading with understanding. This could also be the reason why curriculum materials have much assessment advice but virtually no instructional advice on developing students' comprehension proficiencies (Dewitz, Jones, & Leahy, 2009). What we have learned in the past 25 years is that even small instructional efforts in classrooms enhance reading comprehension. These small efforts include opening the classroom floor for discussion of what has been read (Nystrand, 2006) and asking students to write brief summaries of what the text they just read told them (Langer & Applebee, 1987).

instruction that is needed with the CCSS standards as the guide is more akin to learning to think like a historian (or a biologist, or an economist, and so on). That is because historians know more than historical "facts"; they also understand the various historical methods that historians use to determine what is likely "fact" and what is likely "fiction."

Scholars label this general proficiency *disciplinary thinking*, meaning that people trained for different professions typically learn the ways of thinking that are common in their discipline (Shanahan, 2009). Consider for a moment how a historian, a literary critic, a geologist, and an economist determine the "facts" in their fields. Obviously, literary critics use a sort of reasoning for determining the quality of narrative that is different from the sort of reasoning a geologist uses when evaluating the source of a mineral sample. Additionally, those individuals who have completed much training as a literary critic evaluate differently and more efficiently than those with substantially less training and experience. The same is true of geologists, economists, and mathematicians.

However, it is in K–12 educational settings that students become exposed to the differences in disciplinary thinking. But exposure without much in the way of explicit instruction leaves many students confused and willing to simply accept the information found in a textbook. Too often they have no idea what to do when asked, "Is the information you've read in your textbook actually true?" Developing this skill is necessary to many aspects of adult life, including being able to distinguish 'facts' in a political advertisement from fiction. What we are thinking about here is what Bloom labeled *evaluation* and others have called *critical thinking*. No matter what the label is, knowing how to examine any claim in any field is one of the critical twenty-first century skills that schools must work to develop in their students.

Understanding what has been read is different from remembering what has been read. Understanding is the real goal of reading and of education. While remembering often tags along with understanding, understanding does not necessarily tag along with remembering (although, typically, understanding makes remembering easier).

Engagement and Understanding (and, Perhaps, Remembering as Well)

Engagement is central to all learning. Every athletic coach understands this, which is why coaches frequently can be heard shouting, "Everyone, listen up" or "All eyes on me." The first step in engaging people is getting their attention, ideally their undivided attention. Engaged readers can often be heard to say, "I'm really into this book" or "Time just flies by when I'm reading this book." Unengaged readers more often offer a shrug when asked about a book they are reading, often a book they have been assigned. "Boring," is the most common evaluation when they are asked, "How do you like the book?"

In defense of these unengaged readers and those who reply with a "boring," I must admit that much of what kids are assigned to read in adolescence does not in fact appear very engaging. Perhaps that is why textbooks have so many illustrations, maps, and charts that attempt to garner interest in the textbook. But the issue of engagement involves more than just textbooks; it involves content as well. Most adolescents are studying some set of "required" content, although rarely does anyone attempt to explain why this content was deemed so important that everyone must become familiar with it.

Linking Content to the Lives of Students

Let's discuss why earth science is a required course of study for adolescents. I grew up on a farm but I knew early on that I did not want to be farmer. However, if I had the ambition to be a farmer, then much of what is taught in entry level earth science classes would have provided the background I would later need when I studied soil science at the state university. But I was planning on becoming a teacher, not a farmer—an American history teacher, to be precise. So of what use is earth science to an American history teacher? Not much, unless you really stretch it. However, I am also a home owner with a lawn and shrubs and such, so maybe learning a bit about earth science could help me out there. As a 13-year-old, though, I wasn't much thinking about the lawn I would some day have to tend to.

Perhaps because I attended middle and high school in a rural community, the earth science course I took was often tailored to emphasize knowledge that was linked to agriculture and farming. I recall thinking to myself, "This stuff may be useful some day" as I sat in earth science classes. I also recall the soil science team from the *Future Farmers of America* organization coming to our class and, while blindfolded, determining precisely the kind of soil (dirt) they had been given by the earth science teacher! They were able to determine soil type simply by the feel of it.

Since I grew up in rural Michigan, I also recall the lessons on how the Great Lakes were formed by glacial movement and why the region I lived in had a type of soil that was less suited for growing crops than in other areas of Michigan. So these are two examples of my engagement in my ninth-grade earth science class, an engagement that has allowed me to recall the topics and even some of the demonstrations I observed some 50 years earlier.

Linking topics to be studied to the actual lives of students is one way to build engagement. American history is a natural for such links since all of your students now live in America and therefore have a personal relationship and experience with it. Almost anyone whose descendants lived in the United States in the mid-1800s has someone who was involved in the Civil War, although many are quite unaware of that, as I was as an adolescent. However, had my American history teacher asked me to interview my grandfather about family involvement in the Civil War I might have learned some 30 years sooner that both his father and grandfather had fought with the 81st Ohio Infantry throughout most of the Civil War. By the time I was interested in this information my grandfather had passed away and I located the information on a "family tree" website. So while I know my ancestors fought for the Union army and the unit in which they served, I know little else and have little likelihood of ever finding out much more. My point here is that as a content-area teacher, you must help your students see why understanding earth science or American history is important and how their lives were, perhaps, shaped by the nature of the soils around them or the particulars of their family histories.

Some content teachers can link student imaginations to the material to be studied. For instance, the nonfiction trade book, *The Boys War,* makes the daily life of a 12-year-old drummer boy perfectly clear. Books and videos can help adolescents understand how the climate of arid regions such as the American southwest or South Sudan or the tropical rainforest of the Amazon Basin impacts the lives of people living there as well as what crops are cultivated and the types of shelters people build for themselves.

Writing While and After Reading

Graham and Hebert (2011) note that writing is an "often-overlooked tool for improving students' reading, as well as their learning from text" (p. 4). They suggest that students write about the texts they read, teachers teach the skills and processes that go into creating text, and that schools increase the amount of time students write, especially in content-area classes. Their studies indicate that writing has the potential to enhance reading in at least three ways:

- As a functional activity, when reading and writing are combined, they facilitate learning. Writing about information from an American history text requires a student to record, connect, analyze, personalize, and manipulate key ideas in the text. That is, writing during and after reading fosters learning of the information provided in the text.

- Reading and writing draw upon common knowledge and cognitive processes; therefore, improving students' writing skills should lead to improved reading skills and vice-versa.

- Reading and writing are communication activities and vehicles for better comprehension. Writers develop insights about reading by creating their own texts, which leads to better comprehension of other texts. Reading familiarizes students with different genres and formats used for expressing information.

Further reinforcing this writing/reading connection is research (Pressley, Mohan, Raphael, & Fingeret, 2007) that demonstrated that teaching how to write and edit different forms of expository text improved students' comprehension of their content-area textbooks. Likewise, Langer and Applebee (1987) studied high school teachers who were attempting to integrate writing into their English, science, and history classes. All teachers in the study made more use of writing, with writing used as a tool for evaluation of student learning becoming the primary outcome. This seemed to be a result of student writing about what they had read that suggested major problems with their understanding of the texts. Thus, their teachers used post-reading writing of summaries to reassess the instruction that had been offered and re-teach the material so that students better understood the subject matter. Without the in-class writing assignments the teachers would have simply moved on to the next topic unaware that many students had major misunderstandings about what they had been reading and learning.

Langer and Applebee (1987) concluded, "We learned that subject-area writing can be used productively in three primary ways: (1) to gain relevant knowledge and experience in preparing for new activities; (2) to review and consolidate what is known or has been learned; and (3) to reformulate and extend ideas and experiences" (p. 136). In other words, adding quick writing activities each day to student lessons improved both the quality of the instruction offered and the learning of the subject matter.

It is relatively rare that content teachers ask students to write about what they have been reading in middle and high schools. The composition assignments described above all involved short bits of writing and in each case resulted in improved teaching and learning. Grading some 100 essays is a gargantuan task for a teacher, and perhaps this is why writing is so seldom observed even in English classrooms. But everything that students write does not require grading or even require that the teacher read what has been written. On the other hand, reading even 100 three- to five-sentence summaries does not take long and will provide insights into what students understand from the reading they have completed.

Another alternative role for such writing is partnering students to read the summaries each has just written and then collaborating to create a single summary from both. The goal of each of the writing activities is to learn more about what your students are actually learning so that you can modify your instruction in ways that will clear up misunderstandings after students have read an assigned textbook. The content-area teachers in the Langer and Applebee (1987) study reported that having students write every day improved not only their teaching but also improved the learning that students accomplished.

Teaching Your Students Useful Comprehension Strategies

If you think about it, you probably work in a school where more expertise is needed in developing powerful strategies for students to use in improving their understanding of the texts they are assigned. Most middle and high school teachers are lucky to have completed even a single course on fostering reading growth among adolescents. When teachers have had a course on this topic, it was typically a general methods course enrolling preservice teachers of literally every subject matter. There were future English teachers sitting alongside future earth science and agriculture teachers (and everyone else earning a teaching certificate). Still, even having such a broad course develops a level of expertise that is imperative to effective instruction, and that all teachers of adolescents should develop.

The recent federal model emphasizes that each content-area teacher must take the responsibility for developing the disciplinary reading and writing proficiencies of their students (Kamil et al., 2008). This emphasis seems largely incorporated into the new CCSS framework as well. One official suggested that content-area teachers need to plan for half of their instruction to be focused on developing the disciplinary reading and writing talents of their students. It is felt that disciplinary literacy proficiencies can only be developed by disciplinary experts. In other words, English teachers have little or nothing to offer in the area of reading chemistry or American history textbooks. English teachers must be able to develop the proficiencies their students will need to evaluate, analyze, and summarize the literary texts they read for English class. It is the chemistry teacher who must be able to foster the student literacy development necessary for the student to understand chemistry texts. This is a major new responsibility for every content-area teacher. No longer is a student's difficulty in understanding an assigned textbook someone else's problem; the new framework lays responsibility for such difficulties with the particular teacher who assigned the text to be read.

The specific information on disciplinary reading and writing is too complex to fully cover in this short book. That does not mean that you will learn nothing useful about what you should be doing to improve your students' reading and writing proficiencies. There is a short list of general research-based instructional efforts that can be used across content areas and we will get to those shortly. However, to become expert at improving proficiency in reading a chemistry text, an economics text, or an anthology of short stories, you might select to read one of the papers listed in the accompanying feature box. Each of these papers offers substantive advice on developing disciplinary literacy.

Papers Focused on Disciplinary Literacy for Content Area Teachers

Learned, J. E., Stockhill, D., & Moje, E. B. (2011). Integrating reading strategies and knowledge building in adolescent literacy instruction. In S. J. Samuels & A. E. Farstrup (Eds.), *What research has to say about reading instruction* (4th ed., pp. 159–185). Newark, DE: International Reading Association.

Moje, E. B., & Speyer (2008). The reality of challenging texts in high school science and social studies: How teachers can mediate comprehension. In K. A. Hinchman & H. K. Sheridan-Thomas (Eds.), *Best practices in adolescent literacy instruction* (pp. 185–211). New York: Guilford.

National Institute for Literacy (2007). *What content-area teachers should know about adolescent literacy.* Washington, DC: Office of Vocational and Adult Literacy.

Shanahan, C. (2009). Disciplinary comprehension. In S. Israel & G. G. Duffy (Eds.), *Handbook of research on reading comprehension* (pp. 240–260). New York: Routledge.

Shanahan, T., & Shanahan, C. (2008). Teaching disciplinary literacy to adolescents: Rethinking content-area literacy. *Harvard Educational Review, 78*(1).

Torgesen, J. K., Houston, D. D., Rissman, L. M., Decker, S. M., Roberts, G., Vaughn, S., Wexler, J. Francis, D. J, Rivera, M. O., & Lesaux, N. (2007). *Academic literacy instruction for adolescents: A guidance document from the Center on Instruction.* Portsmouth, NH: RMC Research Corporation, Center on Instruction. Downloaded from www.centeroninstruction.org.

Urquhart, V., & Frazee, D. (2012). *Teaching reading in the content areas: If not me, then who?* (3rd ed.). Alexandria, VA: ASCD.

While experts in different content areas use different text structures to present and argue information, there are a few strategies that seem generally useful regardless of the text to be read. These useful strategies include rereading in order to resolve confusion, a central strategy used by effective readers as part of self-regulation while reading. In other words, effective readers always monitor whether they understand what they are reading. This self-monitoring of understanding is often absent in students who routinely fail to understand what they read. Too often students who have long struggled with reading have also given up attempting to understand what they are reading. They just push on through the text and then, having "read" the text, cannot understand why they fail the quiz. "But I read the assignment," they say. "I guess I just didn't get it." Helping such students learn to know when their understanding is falling short and then working to develop their use of "repair strategies," such as rereading, will be necessary aspects of instruction for every content teacher.

Adolescent readers can experience difficulty understanding even texts that they can read accurately. It isn't just that the students have books that are too difficult for them, at least at the word pronunciation level. Often these students lack the relevant background knowledge, so even though they can read the text accurately they still fail to understand it. Although many students can read the words accurately, they fail to realize that this is but a good first step in understanding what they have read.

Summarizing

Paraphrasing and summarizing what was read to enhance memory and understanding of the content, visualizing relationships and events presented in the text, and note taking and underlining information central to understanding the text are useful strategies that effective adolescent readers use (Pressley, 2006). However, few adolescents have ever been exposed to effective demonstrations of any of these useful strategies (Pressley, Yokoi, Rankin, Wharton-McDonald, & Mistretta, 1997; Pressley, Wharton-McDonald, Mistretta-Hampton, & Echevarria, 1998).

There are several professional texts that you could read to begin developing expertise in fostering use of effective reading strategies. There are also several useful DVD presentations that provide models of effective demonstrations of strategy use by content-area teachers. In the accompanying feature box you can find examples of both useful texts to develop strategy lessons.

Text Resources for Models of Effective Strategy Lessons

Atwell, N. (1987). *In the middle: Writing, reading and learning with adolescents.* Portsmouth, NH: Heinemann.

Beers, K. (2003). *When kids can't read: What teachers can do, a guide for teachers 6–12.* Portsmouth, NH: Heinemann.

Duffy, G. G. (2009). Explaining reading: A resource for teaching concepts, skills, and strategies (2nd ed.). New York: Guilford.

Gallagher, K. (2004). *Deeper Reading: Comprehending Challenging Texts, 4–12.* Portland, ME: Stenhouse.

Tovani, C. (2001). *I read it, but I don't get it: Comprehension strategies for adolescent readers.* Portland, ME: Stenhouse.

Wilhelm, J. D. (2001). *Improving Comprehension with Think-Aloud Strategies.* New York: Scholastic.

What we know is that without effective demonstrations of useful comprehension strategies, many adolescent readers will struggle in school. We also know that when such lessons are made available, struggling readers demonstrate gains in understanding. Edmonds et al. (2009) found a large effect size for comprehension interventions (ES = 1.23), large for adolescents experiencing reading difficulties and larger effect sizes for enhancing the comprehension of pupils with disabilities. They found that,

> A primary finding of this synthesis is that struggling readers can improve their reading comprehension when taught reading comprehension practices. Seemingly obvious, this phenomenon is quite significant because many older struggling readers (grades 6 through 12) are not provided effective instruction in reading comprehension. (p. 292)

In other words, we have too much evidence that adolescents can benefit from useful comprehension strategy lessons and too much evidence that few middle school or high school content-area teachers ever provide these lessons. You can foster the development of effective reading in the content-area texts you assign students to read. However, if students continue without effective strategy instruction you will be less successful in developing their expertise in your content area.

Summary

We know much more about developing the reading comprehension of all students than one would suspect if they only observed the classrooms early adolescents attend. For too long, middle and high school teachers within the content areas have not been encouraged to provide instruction designed to improve understanding while reading the subject-specific texts they assign. The absence of such lessons from grade 5 through grade 12 seems the most likely reason that so many American high school graduates are unprepared for the demands of college reading. Remember, 50 percent of all ACT test takers fail to demonstrate reading levels that would predict that they would earn a grade of C in college classes. And 25 percent or more of all adolescents drop out of school and never take the ACT. These are woeful statistics.

Worse, while the reading achievement of American fourth-graders has been steadily rising for several decades, eight- and twelfth-grade reading performances are basically unchanged since 1970 and school dropout rates remain largely the same as in 1970. As the United States has dropped from number 1 in proportion of students who graduate college to number 16 in the world, policy makers have become worried and are asking what needs to change to make our students competitive internationally once again. Rightly or not they have focused less on instructional quality and more on teacher quality for the solution. Thus, there have been calls for merit pay for teachers who produce good growth among their students and termination for teachers whose students lag behind. All this is primarily the result of so few middle school and high school students participating in any lessons designed to make them more effective readers and more effective at understanding what they read.

Improving the likelihood that students will acquire the knowledge our instructional plans call for means teachers have to work to match the texts they assign students to read against the reading levels of their students and against the levels of prior knowledge of the content that their students possess. Too often too many students in American schools are assigned textbooks they cannot read accurately, fluently, or with understanding. Teachers need to fundamentally change their instructional planning processes to help all students understand and be engaged in their subjects.

Step 1 in instructional planning is deciding what it is you expect students to learn. Step 2 is finding appropriate instructional materials. Note the *-s* at the end of the word *materials*. There are no instructional planning models that skip step 2 and lead to one-size-fits-all textbooks and lessons (Brunn, 2010). Nonetheless, throughout American classrooms filled with early adolescents, teachers still offer one-size-fits-all lessons. Although their colleges derided this approach and encouraged students to create multi-level instruction, many teachers suggest that today, 'No one actually teaches the way our professors taught us.' I will admit that this is true, but this fact should be an indicator that change is needed rather than a reason for teachers to give in to the one-size-fits-all status quo.

Effective Teaching in the Middle School and High School

If you are interested, locate these books for personal reading. In each case they develop for you pictures of the classrooms that were studied. If you want to understand what effective teaching looks and feels like, read these books.

Allington, R. L., & Johnston, P. H. (Eds.). (2002). *Reading to learn: Lessons from exemplary 4th grade classrooms.* New York: Guilford.

Langer, J. A. (2002). *Effective literacy instruction: Building successful reading and writing programs.* Urbana, IL: NCTE.

We can do better. You can do better. It will likely take more planning time on your part initially but once planned multi-level and multi-sourced lessons make effective teaching a lot more likely and a lot easier. Our work (Allington & Johnston, 2002) and that of our colleagues (Langer, 2004; Pressley et al., 1998) has focused on observing those exemplary teachers who actually teach every child without much in the way of one-size-fits-all lessons. What we have learned is that effective teaching is actually easier than the typical teaching that is found in most classrooms because there are far fewer "discipline events" in these classrooms than in other classrooms in the same building. And it is easier because at the end of the day there are more successes to celebrate and far fewer student failures.

Chapter 6

Literate Conversation: A Powerful Method for Fostering Understanding of Complex Texts

In this chapter I will argue that for far too long American teachers have ignored a powerful learning tool: literate conversation. Each of you reading this book already knows how to engage another literate person in literate conversation. If you notice that a friend or colleague has a copy of a book you have already read, you will almost always ask some version of this question: "How do you like it?" Notice you don't say, "Tell me about the plot (or main character, or setting)." Nor do you quiz the person on details from the text. No, you ask the general question, "How do you like it?"

Before this moment it may never have occurred to you that it is the rare teacher who asks students that question. In fact, it is the rare teacher who ever engages students in any sort of instructional conversations (Nystrand, Wu, Gamoran, Zeiser, & Long, 2003). Instructional conversations can be literate conversations. In my mind it would be better if we called them *literate conversation* because it seems as soon as we substitute *instructional* for *literate* it becomes a teacher-led discussion rather than an actual conversation between two literate persons. At the same time, even a teacher-led discussion is an improvement over the 'interrogation' technique often employed by many educators.

Classrom Talk: Interrogation vs. Discussion

The school day is dominated not by literate conversations or even by instructional conversations, but rather by question–answer exchanges where one person (the teacher) asks another person (a student) a known-answer question. School is one of the few places where people are asked a question to which the questioner already knows the answer. There are more effective methods of in-class conversation than such questioning that would be called interrogation outside of school.

Imagine you are sitting in a coffee shop having a cup of coffee when a person at the next table asks you, "Do you know the date of St. Patrick's Day this year?" And, you, who (like me) have little in the way of Irish descendants, might reply, "Sorry, I have no idea." To which the other person replies, "No idea? It's March 17th." Or perhaps if you actually know the date for St. Patrick's Day, you respond with the correct date, to which the other customer replies, "Good job, you really know your stuff."

At this point you may feel like tossing your remaining coffee on him (or her) because either reply just seems rude. It seems rude because it was rude behavior for a customer in a coffee shop. It would also be rude behavior in a church, or in an insurance agency, or anywhere else but in a classroom. In other words, asking questions you already know the answer to is not a good method of engaging people in a constructive discussion. Interrogation is frowned upon in most settings besides schools and police stations. It does not help to form a relationship of mutual respect.

Think about this for a minute. Why is it that teachers are allowed to ask questions they know the answer to but customers in coffee shops are considered rude when their questioning behavior mimics that of the typical classroom teacher? Truth be told, I have no good answer for why it is so common for teachers to ask known-answer questions. Truly, no idea.

What I do know is that asking known-answer questions has been well studied. We know that such questions dominate classroom lessons, and we also know a lot about the structure of such questioning sequences. Cazden (1986) describes this sort of exchange between teachers and their students as a "basic sequence" of common classroom discourse. She describes this event as an Initiate-Reply-Evaluate (IRE) sequence of responses.

In classrooms it is almost always the teacher who "initiates" the exchange or poses the known-answer question. It is the students who "reply" to the question. After the student replies, the teacher "evaluates" the reply (response, answer). The key to the IRE exchange is the "evaluate" aspect. In such exchanges someone—in schools it is the teachers—gets to tell someone else that their answer is correct or not. In most IRE exchanges there is a differential distribution of power, one person holds the power while the other is compliant and accepts the power difference, a relationship that is not conducive to establishing an exchange of ideas.

On the other hand, conversations or discussions are typically entered into with an assumption of shared authority where neither party holds absolute power. In such cases, persons can have a conversation where they end up disagreeing with one another. In schools, jails, and battlefields, on the other hand, someone typically holds the power and the authority to decide what is the right decision or response.

Interestingly, the longer you stay in school the more common conversations become part of your classroom experiences. Think about the graduate school classes, undergraduate classes, high school classes, and middle school classes you attended. At which class level did you engage in the greatest amount of conversation or the greater number of discussions?

Cazden (2001) also argued that teachers give students directions that students then carry out, usually non-verbally. Teachers also ask questions and students answer them, usually in a word or phrase. But these roles are almost never reversed. Students rarely give directions, especially to teachers, and rarely ever ask questions of teachers, except for procedural questions required to get their school work done. Students may give directions or ask questions of their peers, but only if such talk is allowed in the classroom, which it rarely is.

Literate Conversations

What we've learned relatively recently is just how potentially powerful conversations and discussions can be in fostering learning, especially higher-order learning in any subject area (Almasi & Garas-York, 2009; Nystrand, 2006). We've also learned that having students generate higher-order questions improves their learning across content areas (Taylor, Pearson, Peterson, & Rodriguez, 2003). Higher-order questions are those questions where there is no one correct answer, such as: Why did General Grant not pursue the Confederate Army after the second day of the Battle of Shiloh? There are several plausible responses, each supported by some of the data we can still access from that day. But there is no single correct answer because we cannot return to that battlefield and determine just why the Union Army settled in for the evening after defeating the Confederate Army, which moved south into Mississippi to regroup.

Nystrand (2006) largely summarizes much of what we know about the nature of discourse in classrooms that foster high achievement growth. He notes that research identifies discussion, authentic questions, and the proportion of follow-up questions asked as all linked to developing better understandings of assigned textbook content and greater control over course content in the classroom. But he states that observational research also reveals that none of these activities occur in most classrooms on most days.

Literate Conversation and Metacognition

One important aspect of understanding texts that have been read is meta-cognition, or knowing when you don't know. Theide, Griffin, Wiley, and Anderson (2010, p. 331) noted:

> In particular, students who consistently used valid cues—such as the ability to connect ideas contained in the text—had near perfect monitoring accuracy across three different conditions. By contrast, students who consistently used less valid cues—such as the number of big words contained in a text—had consistently poor monitoring accuracy. The key to improving monitoring accuracy is getting people to focus on the more valid cues. Fortunately, we can instruct people to focus on valid cues and monitoring accuracy will improve.

When students are not engaged in useful monitoring of their reading their understanding of the text they are reading decreases. That should not surprise anyone. Literate conversations with peers also seem to foster improved comprehension monitoring. What we know, however, is that teachers can improve the quality of the comprehension monitoring that students do. A first step is to ensure students know why they have been assigned a text to read. The only reason for assigning a text segment cannot be that it comes next in the textbook. What is it that you hope students will learn, or at least think about, as they read the text you have assigned? If you find it difficult to state just what it is, then you should understand why your students are confused and why so many are reading the text simply because it was "assigned."

Think about your own reading for a moment. How many texts do read each day? How many texts do you encounter but elect not to read? You elect not read some texts because you (1) have no interest in the topic, (2) have no background with the topic, or (3) both of these. Literate adults neither read randomly nor engage in much assigned reading. At the same time students do much assigned reading, much of it basically random reading of random passages. I call this *random* because there exist a large number of texts that could be assigned to learn about any particular topic or subject area.

The Ineffectiveness of One-Size-Fits-All Texts

Why so many teachers select just one text for students to read is an essential question we must consider if we ever hope to enhance both teaching and learning. I suppose it could be that many of these teachers work in schools where someone has purchased multiple copies of a single textbook for use in a class. Ordering textbooks this way does make life simpler for district officials but, at the same time, it makes life more complex for students and their teachers. It may be that using a single text makes it easier to locate the students who recall much of the material they've been assigned to read. It also makes creating mindless worksheets and such much easier than if multiple texts were used. But in neither of these cases does the potential negative effects of using a single textbook override the potential of using multiple texts.

Beyond that, it is easier to develop classroom conversations when students have read different texts on the same topic, although multiple texts make it more difficult to create recall questions. If the goal of modern education is to create young adults who can both ask better questions and explore different answers to those questions, then one would think that the era of the single textbook adoption is over. However, that hardly seems the case in the schools I work with.

Maybe the problem is that we are wedged between two quite different views of the purpose of American education. These two views are broadly described as transmission-based education (teachers will tell you what you need to know) and participation-based education (students need to figure out what the answer is).

Transmission versus Participation Pedagogies

Common classroom practices reflect a better alignment with transmission models of learning (filling the brain with data) than with other models of learning that assume that fostering rote recall is not the goal but that fostering improved thinking is. These latter sorts of models have been grouped together as participation models of learning. The goal is not simply recalling whether the Union or the Confederate forces won the Battle of Shiloh during the American Civil War, but understanding the powerful and disturbing message the outcome of that battle sent to the supporters of both sides.

Rote learning of facts is old school. In an example I mentioned earlier, the majority of entering college freshman questioned why using a smart phone to look up answers for a test should be considered cheating. In their "modern" view, since facts are easy to locate on a smart phone, it is a waste of brain space trying to store them. Of course, for many people, such a response seems ludicrous, and many would question how they know that the "facts" they found are actually facts. The students would respond, "How do we know what we read in the textbooks you assigned are 'facts?'"

The college freshmen raise a good point. How many American history textbooks have you been assigned since you began school where the presentation of the discovery of this continent by Europeans basically noted something like, "When the first European settlers arrived the land was largely forest with only a few, scattered native Americans settlements?"

The truth of the matter is that America once had large communities of native Americans, essentially occupying much of the lands along the east coast. In addition, such large native American communities were located throughout the North American continent. In other words, America was far more populated with communities reflecting a far superior organization than we were led to believe from reading our textbooks. You can learn more about these communities in a recent book entitled, *1491: New revelations of America before Columbus,* written by Charles C. Mann. In fact, much of what you think you know about American history is largely untrue and is the result of the long campaign to assert American exceptionalism (Loewen, 2009).

But what if American history as taught in American schools focused more on gathering evidence about historical "facts" instead of focused on remembering a too often inaccurate set of "facts" about America and American citizens? It is just this sort of education that better exemplifies "participation" pedagogies.

Perhaps remembering factual details will become something that "old people" do. However, I doubt this will happen because often an understanding of the facts is required to understand the larger event. At the same time, we have to realize that remembering the facts does not equal understanding the event or phenomenon. Years ago I memorized the basic details concerning the table of elements for my chemistry class. I even remember doing well on a test of all those details. However, I never understood a thing about the table of elements. I'm not sure whether any of my high school classmates learned anything more about the table of elements but for me it was like memorizing the names of all the countries in Africa. I never asked why my teachers expected me to memorize this stuff; I just did it. Neither set of memorized facts have served me well in adulthood. I am not even sure why I took a high school chemistry class except that it was expected of college-bound high school students. Memorizing the African nations in 1963 provided little useful information when I first traveled to Africa in 2005 since most of the nations I had learned no longer existed.

I wish I had had fewer "transmission" teachers and had had more "participation" teachers. The two participation teachers I had in high school (for American history and English) taught me to think, to analyze, to challenge unsupported assertions. Those two teachers provided me with the proficiencies I needed when I got to college. (Thank you, Mr. Morris and Mr. Herweyer) They also set the foundation for the proficiencies I need today as a professor and as a citizen in a democratic society.

How the Internet Changes Everything

The dawn of the internet coincided with the death of traditional journalism. These internet articles (offered as op-ed pieces, blogs, corporate messages, and so on) are not fact checked by one or more editors. Today it seems that getting these comments into the message sphere is more important than assuring the message is accurate. Students of today are confronting the 24-hour information cycle but with little formal preparation for engaging that cycle critically.

Today I read a story in a national newspaper, *USA Today,* about a program using Facebook as a tool for training college athletes about the power of the internet. The gist of the story is that the typical college athlete is truly clueless about the intricacies of social media and about all of the bad things that can happen as a result of even having a Facebook account. Using attractive females as decoys, the company providing the training had the young women request "Friend" status of football players on Facebook before the training session occurred. Most of the players had responded positively to these requests. The young woman entered the session room and then displayed private Facebook page content to all the players gathered for the training session. While wild hoots of laughter arose when the first couple of cases were displayed, by the end of the session it was largely quiet because over two-thirds of the team had "Friended" the attractive young women and, thus, nearly the whole team had embarrassing Facebook moments at the session.

My point here is that while access to the internet, social media, and such have created a world in which many middle and high school students feel comfortable, it is a world they seem to know little about—just like the football players.

While people can seem "out of the loop" if they do not use social media, the truth is that almost any of the social media tools has the power to present to the world a view of every user that was not meant for widespread distribution. What does this mean for schools?

Internet access provides each person with incredible power to explore the world. You have access to hundreds of thousands of websites, each one that has information. Not all of that information—and perhaps not even most of that information—is reliable (reliable here meaning accurate or true). Information, whether found on websites or in textbooks, must always be evaluated for its accuracy and completeness. I'd be happy if our schools only developed each student's proficiencies at evaluating information. However, in most schools judging the adequacy of the information being presented (or read) is rarely the focus of any of the thousands of lessons kids participate in. What our schools do is develop citizens who are more likely to believe almost anything they read than citizens who routinely question almost everything they read. In today's world that means there are far too many citizens who are unprepared to confront life in the twenty-first century.

Recall versus Thoughtful

I am attempting to contrast classrooms where the goal is the simple recall of facts with classrooms that promote the mindful consideration of facts. I believe that if our democracy is to survive, then schools must create citizens who are as skilled at asking questions as they are at finding answers to questions. Life in the twenty-first century finds citizens drowning in data that is provided by every sort of organization from one-person advocacy campaigns to corporate advocacy campaigns. Information generation has exploded and it is the rare individual who can keep pace with the flow of information.

Let me pose a problem here for you. Consider that over the past 40 years the National Assessment of Educational Progress reading achievement scores of American fourth-graders of every ethnic group have risen. Consider also that the average score of American fourth-graders remains largely unchanged. Given these data, politicians argue that American schools are "broken" because achievement is stagnant. This has led to the push for various federal and state education initiatives to improve schools.

But wait! If everyone's scores have been rising, how is it that politicians believe that teachers are no longer as effective as they once were? It is the result of Simpson's Paradox according to researcher Gerald Bracey (2003). As he pointed out, since the NAEP began assessing American students in 1970 the student composition of our schools has shifted dramatically.

The numbers of students of Hispanic heritage has increased dramatically. In the initial NAEP 1971 report there were so few Hispanic students in American schools that the report does not even break out scores for these students. In the most recent NAEP report Hispanic students represented nearly one-quarter of all students assessed. Many of these students live in homes where Spanish is the dominant language and so are placed in English Language Learner (ELL) programs designed to ease the transition into the academic English used in schools. In addition, many of our Hispanic students are the children of low-income parents with limited education.

Perhaps it is the combination of second language learning and poverty that contributes to Hispanic children performing far less well on the NAEP assessments than do middle class Anglo children. The more limited English language literacy development of these students has suppressed the reading performance of American students on average.

In American schools the proportion of students who belong to the highest scoring ethnic subgroup, Anglo students, has been dropping steadily since 1971. It will only be a few years (projected between 2025 and 2030) before Anglo students will represent a minority of all students in school. As we raise the reading levels of today's minority students, we typically raise the reading levels of Anglo students. This is true in the United States also. The addition of many new and lower-scoring minority students has meant that while achievement has improved for everyone, the average reading achievement for all has barely budged. At the same time, the reading achievement gap between students from low and middle income families is now 40 percent larger than it was 40 years ago (NCES, 2011).

In other words, while students today generally read a bit better than they did back in 1970 when the first NAEP assessment was administered, we have made no progress in closing the rich/poor reading achievement gap. Instead, the rich/poor reading achievement gap has simply grown larger over the past 40 years, and it is this gap that creates many of the problems confronting teachers of early adolescents. In general, it is children from low-income homes that struggle in meeting the academic expectations schools have for students.

It seems a sort of double jeopardy, then, that it is in classrooms filled with low-achieving students where literate conversation has almost never been observed (Nystrand, 2006). Fostering literate conversations improves both content learning and reading comprehension. I call this *double jeopardy* because the students who have the greatest need for academic improvement are the ones least likely to engage in classroom practices that enhance learning.

So why is this the case? I will offer four explanations and argue that in most schools all four play a role in limiting access of students to literate conversations. First, there is the influence of the "pedagogy of poverty." As Haberman (1995) has noted, too often teachers succumb to what they see as standard practice in schools enrolling mostly low-income students. When such teachers never observe any other teachers in the school engaging low-income students in literate conversation, they decide that "interrogation" is what has been effective.

Second, it is students from low-income homes who likely have the fewest experiences with literate conversations, whether at school or at home. Thus, getting a good conversation going seems harder in schools enrolling many such children than it is in schools enrolling primarily students from middle-income homes. While this may be the case, fostering literate conversations among low-income students is not really that difficult. Students from low-income families benefit just as much as middle-class kids when teachers add episodes of literate conversation to the daily classroom routines.

Third, many lower-achieving adolescents prefer the low-level worksheets that have dominated their school experiences because these low-level tasks are more familiar. Their preference for these tasks may lead them to resist engaging other students in literate conversations. Imagine what might be the case if all classrooms, beginning in kindergarten, fostered literate conversations! Just because we haven't yet created such classrooms is no reason to delay beginning.

Fourth, because all students have far more experience in school answering known-answer questions, all students need to be eased into literate conversations. This "easing in" is addressed next.

Easing Students into Literate Conversations

Perhaps one of the main issues is that many teachers do not have a good grasp of what comprehension of texts means in practice. Kucan, Hapgood, and Palincsar (2011) involved 60 upper elementary grade teachers (fourth and fifth grades) in completing an assessment of comprehension-related knowledge including analysis of passages and specialized knowledge for fostering reading comprehension, particularly through discussion.

They found only one-third of teachers could engage in the integration and inferencing required to provide coherent statements about the most important ideas in the texts! *One-third!* Only 15 percent of teachers "were able to specify the possible difficulties posed by the assessment texts at a useful level of detail . . .." (p. 71). Too often teachers used very general probes and exhibited a willingness to allow students to focus on tangential ideas rather than the important ideas found in the text.

They noted that

teacher responses across all the responding to students tasks revealed that teachers did not offer the specific kinds of support that students needed in order to explain text information, and instead relied on general probes for more information and rereading. Their responses were more routinized than flexible and opportunistic. (p. 75)

In other words, many teachers need to develop the skills necessary to lead productive discussions and literate conversations.

It is important to note that there is a difference in what students learn from lessons with IRE sequences (where teachers ask known-answer questions) and lessons where teachers offer extended discussion with the teacher and multiple students exchanging ideas related to a topic for a length of time. There is also a difference in what and how much is learned when comparing lessons dominated by IRE exchanges and those where students engage

Teachers Can Assist Students in Their Literate Conversations

The federal *IES Practice Guide* (Shanahan et al., 2010, p. 27) provides a short list of the types of comments teachers might make when students are engaged in literate conversations with each other (and, perhaps, with the teacher). Note how each of these directs students to support their responses and their reasoning.

- What makes you say that?
- What does the author say about that?
- Can you explain what you meant when you said _____?
- Do you agree with what _____ said? Why or why not?
- How does what you said connect with what _____ already said?
- Let's see if what we read provides us with any information that can resolve _____'s and _____'s disagreement.

each other in literate conversations. Both extended teacher–student discussion and student–student literate conversation produce greater content learning and improved reading comprehension when compared to IRE focused lessons (Nystrand, 2006).

If classroom discussions, or literate conversations, improve student learning, why do so few teachers in any subject area engage students in such activities? While I'm not certain, I think it may be because so few teachers ever experienced classroom discussions in their own middle and high school classes. Their ideas about what a classroom lesson is supposed to look like, based on their experiences, constrain them in providing a different sort of experience for their students. In fact, much of what passes as "typical practices" in today's classrooms is simply the remnants of what has been passed along over the years as part of going to school or going to a history or earth science classes (Cuban, 1993). However, while IRE classrooms are certainly the norm in middle and high schools today, we also now have evidence that there are better options that must be introduced.

Integrating student-centered discussion, or literate conversations, into daily classroom routines provides a central option in shifting to classroom lessons that build more and deeper knowledge (and better and deeper understandings of content). Easing students into such classroom routines can begin small and expand over time. It should begin with more teacher scaffolding of discussion while moving on to more student-centered discussions.

Initially, a teacher might begin by simply posing an open-ended question:

We've been reading about the solar system where Earth is located. We've read about new discoveries that have led to redefining that solar system. Take a moment and jot down information that led to demoting Pluto from a planet to a dwarf planet. In a couple of minutes I want you to use your notes to tell me whether you agree with the decision to remove Pluto from the list of planets in our solar system.

Once students have completed their quick-write activity as noted above, the teacher can either offer an open call where anyone can respond or a closed call where the teacher identifies a student to begin the response to the question. In either situation the next step is not to "evaluate" the response but to ask for an extension of the response (e.g., "Tell me more about the third criterion the scientists used to demote Pluto."). These initial introductions to classroom discussion might be organized as whole-class events. Soon though you will want to move to small-group discussion, even of the same question. Class discussions— large group, small group, or online group—are chances for students to compare their thinking with that of other students. Teachers can provide support during group discussion by moving from group to group, modeling questions and comments that deepen the analysis, and encouraging the use of challenging questions that cause students to think deeply (Langer, 2011).

Wonderment, or Open-Ended Questions

Wonderment is a word I created a decade or so ago to describe the sorts of open-ended questions I observed exemplary teachers asking their students. Consider this question frame, "I wonder why General Washington decided to cross the Delaware River and attack Trenton, New Jersey, on Christmas day." Ask this as a question and pair it with "Jot down any reasons provided in the materials you've just read." After giving students a few minutes to write down their responses, you can give the direction to, "Turn to your neighbor and read what you've written and listen to what your neighbor has written." All this sets the stage for a teacher-led discussion on the topic.

Wonderment questions are designed to foster thinking, to foster consideration of "facts." There can be no single correct answer to a wonderment question, but there can be answers that are more or less based in the evidence available.

The goal here is to get students to actively think about the topic. Wonderment queries move students away from simply remembering "facts" toward considering "facts." Although we may never know why Washington decided to attack on Christmas day, there are several potential reasons historians have explored and the goal here is to move students to also generate explanations.

Taylor, Pearson, Peterson, and Rodriguez (2005) noted that time spent in classrooms with teachers asking and students answering low-level recall questions undermined efforts to improve both teaching and learning. They noted that, "high amounts of mechanistic practice on comprehension skills are taking time away from other important comprehension activities such as higher level talk about texts and use of comprehension strategies during reading" (p. 57).

Wonderment queries should stimulate thinking and foster hypothesizing about an event or a person's actions. Hypothesizing is what historians and other scientists do regularly. Examining the evidence that supports or undermines a given hypothesis is at the center of virtually all scientific thinking. We can foster growth in this higher-order cognitive function, but currently we rarely engage in instructional routines that lead to hypothesizing or hypothesis testing. In short, classroom activities that require thinking, as opposed to remembering, are relatively rare classroom events.

Fostering Engagement

Fostering student engagement in discussion is a critical teacher capacity. Demonstrating how a literate conversation might develop, asking open ended questions, providing probes, and modeling productive conversations about a text are all part of fostering this engagement. In addition to improved reading comprehension, literate conversations promote social acceptance and belongingness among class members. Classes where discussion was common had fewer social isolates and fewer social stars in contrast to classes where teacher interrogation dominated (Okolo, Ferretti, & MacArthur, 2007). Working in small groups facilitated conversation, as did "liking" other group members. Helping students understand that contributing was everyone's responsibility and staying focused on the conversation were also seen as requirements for successful conversations (Almasi & Garas-York, 2009).

When it comes to grouping students for discussion, remember that the dynamics of a group are created by group members interacting with each other. I suggest you begin by asking kids to create their own groups, taking care that every student is in a group. In the initial discussions it may be useful to also assign students different roles to play.

So, for small conversational groups you might want to consider using Reciprocal Teaching (Palincsar & Brown, 1984), a research-based form of cooperative learning. In reciprocal teaching, students read sections of the text silently, and then take turns leading a discussion of their material that includes questioning, summarizing, clarifying, and predicting (Rosenshine & Meister, 1994). One good treatment of reciprocal teaching can be found in Oczkus' (2010) small book on the topic.

Essentially, reciprocal teaching involves assigning students one of five roles: predictor, questioner, summarizer, clarifier, and discussion director. Each role has certain responsibilities that foster student engagement in discussion activities that replace the traditional worksheets too often found in classrooms. The reciprocal teaching routines provide a bit of structure and guidance for students venturing into classroom discussions. Some evidence suggests that the use of reciprocal teaching engages more students more often than use of a whole-class discussion routine. Other studies demonstrate that adding reciprocal teaching routines as regular classroom events improves student learning (Palincsar, 2007).

As the small groups meet to read and discuss a text, you should be up and about the room, away from your desk and away from the front of the room. Move from group to group and observe group interactions. You may even want (or need) to step in and provide guidance for the members of the groups.

Useful Tools for Developing Powerful Literate Conversations

Peterson, R., & Eeds, M. A. (2007). *Grand conversations: Literature groups in action*. New York: Scholastic.

This short professional text is focused on developing useful conversations about literature that students have read. However, it remains a useful introduction to the idea of how to organize such conversations in any classroom.

Oczkus, L. D. (2010). *Reciprocal teaching at work: Powerful strategies and lessons for improving reading comprehension*, (2nd ed.). Newark, DE: International Reading Association.

This small book provides an introduction to using reciprocal teaching routines in your classroom, and suggests practical and powerful ideas for enhancing content-area lessons.

Tovani, C. (2012). *Talk to me: Conferring to engage, differentiate*. Portland, ME: Stenhouse.

Tovani, C. (2003). *Thoughtful reading: Teaching comprehension to adolescents*. Portland, ME: Stenhouse.

These two DVDs feature middle school teacher Tovani as she goes about developing adolescent readers and writers. Both provide teachers of adolescents powerful models for fostering an understanding of texts.

There isn't much magic involved here, just supporting students as they attempt to fulfill their various roles in the reciprocal teaching activity. At times it may be necessary to remind students to turn back to the texts they've read to support assertions they are making. You may also need to remind some students that being respectful to everyone is also a necessary condition of good discussion. While being respectful doesn't mean agreeing with everything others say, it does mean that supporting your concerns about an idea someone has raised has to be more than uttering, "That's just stupid."

One way to enhance the quality of the discussions is to model appropriate verbal interactions. You can provide the model during discussions that you lead or create a classroom wall chart that suggests appropriate verbal statements. For instance, you can model saying, "I disagree with your statement because page 321 of the text we just read says _____" Or, "I'd like to expand on the point you made by noting that this text also says_____" In other words, provide students with the verbal models we use when engaged in, for example, a polite disagreement with a friend. Each of you reading this knows how a normal discussion goes and how to argue a point without offending the other member(s) of a group. Help students see this by putting such practice into play in the classroom.

Think–Pair–Share

The smallest group is two students. Pairing students together to discuss what they have read provides the simplest format for initiating classroom conversations. Allowing students to self-select their partners has both advantages and disadvantages. As Almasi, Palmer, Madden, and Hart (2011) note, friends find it easier to initiate discussions between themselves than with strangers. So the advantage of Think–Pair–Share (TPS) is that getting conversations off the ground is easier if students select their conversation partners.

However, there are also disadvantages of using friends as partners. The first is that some students may have no friends in the classroom and asking students to self-select conversational partners almost always leaves someone out. (Often several students may get no invitations to converse with a classmate.) One positive aspect of TPS activities is that students make new friends when they engage in conversations with students they don't know well (or may not know at all).

A second potential disadvantage is that friends often share a common background and so their discussions can be bland and neglect to address issues that the friends agree on. Mixing up students of different social classes, different home languages, different academic achievement levels, and so on offers possibilities of real discussion of critical issues found in a text. However, it is not always easy to get a high achieving student and a low achieving student to actually discuss any issue. Everyone has learned over the years the persons who always seem to get the answer correct when teachers ask questions during class time or on an exam. In such environments it is not unreasonable to assume that many lower-achieving students will allow the higher achieving students to take the floor and determine the nature of the discussion.

My recommendation is to experiment. Try friend pairings and ensure that all students are selected for a pair. (Or you can simply gather the names of student pairs in writing before the event and match up kids who don't name another student who they plan to work with.) After a few experiences with friends as conversation partners, mix students up a bit. Finally, have students simply look left or right, front or back, to locate their next conversation partner.

Ban Questions with One-Word Answers

For conversations to be productive they must not be allowed to mimic interrogations. I mention this because, too often, students have existed in classroom environments where interrogation has been the primary means of interaction, and they model the interrogation routines when we ask them to TPS. Your students will likely need some modeling to ask questions that require more than a single word as the answer. You can model this during teacher-led classroom discussions. I will note that even today I find it useful to develop two or three such questions before I initiate a teacher-led discussion.

William Goldsmith, a fifth-grade teacher in the Orange County, Florida, public schools, writes about how he has honed the TPS process, focusing

Explain Your Thinking

Partner A might begin by saying: "I think _____ because _____."
Partner B could respond by saying: "I heard you say _____. I agree/disagree with you because _____."

Goldsmith (2013) offers a second useful support to use as you begin to create classroom conversations. He suggests that when students respond to a question with, "I don't know," you don't let them off the hook by moving on to another student. Instead, you might allow that student to turn to a friend for advice on the answer. Asking the first student to then restate what his or her friend said and following that with, "Do you agree? Why or why not?" pushes all students into the conversational stream.

Finally, Goldsmith offers this advice: Use a randomized system for calling on students instead of asking students to raise their hands to answer. He notes that such a process creates greater on-task attention in classrooms while also allowing every student a chance to participate. This is especially useful at the end of a TPS routine where you ask students to share with the whole class what they've been discussing and what they agreed on. Continued use of the hand-raising routine produces a classroom that is two-tiered: one tier of students who know the answer and another tier of students who do not. Your goal is to create a classroom where all students are not only involved but also learning.

Remember that it is when students are talking to each other that learning occurs. As adults we talk through difficult things we are learning. Allow your students the same privilege.

You can keep the initial conversational periods short—say, 3 minutes—and gradually lengthen the time period. You can also go from pairs to triplets or foursomes as conversational groups. As students become more comfortable and more acquainted with literate conversation, you can move to larger group sizes. The largest groups size I recommend is five students.

You may want to address the volume of the talk that occurs during TPS activities. I've found that modeling "whisper talk" is one way to tackle the problem of a too-noisy classroom where the volume is too loud for anyone to hear his or her partner.

especially on his ELL students. He has posted an anchor chart on his classroom wall that provides a set of words that students can use when engaged in TPS.

You can follow up on the TPS experience with a question such as, "What did you guys notice when you discussed this story/chapter/section?" You might follow their response by asking, "Did anyone else notice this same part of the text you read?"

Professional Texts on Fostering Comprehension

Daniels, H. S., & Steineke, N. (2013). *Texts and lessons for teaching literature.* Portsmouth, NH: Heinemann.

Tovani, C. (2001). *I read it, but I don't get it: Comprehension strategies for adolescent readers.* Portland, ME: Stenhouse.

The TPS routine can also be used to have students compare notes they've taken about a text or annotations they have written while reading. In fact, turn-pair-share can be used to initiate discussions both longer and shorter. It is largely up to the teacher to decide when a turn and share opportunity might be useful for fostering discussion and, of course, improved learning.

You can extend the usefulness of turn and share time by asking students to co-construct summary statements for the section of the text that has been read or to jointly provide examples from the text that support the argument they've made. Just remember to be out and about your classroom as the turn and share activity is pursued. Again, your role here is to monitor, teach, and inject an idea into the conversations you are observing.

Find the Experts

Smokey Daniels and Nancy Steineke (2013) provide a number of useful activities with texts of various sorts that you might use to foster discussions in your classrooms. One activity they suggest is "Find the experts" in your classroom. They provide a lesson design using this for the book *To Kill a Mockingbird* by Harper Lee. In that lesson they list a number of items that you might want to identify students as experts on—for instance, collard greens, or someone who has visited Alabama or Mississippi, knows about head lice, collects coins, or takes care of younger siblings, and so on. You simply list these on the board or large paper chart and then let students discuss each item in pairs. You could distribute the list of items on a sheet of paper and ask each pair to indicate if there are any items on which one of them, or both, feel as though they were experts. Not every class has an expert for every item but many do and many classrooms have multiple experts on some items.

You use the expertise of your students when you encounter an example of the item while reading *To Kill a Mockingbird*. Ask them to tell the class about collard greens or about head lice and so on. Make sure class members know who is expert on which items, perhaps by displaying the list of items with the local experts listed for each item. Make sure students know that when they are having difficulty in understanding something written about an item, they can visit with a local expert in an attempt to find clarification.

Summary

Engaging students in literate conversations is a powerful, but too often ignored, tool for improving student learning. Such discussions have the potential to help students put into words what they have been reading (learning). It seems odd (or weird, if you prefer) that classroom discussion seems such a rare event. Discussion is a way to get students talking about what they are reading and learning. This talk also makes visible the misunderstandings some students may have as they read content texts. It is this potential—observing misunderstandings—why teachers must be up and about the classrooms during peer discussions.

However, as Leigh Hall (2012) has observed, differences in reading comprehension of students means that you should not be surprised if all conversations are not equal. At the same time, when conversations seem deficient, it is the nature of that deficiency that becomes the focus of classroom lessons. Problems that do occur during discussion sessions may also be addressed by the classroom teacher, literally on the spot, as the teacher moves about the classroom. Whether to address the problem at the moment or later on depends largely on what deficiency was observed. Better readers seem to be the group most comfortable with classroom discussions and the group most likely to make the session productive. This should not surprise us. What it means, simply, is that better readers are generally better at doing school tasks, in this case both reading assigned texts and discussing those texts.

It also means that students who struggle with reading or discussion or both need instructional attention. One aspect of that instructional attention is ensuring each student has a text that they can actually read accurately and with understanding. Too often the classroom breakdown of conversational groups is related to expecting students to discuss texts that they cannot read.

Likewise, when a text that has been read contains many new words and new ideas unfamiliar to some students, it is tough to get a good discussion going if only because the students were overwhelmed by the new words and the new information. This is when using pre-teaching concepts and explaining vocabulary introduced in the chapter is most appropriate. In other words, productive talk about texts is more likely to occur when students understand the text they have read. Ultimately, understanding of the text is facilitated by the discussion and conversations students have with each about what they've been reading.

In the end, it is you, the teacher, who can create classrooms where students learn to do much more than recall some details about topics and events—the outcome for most students in most schools. The recently adopted CCSS focuses attention on developing students' proficiencies reading texts that are more complex than those currently offered in American schools. Literate conversation is one strategy to foster such development. In the end, students learn what they are taught, but unless we provide a greater focus on thinking about the ideas found in the texts students read, they will recall some of the things they read but never actually consider what they read with any rigor. It is the teacher who can change the lessons and the learning. The kids are just waiting for this change to happen.

Chapter 7

Getting the Gist of It All: Summarization after Reading

We cannot continue to believe that what students are supposed to learn in school is a "basket of facts." Authentic learning is the complex, interrelated conceptual network that supports students in establishing themselves as "educated" and that will continue to grow and change as students acquire additional expertise on a topic (Anderson, 1984; Resnick, 2010). In other words, a primary reason so much of what you have already "learned" in school has already been forgotten is that the "basket of facts" model represents shallow learning, the sort of learning that allows students to hold "facts" until the test and then delete them from their memories. At the root of this shallow learning lies the known-answer questions that American students are inundated with day after day. These questions represent the one thing students have learned to do best: how to answer low-level literal questions after reading a text.

Allington and Weber (1993) noted there was little empirical evidence suggesting that the ability to answer the questions that teachers ask students after a text has been read was related to other assessments of students' understanding the text. In other words, being able to answer the low-level literal questions that teachers ask and that dominate students' classroom lessons is largely unrelated to more complex measures of learning, such as students' summarizing a segment of text they have just read. Likewise, the inability to answer low-level literal questions is largely unrelated to a student's ability to summarize. The research is similar on activities such as completing worksheets or copying definitions of vocabulary, two very common classroom tasks. In other words, much of what was common practice in classrooms 50 years ago (when I was attending public school), and still remains common today, exhibits no relationship for students to actually understand what was read or what was taught.

Close Reading and Summarization

There seems to be no way that shallow learning can continue to be the accepted outcome of schooling. The recently adopted Common Core State Standards put so much emphasis on deeper learning and on developing proficiencies in defending responses, especially with reference back to the texts that is being discussed. Likewise, the new assessments that accompany the CCSS require that students demonstrate their thinking along with referencing the text in their responses to the questions that are posed.

Close reading is emphasized in the CCSS. Close reading was a popular methodology a half-century or more ago. But, as Hinchman and Moore (2013) note,

> As veteran literacy educators, we are surprised that close reading has become a principal aspect of reading in the CCSS because it has received little notice in recent professional and research literature devoted to adolescents' literacies. Close reading has been ignored by current high-profile syntheses of literacy research (e.g., Carnegie Council on Advancing Adolescent Literacy, 2010; Duke, Pearson, Strachan, & Billman, 2011; Edmonds et al., 2009; Kamil et al., 2008), and we have been unable to locate individual empirical studies that overtly investigate its use with youths. (p. 443)

You might be wondering, as I have, how close reading became the new goal if there exists no research base supporting the practice. The best explanation I can provide is that it seems that the authors of the CCSS simply returned to their school days and resurrected close reading as a preferred school practice. Close reading was popularized through books such Adler's (1940) *How to read a book,* a text written to assist everyone at developing higher level literacy proficiencies. High level literacy proficiencies meant reading a book the way a college English professor might have read it. However, as Hinchman and Moore (2013) noted, close reading fell by the wayside for decades, perhaps caused by the emergence of constructivist theory and research on the powerful role that prior knowledge plays in understanding texts (Anderson, 1984).

Close reading took many forms but in all cases it involved reading and rereading texts to establish meaning. It did not allow for the use of a person's world knowledge or their knowledge of a historical era to establish meaning, which was found in the text by reading and rereading the text. Today, most psychological theories of learning emphasize the role that prior knowledge, or schema, plays in learning new material. Their argument goes something like this:

> *Learning is adding new information to your existing prior knowledge. As you read more about trees you acquire more detailed information about trees. The new information that you encounter must be worked into whatever prior knowledge you have on the topic.*

The developers of the CCSS have been critical of many modern lessons, and argue that often teachers summarize the key information in the text before assigning the students to read the text. Thus, close reading seems to be as much a backlash against current practices that are viewed as unproductive. The CCSS authors rely largely on anecdotes and a video clip or two to argue that educators generally are doing all the work for students. It is this vision of the teacher doing all the analytic work that seems to drive the CCSS interpretation of why so many students do not develop strong enough reading skills to be successful in college.

I suppose that this vision of the teacher doing all the analytic work might have a bit of truth to it, but the substantial focus on low-level tasks and the lack of either discussion or writing, demonstrated by a wealth of research, seem a more likely explanation for college difficulties to me. College level work doesn't involve worksheets or fill-in-the-blank tasks but rather involves students engaging in a substantially greater volume of reading with far less teacher support. College work involves

Resources for Close Reading Lessons

These resources are recommended by Hinchman and Moore (2013) as possible sources for videotaped lessons involving close reading:

- Council of Chief State School Officers: Common Core Implementation Video Series:

  www.ccsso.org/Resources/Digital_ Resources/Common_Core_ Implementation_Video_Series.html

- Engage New York: www.engageny.org

- Student Achievement Partners: www .achievethecore.org

much more independent responsibility than the work most students have done during their years as adolescents in American schools. It is this independence of effort along with a substantial increase in reading volume that leads too many students to fail once they have arrived at college.

The CCSS seems to recognize that most adolescents fail to read, write, or think very much for school. So while there has been much attention paid to the close reading demanded by CCSS, I will argue that we must pay more attention to the use of multiple texts representing multiple points of view. More attention should be paid to evaluating the evidence presented in the texts assigned or selected, meaning more attention paid to thoughtful literacy and less attention to regurgitation literacy.

With the CCSS, once a reader has discovered the meaning of a text or a text segment, then the text could be summarized. The traditional method for teaching summarization fits in with the CCSS framework only because summarizing a text typically does not involve including information not expressed in the text. However, the ability to develop a reasonable summary does seem related to a reader's prior knowledge of the topic discussed in the text (Pressley & Afflerbach, 1995).

We do know that the ability and the proclivity to summarize what one is reading is strongly related to understanding and long-term learning. We also know that far too many adolescents (and early adolescents) are not very adept at developing adequate summaries after reading, and we have known this for quite some time.

Over a quarter of a century ago, Applebee, Langer, and Mullis (1988) noted that a majority of adolescents performed adequately on multiple-choice items after reading passages on the National Assessment of Educational Progress (NAEP) but these same students failed to perform adequately when asked to summarize or interpret passages they had read and most were unable to explain or defend their choices on the multiple-choice task. Perhaps these results simply demonstrate the old adage, "Kids are more likely to learn what they are taught than what they are not taught." In other words, American students perform reasonably well on low-level literal questions posed in multiple-choice or fill-in-the-blanks formats, but they routinely fail at writing summaries of what they have read or orally defending a response they have made. This suggest to many outside the educational establishment that our schools and teachers are preparing students to be skilled at something few still appreciate. Further, they argue, our schools are not preparing students for the actual demands of college or careers:

> These findings are disturbing. . . . Students in American schools can read with surface understanding, but have difficulty when asked to think more deeply about what they have

read, to defend or elaborate upon their ideas, and to communicate them in writing. (Applebee, Langer, & Mullis, 1988, p. 25)

For the past 25 years federal education officials and business leaders have been arguing for changes in schools and lessons. Schools and lessons need to leave the nineteenth century and enter the twenty-first century with classrooms that foster higher-order thinking, collaborative work, and development of problem solving proficiencies. Today in most classrooms, a teacher from the nineteenth century could step in and complete the lessons being offered. Indeed, the nature of lessons offered today have changed little since the 1800s (Cuban, 1993).

The Gist of It All

When it comes to demonstrating an understanding of what was read, there may be no better assessment than evaluating whether the reader can express the "gist" of the text. This understanding could also be labeled as "getting the main idea" or "understanding what you've read." We usually assess this sort of understanding not with multiple-choice or fill-in-the-blank tasks but by asking the reader to tell us what the text was about. We might ask them to "summarize" the text or to compose a summary, perhaps even specifying a length limit (e.g., "Summarize this section in a single sentence.").

When we do recreational or voluntary reading, we are not surprised when someone asks us to tell them what the book (or article, letter, blog, etc.) we have just read is about. What the person wants is a summary or at least the main idea of the text. The most common comprehension test we face is telling someone else the gist of a text. In such tellings (or retellings) we don't typically focus on details (or facts) but instead we focus on the "big picture" and retell only a small aspect of the text that includes the primary arguments or actions presented.

I vividly remember the only examination I ever failed in my school career. It was the midterm examination for a college course on the Civil War. (I was a history major.) I truly enjoyed the professor and the course and had read all the course materials, and more. I read them the same way I had read in high school: I had paid attention to details! I had created notes cards with all the various names and dates of all the battles we had read about. I studied those cards. But the exam was only a single question: "What were the political and economic impacts of the first Battle of Bull Run (also known to Southerners as the Battle of Manassas)?"

I recall writing for the full 90-minute class period. I wrote about everything that I had studied: pages of facts about the battle and the generals and units that had been involved. But I failed the exam because, as the professor noted on my exam paper, "You failed to answer the question." At first I was stunned at my grade. I thought that knowing exactly how many civilians were killed by a madly retreating Union army as it literally raced away from the battlefield couldn't result in a failing grade. How can knowing how many soldiers Union General Irvin McDowell lost that day not count for something?

But after a day of self-pity, I acknowledged that I actually did not answer the question. It also became clear to me that I could not answer that question because I had paid so little attention to those big ideas while I was reading and creating note cards to study. As I thought about the course and the lectures and discussions we had been having, it finally dawned on me that I had been paying too little attention to the "big ideas" I was being exposed to (Burke, 2010). I think it was that day that I concluded that I needed to study differently from the way I had been studying. I needed to pay less attention to details and more attention to big ideas and to defending the arguments I was trying to make.

The good news, at least for me, was that I aced the final exam and earned a final grade of C and acquired a new appreciation for studying American history. I must also admit that even though I read a number of books each year on the Civil War, to write what I just wrote now required a quick check with Wikipedia where I learned that it was McDowell not McClelland who commanded the Union army at that battle. I'm sure years ago I had that information on one of my note cards as I prepared for that exam, but today I failed to retain that "fact" and had to rely on technology to supply the general's name. Details are quickly forgotten by all of us but the "big ideas" seem to remain forever. As I read the Wikipedia entry on the First Battle of Bull Run, I didn't find anything that contradicted any of the big ideas I still retained, 48 years later!

Think of all the "facts" you have forgotten but once knew well enough to answer an exam question. I can even tell you which high school courses I've forgotten the most about (geometry, chemistry, government) because these were the courses where I never encountered thinking (as in, "Think about this for a minute."). Perhaps because most students in those classes were never given the opportunity to think about a subject or to talk about a topic, few (including me) likely recall little of what filled our notebooks all those years ago.

Why Early Adolescents Have Difficulty Summarizing Expository Texts

When we think of a summary of a narrative text, a novel, or a short story, for instance, we expect that the summary will include information about the setting and the characters, as well as the problem encountered, attempts at resolution of the problem, and finally, the actual resolution. In elementary grades much work is often done with students completing graphic organizers (Kamil, 2004). One graphic organizer for summarizing a narrative is a "story map." After completing a story map organizer on a story that has been read, students are expected to use it to construct a short, written summary.

Most early adolescents have had some experience with summarizing narratives, or stories. However, instructional activities involving summarizing expository, or informational, texts have been relatively rare in the elementary grades. Indeed, even reading expository texts has been relatively uncommon in early elementary grades. Duke's (2000) classic study of texts used in primary grade classrooms reported that students in those grades spent less than 5 minutes a day reading expository texts. She also noted that schools with many students from low-incomes families spent even less time (90 seconds!) reading expository texts.

However, when early adolescents reach the upper elementary and middle grades, school reading demands shift perceptibly and almost overnight expository texts become the majority of assigned reading for early adolescents. This shift away from a school day dominated by narrative texts or stories to school days where expository texts dominate has been labeled "the fourth grade hump" (Chall, 1987). In fact Chall argued that it was this shift that made the transition to the middle grades so difficult for many students.

Expository texts present information in a variety of styles with or without a variety of adjunct textual aids (photos, line drawings, models, bar graphs, timelines, etc.) that are designed to enhance a reader's understanding of the text. There is no graphic organizer similar to the story map that students or their teachers might use for the multiple expository texts assigned during a school day. Expository texts may be written in several different styles, such as cause-effect, problem-solution, a list of characteristics, or a chronology of events, to name a few of the most commonly used disciplinary styles. A single content-area expository textbook (e.g., general science, biology, American history, algebra, etc.) may contain each of these common text styles or structures.

Teachers of early adolescents can expect that most of their students will not be familiar with any strategy for summarizing expository texts because little use is made of such texts until fourth or fifth grade. Yet summarizing what you have read is central to demonstrating an understanding of a text. Thus, a major aspect of developing early adolescents' literary proficiency involves teaching them the strategies needed to develop summaries, especially summaries of informational texts.

We know that early adolescents can acquire the ability to summarize what they have read. It is the teachers of early adolescents who are the ones to ensure that the needed strategies are taught and not just assessed. It doesn't seem to matter much what the teacher's content area is (e.g., science, social studies, mathematics, English), or whether they are reading specialists or special education teachers providing instruction in the needed strategy. Almost anyone could teach these strategies but too often early adolescents push forward trying to complete assignments where summarizing is expected but who have never had a single lesson on how to summarize.

At this point I must also note that English teachers are not very good at teaching useful strategies for summarizing scientific texts for the same reason science teachers are not very good at developing literary analysis. English teachers are not experts in science and science teachers are not experts in literary analysis. What seems clearer now than ever is that the various teachers students encounter every day must shoulder the responsibility to develop in their students the specific summarization strategies appropriate for their various disciplines.

Disciplinary Reading as a Focus

One important aspect of disciplinary expertise (such as completing an American history major and becoming certified as an American history teacher) is that disciplinary experts understand how to read in their discipline. This means that history teachers understand how to read historical texts, science teachers understand how to read scientific texts, and so on. My college experience led me to learn to develop summaries as I read historical texts and to begin to think about the big ideas found in a text.

Shanahan (2009) reviews what we know about disciplinary literacy. She notes that the available research indicates "that the disciplines of physics, history and mathematics differ in the way information is represented in text and in the way experts approach reading" (p. 250). In other words, experts in different fields use different strategies when reading texts in their disciplines. Experts in some fields pay more attention to sourcing while experts in other fields pay more attention to proofs presented. But as Shanahan also argues, we know actually very little about how experts develop their preferred reading strategies. We know even less about how to best assist early adolescents in developing the sorts of reading strategies experts prefer. But we do know a few things that we should pay more attention to when we design lessons for our students.

Building Readers' Competence with Expository Texts

While we have relatively little research on how best to develop disciplinary literacy, we do have studies that demonstrate that we can improve the proficiencies of early adolescents with reading expository texts. Faggella-Luby, Craner, Deschler, and Drew (2012) argue that while disciplinary literacy is a "potentially powerful idea, [it] cannot replace general strategy instruction for all adolescent learners because adolescents who struggle with reading and writing do not possess the foundational skills and strategies necessary to learn proficiently" (p. 69). Struggling readers are simply not very expert at reading anything with understanding, especially deeper understanding. Struggling early-adolescent readers need to learn proficient reading strategies that will only come from powerful reading instruction that can profitably produce better understanding of the texts they read. We already have studies demonstrating how to foster such development. For instance, Gaffney, Methven, and Bagdasarian (2002) focused on providing tutoring for struggling early-adolescent readers using expository texts that were selected as easy enough for their comprehension.

Tutors were to select texts that were intrinsically interesting and well written. Tutors asked themselves . . .

Do I find this interesting, engaging, clear . . .

Tutors oriented students to texts with directions similar to these:

This is about . . . and you will learn.
This part is an explanation of . . .
This passage is an introduction to . . .
You may need to read this part more than once to find out . . .

As students read, tutors might ask,

Can you explain that sentence in your own words?
Do you know what that means?
Are you thinking about . . .
Do you need some help?

If a student seemed to be having trouble with the text they were reading the tutors would ask or say:

Did you understand that part?
Don't continue to read if you are not sure you are understanding what you just read.
Take some time to think about what you just read, especially at the end of a sentence.
When you don't understand, be sure to stop and think. You may need to read some of it again.

As you can see from the types of prompts that were provided by the tutors, a central aspect of this tutoring was supporting struggling readers as they began to develop self-regulation skills as they read. Too often struggling readers just give up when they run into difficulty while reading a text. Many of these readers have never developed useful strategies for puzzling through difficult text. By asking, prompting, and modeling the sorts of strategies that good readers use, the tutors were able to improve the development of struggling readers.

Ten tutors provided such support over 3 months, for 30 to 40 minutes four times a week. They used three to four expository passages for each lesson, with varying dimensions, styles, and topics. Having students write a couple of sentences, discussing what was read, offering lessons on decoding big words, ensuring a focus on self-monitoring, providing explanations of text features, and so on, were components of the tutoring sessions. In other words, tutors attempted to provide their students with instruction and support that would ensure they were understanding the texts that they read.

This targeted tutoring was enormously successful. The students who were tutored made gains of 1 to 7 years in reading proficiency over a single semester of tutoring. At the end of the 3-month tutoring period, half of the students tested as reading on grade level while before the tutoring sessions they were reading 2 to 3 years below grade level. I describe this study in some detail because it provides powerful evidence that there are strategies available that schools could implement with struggling early adolescents.

Classroom teachers of various content areas could use the same prompts and cues that the tutors provided. While this will not likely produce the same sorts of gains as the one-on-one sessions, you may be surprised at the growth that you do see. The focus on expository text targeted the types of texts students had the greatest difficulty reading with understanding. Your intervention could do the same and provide the prompting whenever students seem puzzled by the assigned readings, and you could tailor the support so that you provided it only for the students who needed it.

The strategies used in this study accelerated reading development in a relatively short period of time and helped struggling readers become achieving readers. Virtually all schools could provide similar support, although too few of our school systems have implemented any of the several proven strategies.

Modeling the Thinking that Underlies Summarization

As with all mental activities, the simplest way to develop student proficiency with summarization is by modeling it for students. Summarization is basically a select and delete strategy. To develop an effective summary of a text the reader must decide what portions of the text will be deleted and which portions will be included. This process of selection and deletion is purposeful because creating an effective summary is more than randomly selecting things to be deleted or included. Teachers can offer a think-aloud version of the process they use to select and delete information found in the text.

As an example, let's imagine that you will be using the passage featured below in your think-aloud model of writing an effective summary sentence. In a think-aloud you simply provide students with your thinking as you read and then develop the summary. You describe why some information is being deleted and why other information is being included. I've attempted to illustrate how you might do a think-aloud with this sample passage in which I summarize a paragraph in a sentence. I do this because it is easier for students initially to get the sense of what to do with shorter passages that result in shorter summaries.

First, I will project the passage up on a screen (or wall) using a document camera or some other means. I want everyone to be able to see the passage and to observe me as I delete and select aspects of the text to include in my summary. Using a document camera allows me to model deleting text by simply drawing a line through it. For text I select to include in the summary I can use a highlighter to mark it. (I could probably offer the lesson with either the cross through or the highlighting strategy.)

Text to Be Summarized

Consider the Amami rabbit (*Pentalgus furness*) that lives on only two remote islands near Japan. It has short ears, short hind legs, and a short tail. At the same time it has huge and formidable front claws. It relies upon a unique method for communication involving both vocalization and drumming its hind feet on the ground. The Amami rabbit is active during the nighttime. As it is getting dusk it will appear at the entrance to its burrow and loudly call out across the valley. It then thumps its feet several times using the thumping sound to further signal its intentions. However, because of severe habitat loss and new predators fewer than 5,000 of these rabbits survive today and their numbers are continuing to decline.

Summary Sentence 1: Only about 5,000 Amami rabbits survive on two islands near Japan.

Summary Sentence 2: While the Amami rabbit doesn't look much like the rabbits we know it is nearing extinction on two islands near Japan.

Summary Sentence 3: Because of severe habitat loss and new predators fewer than 5,000 Amami rabbits survive on two islands near Japan.

Second, once it is displayed for everyone to see, read the passage aloud to your students. Then make a first run at deleting information, explaining why you are doing so as you draw a line through it.

Third, again reading aloud, read everything you have not yet deleted. Using the highlighter mark any segment of the text you've read that you think needs to be included in the summary. Again, think out loud for your students as you are doing this.

Finally, take what you have selected and work it into a single summary sentence and write this sentence on the bottom of the document. I usually write two or three versions of summary sentences to illustrate that there is more than a single correct summary. You can see from the sentences I wrote for the sample that each sentence basically conveys the same information but that each expresses it differently.

Understand that providing a single example of summarizing with an accompanying think-aloud will not be sufficient to foster much development of your students' abilities to write a summary. As I have noted, the single paragraph with a single sentence summary is probably the easiest for students to learn. But you will need to plan doing a dozen or so of these short summary modeling demonstrations before you can expect your students to begin to demonstrate that they too can summarize (a short paragraph in a sentence).

As you provide additional example summaries for your students, remember the most effective instructional routine is (1) you demonstrate and explain, (2) you share the demonstration and explanation duties with your students, and (3) you expect your students to develop summaries on their own. This is the "I do, we do, you do" framework for effective skill and strategy instruction. This is a powerful form of "scaffolded instruction" (Palincsar, 1986). In the first step you begin by providing the scaffolding to demonstrate just how you develop a summary. Then in step 2 you share the work of scaffolding with your students. At times you are still modeling the process and at other times you are asking them to model the process. With sufficient scaffolding and practice all of your students will move on to step 3 and over time develop summarization proficiencies.

I usually have pairs of students collaborate when we've moved into step 2 (the *we do* step). I do this because just talking through a text with another student typically makes it all come together faster than having students practice alone. As they work you can move about the classroom noting what sections have been crossed out and engaging students in a discussion about their decisions. The point here is to get them verbalizing why they are making decisions to delete. I don't tell them "bad choice" but simply ask, "Why did you delete that section?"

After a few weeks of moving through a number of tasks with step 2, *we do,* your students are ready for you to make a bit more complicated. At this point you move to step 3, *you do.* If your students manage this work without much difficulty you can quickly move on. Now you introduce summarization of texts longer than a single paragraph.

Once your students have acquired the ability to write summaries of short texts (e.g., paragraphs), you will need to repeat the three-step process with longer texts. I suggest moving next to sections of informational text, perhaps three or four paragraphs long, for the next modeling and demonstration activities. Sections in textbooks that are set off by headers usually provide useful texts for use here. The steps remain largely the same except you no longer are trying to compose a single sentence summary (although this is a possibility for some texts).

As you walk your students through a demonstration of reading three or four paragraphs, you will still engage in the select and delete system. I usually simply highlight parts of the text I plan to include in the summary sentences. In other words, I model selection only and by default automatically delete (or don't select) some aspects of the text. Summaries are still brief, maybe two or three sentences in length, although there are texts where four or five paragraphs can be summarized in a single sentence.

Don't be surprised when your students seem to catch on to what you are demonstrating more quickly than they did during the introductory summary lessons with a single paragraph. You will now be demonstrating basically the same process but with longer text samples. In the first step you simply project the text on a wall or screen where everyone can see it and then select those segments you will include in the summary sentences. Take that highlighted information and compose a two or three sentence summary, and then compose another two or three sentence summary that differs in form more than in content. The goal is to show that you are not looking for the single correct summary but rather a summary that includes the most relevant information.

The final stage of this summary writing adventure is helping students learn how to summarize longer sections of textbook, not a whole chapter but a major section of a chapter. Developing this proficiency is essential if we expect students to independently learn from assigned texts. Because so few students ever receive demonstrations of the sort I have outlined, few students are very good at developing summaries of any informational text they read. In the end, though, it is the information from the summaries we develop (even though we may not write it down) that will stick with us over a lifetime. However, much of what we read is quickly forgotten even if once acquired when we never summarize as we read,

Composing Summaries

Once your students are familiar with summarization (i.e., after you have modeled and demonstrated summary writing) you can use student-generated summaries of text segments read as a task to promote greater content-area learning. A number of years ago Langer and Applebee (1987) published a small book entitled *How writing shapes thinking*. This is a book-length report of a study they did with English, social studies, and science teachers of adolescents over a 2-year period. Each of the teachers was selected because each was effective and the goal of the study was to further enhance teaching as well as student learning.

They learned that simply providing teachers with new instructional tools did not actually improve teaching or learning very much. While the teachers did use writing activities, they often had their own purposes for the assignments. As one teacher noted, "Before I asked my students to write summaries about what they had read, I had no idea many of them had no idea what they were reading." Writing became a sort of "every pupil response" activity that provided teachers with greater insights into the problems the students were having with the assigned texts. However, this additional information did not always, or even typically, lead to the "big idea" lesson frameworks that Langer and Applebee had hoped for.

Lessons involving writing fostered greater learning than lessons involving reading and studying only. Different kinds of writing focused attention on different curriculum features. Short-answer essays required little rethinking as students simply turned to the text to summarize what they had read. Analytic writing activities required more time so less information was covered but the active rethinking of the information led to longer duration of learning.

Langer and Applebee (1987) concluded,

> We learned that subject-area writing can be used productively in three primary ways: (1) to gain relevant knowledge and experience in preparing for new [instructional] activities; (2) to review and consolidate what is known or has been learned; and (3) to reformulate and extend ideas and experiences. (p. 136)

However, they also noted that

> Across time, while all of the teachers moved toward a new conceptualization of writing as a tool for learning some of the time—none of them incorporated new approaches to writing and learning all of the time. (p. 85)

Perhaps if the study has lasted longer, there would have been more use of writing activity put in place, but perhaps not. While the content-area teachers appreciated the information that having students write, even quick writes, provided them, they did not seem to fully accept the potential roles that such writing might play in their classroom.

Summaries as Quick Writes   A quick write is just that: a quick write. Once your students have largely mastered developing summaries of texts they have read, you should consider having them use what they now know as they read assigned texts. You would have students develop summaries as they read the texts you are using in your class. For instance, they could develop summary sentences for each section of the text they read.

I suggest that you begin this activity with in-class reading and summary writing. Pair up students and have everyone read the assigned segment of the text. Then have the partners work together to write a summary statement. Once they have read the text, the quick-write summarization should take no more than about 3 minutes. You can then ask different pairs of students to read their summaries aloud. Ask three or four pairs to read what they developed. As these students read, have the other students just listen and compare what each pair wrote to their own summaries.

Now select one of the summary sentences one pair wrote as a model summary, and write that summary sentence on the chalkboard or white board where everyone can see it. Ask students whether they would alter/edit that summary by deleting or adding a word or phrase. Have them develop their edited summary sentence and select one or two pairs to come to the front of the class to write their summary sentence under the one you selected. Have the students describe what they added or deleted and why they did so.

Initially, while you may be surprised by what students included or excluded from their summaries, let the group work at perfecting the summary sentence. Remember, students learn best by doing, not by looking at red check marks on their work. Over time you will find students get better at writing summary sentences, and do it faster, too. Once this happens you can ask them to write longer summaries of longer segments of texts. And you can expect that they will learn more from the texts that you assign.

The key point here is that summary development is not something students learn in a single lesson or even in a single weeks' worth of summary writing lessons. Summarization is one of those essential but complex strategies that takes time to develop and even more time to perfect.

Higher-Order Questions and Summarization   While we have good evidence that most classroom teachers ask their students lots of low-level literal questions, the evidence also indicates that—perhaps because of the focus on low-level literal questions—few teachers ask any higher-order questions of their students. This is similar to the fact discussed in the previous chapter about classroom discussion. A few teachers use higher-order questions and a few teachers engage students in conversation about the text that was read. However, in both cases it is very few teachers who routinely offer either task to students. And, as was the case with discussion, we know that when teachers do ask higher-order questions, the reading and writing skills of their students improve (Taylor, Pearson, Peterson, & Rodriguez, 2003).

The authors contrast the types of questions asked by more effective and less effective teachers. Many more of the more effective classroom teachers (46 percent versus none) engaged their students in discussions of what had been read and many of the more effective teachers (46 percent versus 8 percent) asked students higher- order questions about theme compared to the less effective teachers. Many more of the less effective teachers (92 percent versus 46 percent) asked low-level questions about events or characters mentioned in the text. Oddly, though, the proportion of time devoted to higher-order questions and to discussion decreased as the students moved through the grades. Thus, effective primary grade teachers were more likely than upper elementary grade teachers to provide opportunities for students to engage in these powerful routines.

As Taylor et al. (2003) noted,

> *One consistent finding is that higher-level questioning matters. The more a teacher asked higher-level questions, the more growth the students in her class experienced on a variety of measures. The teachers who asked more higher-level questions appeared to understand the importance of challenging their students to think about what they had read. (p. 22)*

Higher-order questions are simply questions that cannot be answered with a single word or short phrase or by a quick reference back to the text. Questions that begin, "I wonder why . . ." or "Did anyone notice . . ." are far more likely to promote understanding because students must think before they respond. They also promote student engagement in problem solving. If there is only one answer and that answer is in the book, then there is little reason to think. Instead, when confronted with a barrage of low-level literal questions, students essentially turn off the thinking part of their brains and concentrate on the recall strategies they have acquired.

I believe that this enormous expansion in the focus on recall questions comes from our ever increasing reliance on group achievement tests. In this case I am thinking primarily of those nationally normed tests and those state tests that proliferate in American schools.

I never took a standardized test until I sat for the SAT exam during my junior year of high school. How did anyone know whether I could read or not since I had never taken a reading test? I assume my teacher, Mr. DeGraw, knew I could read because he saw me reading every school day and he interacted with me on my reading. Based on those interactions he determined I was a reader. I read well enough, in his mind, that he recommended that I be placed in the college prep track when I left elementary school. Now, today, as a college graduate (and a college professor), I remain a reader. Would I have been any better off if I had taken standardized reading tests? If my teachers had my standardized test scores, would any of them have been better able to teach me?

I worry about all the testing going on in our schools today because most schools seem to be drowning in data, much of which provides no good evidence that students can or cannot read with understanding. None of that data tell schools whether their students are engaged readers who read voluntarily, for instance. I worry most about the lack of assessment strategies that assess students' understanding of what they have been reading. I know almost all of the state and national tests report "reading comprehension" performances, but there is just something wrong about relying on students' abilities to respond correctly to low-level multiple-choice and literal questions as our most common strategy for evaluating understanding.

What bothers me is that too many people actually believe that the ability to locate the correct answer to a low-level question while looking back at the text is somehow related to readers understanding what they have just read. I understand the difficulties of developing tests that measure students' abilities to problem solve or to summarize but just because a task is more difficult to develop should not be a reason for ignoring tasks that do measure problem solving and summarizing.

For 40 years the federal government has developed reading and writing assessments that actually seem to provide information of student abilities to

The Usefulness of Testing

Nancy Allison (2009) writes that "schools now do a lot of testing which typically tells us who passed the test and who failed. The only problem is we don't know why" (p. 154). She notes that we have to get to know each student to make sense of testing data and to plan appropriate instruction. However, if students understanding texts is what you are interested in, you may find that traditional standardized reading tests provide little useful information beyond the fact that these students might read several years below grade level.

I suggest that if learning which students understand the text they are reading is your interest, then preparing your own personal assessment of understanding may provide more useful information. This assessment could be scheduled early in the school year and be composed of passages drawn from the texts you plan to use. Give students copies of those text samples, have them read the passages silently and then construct a summary of what they have just read. You may find, as the teachers in the Langer and Applebee (1987) study found, that many students don't seem to have any real idea of what the texts they are reading are actually about. You may find odd details in their summary from text and even an attempt to draw a conclusion about the content of the text. Usually what content teachers find is evidence that they need to begin summarization lessons immediately.

problem solve or summarize. It was those data that Langer and Applebee were examining when they wrote about how poorly American students performed on tests that went beyond the literal and obvious. I am hoping that the new assessments that have been developed to accompany the implementation of the CCSS will incorporate the sorts of tasks used for years on the National Assessment of Educational Progress. However, given that the nation's two largest test makers are producing the new tests, I worry that the new tests will look much like the old state tests and will still fail to reflect much of what we know about measuring understanding.

Commercial Core Reading Programs and Comprehension Instruction

While commercial instructional materials often contain a lesson on summarizing and, perhaps, a few worksheets for students to complete, every commercial program typically fails to develop the ability to write summaries. In an effort to "cover" every skill and strategy ever imagined (or listed on a curriculum framework), commercial materials are simply not very effective at developing the few strategies every student needs to acquire. There is no evidence that the folks who create commercial materials are familiar with the research on comprehension strategy development (Dewitz, Jones, & Leahy, 2009).

In their analysis of the five commercial core reading programs used in the upper elementary grades, the authors noted that while opportunities for discussion were nearly absent all programs contained what seemed an unending supply of low-level literal recall questions. (Over half of all teacher moves in the majority of the programs involved asking students low-level literal questions.) Not only were discussion questions largely missing from the available commercial reading programs but so were higher-order questions and summarization. Guided practice and the research-based design feature of the gradual release of responsibility to the student for using the skill or strategy were also absent (Pearson, 2009).

The researchers also noted that, "The claim that these core programs are research-based is built more on the teaching of the same skills and strategies found in the research than on the use of the same instructional methods or the same intensity of instruction" (Dewitz et al., 2009, p. 121). They concluded their report by noting that there was no virtue in teaching with fidelity using flawed commercial core reading curriculum materials.

The point here is that using a commercial core reading program with early adolescents will not likely lead to much improved summarizing because most of what we know about developing reading and writing proficiencies in these students is absent from most commercial products your school might purchase. In the end, the only real hope for struggling early-adolescent readers is their teachers. For this hope to result in better readers, those teachers will necessarily have to know how to structure lessons so essential reading and writing strategies are effectively developed in every class, every day. That is the challenge facing you.

Summary

Summarization is one of those essential strategies that good readers develop. It is also the single most common comprehension task we are given once we leave school. Whether a friend is asking about the novel *Bring up the bodies,* or our boss is asking about our review of two competing systems for tracking the company's shipments, they both want a summary.

We can develop our students' proficiencies with summarization. However, for too long our lessons have been more likely to assess our students' summarizing abilities than to provide support in fostering the ability to summarize. As we move into this new era of the CCSS, developing proficiency in summarizing rises to the top of the list of tasks facing all teachers, especially teachers of struggling early-adolescent readers.

Improving your students' proficiency with summarizing will require more opportunities:

- to respond to higher-order questions
- to engage peers in discussions of what has been read or written
- to participate in lessons that provide demonstrations of how one creates a summary
- to have the opportunity to participate in scaffolded lessons where the students take on more and more responsibility for developing summaries of what they have read.

In the end, all students need to develop a proficiency with summarization. After reading a text, summarizing is the essence of understanding. While all students can learn to summarize, for this to happen educators will be required to offer instruction in summarization, something that is too uncommon in today's classrooms.

Chapter 8

Pulling It All Together: Effective Instruction All Day Long

Tyrone is a struggling sixth-grade reader. His current reading proficiency is more like that of a beginning third-grader than that of a mid-year sixth-grader. It's not that Tyrone cannot read—he can—but he cannot read sixth-grade–level texts. He cannot read the words in sixth-grade texts accurately, fluently, or with comprehension. Nonetheless, Tyrone has a backpack full of sixth-grade–level texts. He has a sixth-grade literature anthology, a sixth-grade science book, a sixth-grade global studies book—and an eighth-grade reading level novel that his district expects all sixth-graders to read.

But Tyrone cannot read any of these books. Why would anyone give Tyrone books they must know he cannot read? Why doesn't Tyrone have a desk filled with books written at a third-grade level that cover the core curriculum content for the sixth grade? It isn't that such texts are not available nor is it true that such texts are substantially more expensive than purchasing the books that Tyrone cannot read.

So why is Tyrone's backpack filled with books he cannot read? I will argue that it is primarily because school districts think of intervention for struggling readers—if they have thought about their struggling readers at all—as something accomplished in a session outside the regular classroom. This would be a session one period long taught by someone other than Tyrone's classroom teacher. School districts have adopted this model, I believe, because federal education policy has long supported such designs by funding supplementary reading instruction provided by special education and English language learners specialists (Allington, 2010). To this list we can add paraprofessionals who are funded by the same federal programs that fund the specialist teachers.

These various federal programs have been having almost no significant positive effects on struggling early-adolescent readers' reading development (Wanzek et al., 2013). While other scholars have reported slightly larger effect sizes (e.g., Flynn, Zheng, & Swanson, 2012; Scammacca et al., 2007), even in these cases older struggling readers who make some progress in reading development only rarely achieve grade-level reading performance.

There are several reasons why interventions currently available for older struggling readers fail to accelerate these students' reading development to grade level. First, it may simply be that reading intervention in middle and high schools is a case of too little, too late.

Few older struggling readers ever receive much academic support. Few of the studies analyzed in these reviews I just noted have provided even a full year of reading intervention for older struggling readers, and few provide more than one period a day for the intervention. However, the few studies that describe longer and more frequent intervention efforts show that they have produced better outcomes than the more typical, shorter intervention efforts. However, most older struggling readers never have the opportunity to participate in these more substantial attempts to improve reading proficiencies.

A second reason most older struggling readers continue to struggle is because we design our most common interventions for older students to focus primarily on developing decoding skills. These are the students who struggle with *Wilson Phonics,* with *Language!,* with *ReadWell,* and with other commercial programs targeted to improving students' decoding. None of these programs have a reliable research base demonstrating positive effects in improving reading proficiency. If decoding were the primary problem that older struggling readers exhibited, then using such commercial products might make sense. However, three studies have all consistently demonstrated that weak decoding proficiencies characterize only 10 to 15 percent of older struggling readers.

Most older struggling readers actually struggle with the meaning of vocabulary, weak comprehension skills, and limited world knowledge (Buly & Valencia, 2002; Dennis, 2013; Hock & Brasseur, 2009). Perhaps if interventions for early-adolescent struggling readers were designed to match student needs, fewer struggling readers would continue to struggle. As Torgeson and Hudson (2006) argue, "The most important factor appears to involve difficulties in making up for the huge deficits in accurate reading practice the older children have accumulated by the time they reach later elementary school . . ." (p. 147).

Rather than assuming that early-adolescent readers have a decoding deficiency that underlies their reading difficulties, we now have sufficient evidence from the research that the weakness causing their difficulties is limited reading practice, especially accurate reading practice. Extensive reading practice builds most of a student's vocabulary and world knowledge (Nagy, Anderson, & Herman, 1987; Stanovich, West, Cunningham, Cipielewski, & Siddiqui, 1996). Following this research evidence then will lead back to the basic arguments you've been reading in this book.

A third factor to consider is that early-adolescent struggling readers have typically been struggling with reading (and with schooling) for 6 or 7 years— literally for all of their lives as students. Although almost all of them have participated in various programs targeted to solving the reading problems, they are still well behind their peers who are reading on grade level. In too many cases they have made the logical decision to stop trying. Think about it: How long would failing in a pre-med college curriculum take to convince you to change your major? My experience as a college professor suggests that failing all of your first-semester pre-med courses would undoubtedly lead you to change your major.

Instead of providing Tyrone with a backpack full of books he cannot read we might, instead, provide him with a backpack full of books he could read accurately and with understanding. These would be books that provide information of the sort needed to pass seventh-grade science or social studies courses. We could also provide Tyrone with books on topics that interest him, topics that may vary from those covered in his content classes.

We also know from the research that wide reading develops most of the meaning vocabulary that students acquire each year. We can expect to see the vocabulary deficits researchers observe when the struggling students read much less than the achieving readers. We can also expect that limited reading will create students who lag behind achieving readers in the amount of world knowledge they acquire. Lessons that focus on decoding put almost no emphasis on comprehension. Thus, struggling readers in typical intervention programs will be provided with fewer lessons on comprehension, especially higher-order comprehension, and this will lead to diminished reading comprehension proficiency (Lent & Gilmore, 2013).

My point, expressed throughout this book, is that the very lessons schools have provided early-adolescent struggling readers are more likely to perpetuate the reading difficulties the students exhibit than to resolve those problems and turn those students into achieving readers. We will continue to have—and to create—a significant supply of struggling readers as long as we continue to ignore the research and design programs that involve struggling readers engaging in little accurate reading with little emphasis on higher-order understanding after reading.

Fight or Flight? Responses to Underachievement

Consider a 12-year-old student who has never read on grade level, who has been receiving special education resource room support for the past 5 years, and who is still earning mainly Ds and Fs. Think for a minute about his mindset as he enters your middle school classroom carrying a backpack filled with books he knows he cannot read. Is it reasonable to expect that this early adolescent will be an excited and engaged student in your class? Or is it more reasonable to expect that he will find a seat in the back row and simply pull up his hoodie and pretend to be asleep? Or that he will enter your classroom with much fanfare after the final bell has rung, working hard to demonstrate that he is a tough guy and cares not a whit about what you think?

This is the question that Tyrone must answer as he enters your classroom. Who will he be today?

Luckily for every middle school teacher, most of our Tyrones choose to pull up the hoodie in an attempt to escape notice. However, as long as Tyrone stays unengaged in class, he will remain on the pathway that leads to dropping out. For adolescents who have never been successful in school, dropping out is a logical response to the daily humiliation of being unable to do the work they are expected to do. Tyrone can also take on a tough guy stance and work to make your life hell through repeatedly misbehaving in various ways. Again, such behavior can be seen as a logical response in our fight or flight thinking that underlies the responses all humans make when confronted with challenges.

Too Few Teachers with Expertise in Teaching Struggling Readers

Few middle schools and high schools have teachers with extensive expertise for teaching struggling readers. Thus, in too many middle and high schools the teachers staffing reading intervention programs have certification in physical education, art, or social studies, but have never had even a single course focused on teaching early adolescents to read. Worse, in too many schools we observe paraprofessionals monitoring struggling readers as they engage with a computerized intervention program. These paraprofessionals are staff that research has demonstrated are ineffective at accelerating reading development! Is it any wonder that so few older struggling readers ever become grade-level readers? These readers are largely unmotivated and have been struggling since they first set foot in school as kindergarteners. Because they are not voluntary readers, they have accumulated far less practice in reading than the achieving readers. In other words, they often are doing nothing to help themselves become better readers.

These struggling readers have been attending school in an era focused on excellence more than on equity. Their teachers have been under pressure to raise the achievement of all students with little concern given to struggling students. This is the era of widespread expansion of advanced placement courses. This is the era of creating greater academic demands on students with little regard for the students who were struggling under the older, less demanding standards. This is the era when classroom teachers are blamed simply because these struggling students exist in our schools. In short, there has been very little effective policy or practice provided for struggling readers or for the schools and teachers who must work to educate these students.

The good news is that we can do better when it comes to educating our struggling readers. First of all, there are now fewer struggling early-adolescent readers than at any time in our nation's history, largely because our K through fourth-grade teachers—along with early-intervention reading programs—have been more effective in addressing the instructional needs of these students. While there is much left to do during the K through fourth-grade years, students in those grades are reading better than ever before. However, the recently adopted Common Core State Standards (CCSS) will raise the difficulty levels of the texts students will be reading. The ultimate goal is that graduating high school seniors will improve their reading level by two or more grade levels.

This improvement, it is argued, will result in more students becoming "college and career ready." Currently, only about one-half of all high school graduates read well enough to handle the demands of college courses. Consequently, only about one-quarter of high school graduates earn a 4-year college degree. While roughly three-quarters of high school graduates attend college, most of them never complete the coursework required to earn a 4-year degree. The folks who have brought us the ACT and SAT examinations note that they can quite reliably predict who will and who won't complete that 4-year degree based simply on the reading scores they earn on those tests (Pearson & Hiebert, in 2013). We will now examine what the CCSS will change if implemented with fidelity.

The CCSS and Early Adolescents

The CCSS marks a turning point in American education. While our schools have, until recently, increased the proportion of students who are awarded a high school diploma, those increases seem to have come at a cost over the past 50 years of less-demanding middle and high school curriculum materials. When I graduated from high school only about half of all students received a high school diploma. At one point in the 1990s that proportion had risen to 80 percent, but since the 1990s the dropout rates have increased, perhaps because our schools have adopted more challenging curriculum requirements.

Over this same time period the reading levels of fourth-graders have also been rising while middle and high school reading levels have remained largely stagnant. Thus, one way to consider the CCSS is to note that students in middle and high schools will be expected to improve their reading achievement more dramatically than is currently the case. Put another way, currently the reading achievement of fifth- to eighth-grade students grows more slowly than it does for students in K through fourth grade. The reading achievement of students in grades 9 through 12 grows more slowly than the growth in grades 5 through 8.

This probably should not be surprising since from grades 5 and onward, reading instruction shrinks with every year so that by ninth grade few schools

Textbooks today are not easier than textbooks textbooks used in earlier eras. A primary rational offered by CCSS for advocating for more complex texts was that school textbooks have been getting less complex (easier to read) over the past century. The problem with this assumption is that the evidence available indicates that it is simply wrong. As Gamson, Lu and Eckert (2013) have recently reported, 4th grade texts are more complex than they have ever been in the past 50 years and 6th grade texts are at least as difficult as they were 50 years ago. Thus the evidence seems quite clear, textbooks used in middle and high schools today are not less complex than in earlier eras.

(Gamson, D. A., Lu, X., & Eckert, S. A. (2013). Challenging the research base of the Common Core State Standards: A historical reanalyis of text complexity. *Educational Researcher, 42*(7), 381–391.)

have a reading improvement course. Of course, those ninth-grade students do take an English class (along with a number of other classes where reading is required), but it is only in a very few of those English classes (and even fewer of the other classes) where lessons designed to improve reading performance are offered. It is largely the case that by grade 4 or 5 students are considered to have "mastered" reading and so reading instruction is no longer necessary. This of course isn't true, but it is too often incorrectly "assumed" to be true.

This represents quite a shift from 40 years ago when all commercial reading programs were designed as K through eighth-grade programs and when virtually every fifth- through eighth-grade student participated in at least one 55-minute period of reading instruction per day. For reasons I do not fully comprehend those reading classes have largely vanished from middle schools. Teacher certification also changed over that same time period. I was certified as a K–8 teacher through my elementary education teacher education program. Today that certification is more likely to be K–4 or K–5 than K–8. As the nation moved to make schooling more rigorous, teacher certification and teacher education were altered in ways that reduced the likelihood that teachers of early adolescents would be well prepared to teach their students essential reading strategies.

Those teachers—many lacking any academic preparation in reading instruction—began to believe that such instruction was either (1) not their job or (2) unnecessary for young adults. Today it seems the CCSS is suggesting that every middle and high school teacher will develop the reading proficiency of their students. Today the focus is on what is labeled "disciplinary reading," the sorts of reading that folks do "in a discipline" (Shanahan, 2009). We know that experts in various disciplines, or content areas, approach texts differently. Anthropologists, for instance, have a common set of strategies they use when reading anthropological texts. These strategies differ, for example, from the strategies used by chemists reading texts on chemistry topics. Thus, the argument goes, "Only chemistry teachers can teach students how to read chemistry texts."

While I believe there is some truth to these assertions, I remain unconvinced that we will observe chemistry teachers allocating half of each class period to instructing students on how to read chemistry texts. At the same time there is much that teachers of chemistry (or social studies, or science, or mathematics) could be doing every day that will improve their students' abilities to handle content-area texts as they improve what they learn from those texts. It is those instructional routines that have been the focus of this text.

What Some Schools Are Doing to Meet the New Challenge

Mueller (2001) describes the various efforts at Michael Webster School in New Hampshire where the reading program for struggling adolescent readers incorporates the following courses.

First, there is an elective course entitled "Reading Workshop" that all struggling readers can choose. The student-teacher ratio in this class is ten to one or better. Students see reading modeled by adults through read-alouds, shared reading, and group sharing. The focus is on encouraging students to read for pleasure at—not above—their reading level so the classroom is stocked with an array of below grade-level books. There is no stigma attached to the course because it is just another freshman elective. Student reading levels increase steadily with 75 percent of participants exiting at end of the year with reading achievement at grade 8 or above as assessed on the Nelson-Denny reading achievement test. It is a one-and-a-half hour block scheduled every other class day, with a schedule that looks like this: 9:50–10:10 mini-lesson; 10:10–10:25 teacher read-aloud and discussion; 10:25–10:55 silent reading of self-selected texts; 10:55–11:05 journal work; and 11:05–11:20 book share/homework review. In other words, the focus is on engaging these struggling readers in lots of successful reading experiences.

Webster School has also offered a number of other courses for struggling readers. "Literacy Tutoring" pairs a high school student with elementary struggling readers and includes weekly sessions for the older students with a mentor teacher on appropriate instructional interventions they might use with their younger tutee. Webster also offers "Oral History" (linked with the Foxfire program) where students interview senior citizens about town history and then write up what they have learned and present it to their classmates and often others. It offers the "Independent Learning Seminar" with a focus on learning and applying reading strategies in their content-area reading assignments. This course is designed for kids who get the words mostly right but have difficulties with comprehension. This course is linked to content-teacher support. "The Play's the Thing" is another Webster course that focuses on developing fluency and automaticity by working with play and movie scripts.

Mueller (2001) describes "Reading Rebound," a one-on-one tutoring program for early adolescents at Webster School. This

We Teach Kids to Hate School

"Children are not born hating science or social studies or even reading. We create that dislike by how we teach and what we make students read" (Wolk, 2010, p.11).

program focuses on cognitive skills while students read high-quality literature that is written at the student's reading level, with repeated readings to build fluency, writing activities that reinforce the reading skills (including word recognition), ongoing process assessment, and additional readings outside the program. The teachers drew on "Reading Recovery" tutoring design in planning this effort.

Each of these courses focuses on finding texts that struggling readers can read and topics they want to read about. If every American middle and high school had such offerings, struggling early-adolescent readers would have some hope of learning to read at their grade level. Unfortunately, most middle and high schools offer none of the courses that are available to readers at Webster School.

Brozo and Hargis (2003) describe a case study of change that occurred in one southeastern U.S. high school where 35 percent of students read a year or more below grade level. The researchers first analyzed student reading proficiency with teachers and administrators. Prior to this, teachers had no information on student reading abilities. The reading test results produced a shift in many teachers' thinking about their students. An eleventh-grade mathematics teacher, for instance, altered his view of one student who read at the fifth-grade level and was having difficulty in his mathematics class. And the same was true for an English teacher who reconsidered the reasons another student was performing poorly in a tenth-grade English class. The school focused on three initiatives: (1) increasing the amount of silent reading in classes, (2) reading adolescent literature in content-area classes, and (3) making alternatives to textbooks available for struggling readers. They also added a "Reading Buddy" component for students with very low reading achievement, such as those with disabilities.

To support increased silent reading, class sets of young adult novels and magazines were created and placed on racks in every teacher's classroom. Drop boxes were added to halls to encourage kids to donate paperbacks for this purpose. A daily 25-minute homeroom period was established to support self-selected silent reading of both books and periodicals. The increasing use of young adult books in content classes fostered an increase in silent reading. In tenth-grade biology class, for instance, students read *The Beggar's Ride* (Kress, 1996) as they studied genetics and genetic engineering. In a geometry class students read *Visions of Symmetry: Notebooks, Periodic Drawings, and Related Works of M. C. Escher* (Schattschneider, 1990). In an eleventh-grade history unit on World War II, students could read *Jacob's Rescue* (Drucker, 1994), *No Pretty Pictures* (Lobel, 1998), or *The Night Crossing* (Ackerman, 1995) during their study of the Holocaust, and they could elect from several picture books including *Rose Blanche* (Innocenti, 1998) and *Tell Them We Remember: The Story of the Holocaust* (Bachrach, 1994). Approximately 15 minutes of daily class time was set aside for reading these texts beyond the time spent on the traditional textbook that was also used.

Alternatives to traditional textbooks were also found on the internet. Whether they were searching for readings for world geography, chemistry, or American history, teachers found a wealth of text sources on the internet that proved more manageable for many students (for both good and poor readers). Post-testing showed over half the students increased reading levels by two or more grade levels in a single year and virtually all students gained at least a year in reading achievement.

Finally, Ivey and Johnston (2013) write about the program that four eighth-grade teachers in a southern middle school have voluntarily put in place. They report on a study of this program during its third year of operation and focus primarily on student engagement and agency. They note substantial improvements were made in the numbers of students who passed the eighth-grade reading examination as compared to the numbers of students who had passed the seventh-grade examination the previous year.

The teachers in this school moved away from the traditional texts used in middle school English classes. Instead of an anthology with excerpts from classic literature and whole-class texts where everyone reads the same books, these teachers put in place a self-selected reading program. They outfitted their classrooms with between 150 and 200 "edgy" books across a range of reading levels. This supply of books was replaced several times throughout the year with a similar collection of different titles.

These teachers taught 90-minute classes that were filled with multiethnic students, many from low-income families (47 percent of students were eligible for free lunches). During class periods students read the books they had selected and engaged each other in conversations about those books. Teachers moved about the classroom engaging students in conversations about the books they were reading or providing short mini-lessons to individuals when needed.

Ivey and Johnston (2013) note that improved reading test scores is only one of several different data sets that one might consider when evaluating this program. They focus on developing "personhood" or developing literate citizens who participate with a wide range of others, many of whom were new to their circle of friends.

Samples of the Edgy Titles Used in the Ivey and Johnston Study

Anderson, L. H. (2007). *Twisted*. New York: Viking.

Chaltas, T. (2009). *Because I am furniture*. New York: Viking.

Deuker, C. (2007). *Gym candy*. New York: Houghton Mifflin.

Hopkins, E. (2004). *Crank*. New York: McElderry Books.

Scott, E. (2008). *Living dead girl*. New York: Simon Pulse.

Sitomer, A. L. (2007). *Homeboyz*. New York: Hyperion.

Strasser, T. (2009). *Wish you were dead*. New York: Egmont.

Van Diepen, A. (2006). *Street pharm*. New York: Simon Pulse.

The researchers noted that these students made substantial progress in developing strategies needed to be a proficient reader. In fact they note:

> Strategic behavior for these students though, appeared to be less the result of strategy instruction than a response to their own need to make sense. Their reading processes suggest that although it is possible to teach particular strategies, instructional time might be better spent supporting engaged reading, a context in which students are more likely to actually become strategic. (p. 273)

They also document the increasing agency and self-regulation that self-selected reading developed. In short, they make the case for a very different sort of structure for middle school English classes.

How do you get middle-school kids—typical kids, not science prodigies—interested in learning about cells? At Westlane Middle School in Indianapolis, Indiana, science teacher Bill Pitcock has found one method that so excites his students that they pepper him with pleas: "When can we start learning about mitosis?"

He does this with novels that his students select to read. Instead of relying just on the textbook or a lecture to explain cell division, DNA, and other concepts, Pitcock lays out an array of interesting reading, including young-adult thrillers like *Code Orange* and *Double Helix,* along with memoirs like *The Immortal Life of Henrietta Lacks.* Each of these books present information about cell topics. His goal is to develop an interest in science and the motivation to study science topics, and he has found novels help him attain these goals.

Reading Proficiency and Dropping Out of School

I included these four projects as examples of what schools could be and what schools could do to address the problems that struggling readers encounter every day. These are problems serious enough to cause 7,000 to just quit school every day. They decided to quit because they were tired of trying to deal with too hard texts and being embarrassed day after day because they could not do the work, and they could not read the texts they were assigned. Today 25 percent of all freshman quit school before they reach the twelfth grade. These are typically the same kids who entered high school reading at the sixth-grade level or below. Unlike Sisyphus who kept pushing the rock back up the mountain, these students elect to let the rock sit and go on to other things.

After a century of ever-increasing high school graduation rates, American schools now can observe the reversal of this progress in rising dropout rates. This alone should be enough to tell us that something is very wrong with the schools we have. At the same time that ever more students are giving up on schooling, our society has embraced a new goal of having every student become college and career ready.

Accompanying this college and career readiness initiative is the CCSS. While I like the seeming simplicity that the CCSS represents when it comes to defining reading and writing, I worry that too much attention is being paid to one aspect—text complexity. I worry because what research tells us quite clearly is that giving early-adolescent struggling readers grade-level texts is not a path to success (O'Connor et al., 2002; O'Connor, Swanson, & Geraghty, 2010).

If the CCSS leads to schools where opportunities such as those described here are common, I will judge that a good thing. If, on the other hand, schools simply purchase new and more difficult texts, then I expect we will see the dropout rates continuing to rise. That will not be a good thing.

What the CCSS Assumes Will Accompany Those More Difficult Texts

If you have not read the full set of CCSS documents, now is the time. As you read those materials notice how often notions of project-based learning, student choice, extensive and engaged reading, and differentiated lessons arise. The CCSS does not suggest that a one-size-fits-all curriculum is worthwhile. What the CCSS does suggest is that every teacher an early adolescent encounters has responsibilities for fostering the student's growth and development as a reader and writer. It is no longer the responsibility of the English teacher (or of the reading teacher or of the special education teacher) to teach the strategies every reader and writer needs to know. There is a role—an important role—for every middle and high school teacher when it comes to preparing college- and career-ready readers and writers.

The CCSS assumes that no teacher will ever say (or even think) that if their students cannot read the texts selected then they don't belong in that class. Instead, the CCSS assumes that every teacher will be locating a variety of texts that present the content to be studied, texts that vary in their complexity so that all students will acquire greater content knowledge as well as greater literacy proficiencies. The CCSS also assumes that every teacher will sufficiently support students so that they can read the texts with higher-order understanding.

While readers may be aware that too many early adolescents experience difficulties reading the texts they are assigned, most are unaware that American students do not read nearly as poorly as is often suggested. Internationally, American students, even at the high school level, read as well as the average high school student in the 32 industrialized nations that participate in the international assessment plan (Fleischman, Hopstock, Pelczar, & Shelley, 2010). However,

This quote comes from English teacher Jeff Wilhelm. He teaches eighth-grade remedial reading and inclusive language arts classes and has written several books about his teaching.

If literature does not speak to student lives, then what good is it? If students don't come to love reading now, when will they ever read later? If I cannot help students to read better, with more purpose, better attitudes and greater power, then what good am I? I am sick and tired of teaching the "classics" and blaming kids who can't answer my questions as "lazy" or "below grade level." If I am really going to be worthy of the title "teacher" then I had better start understanding what this act of reading is all about, and I'd better find out how to let kids in on the secret (Wilhelm, 1997, p.16).

reading as well as the average student in international comparisons does not sit well with folks who consider America the preeminent international power. In addition, while American high school students have not improved their reading proficiency, students in these 32 industrialized nations have. So while American students could be viewed as typical of adolescent readers, they do not stand at the top of the international rankings.

American educational policy makers have urged adoption of the CCSS with its focus on having students exit high school reading at roughly two grade levels higher than is currently the case because, today, rather few high school seniors read well enough to be successful in college.

With the new national goal of all students becoming college- or career-ready, it may be useful to see if we are close to that goal. The most recent ACT report suggests, when it comes to college readiness, that American students are still falling way short. Only a quarter of the ACT test takers in 2012 earned scores high enough in all four areas the ACT assesses (reading, English, science, and mathematics) that they can be expected to earn at least a grade of C in college courses in these areas (Adams, 2012). Just above half (52 percent) of ACT test takers earned reading scores that indicated they can handle college reading assignments and 46 percent earned mathematics scores high enough to be expected to earn a C in college mathematics courses. Fewer than a third earned science scores high enough that a C grade could be expected, while two-thirds earned English scores that met that criteria. But when scores high enough to achieve a C grade in all four areas was the criteria, only a quarter of the test takers earned such scores.

The performances look worse when you examine scores by ethnicity. Only 5 percent of African American and 13 percent of Hispanic students achieved the benchmark scores. In comparison, 42 percent of Asian American and 32 percent of white students met the standard. In other words, American schools seem to be working to prepare students of some ethnic groups for college better than students of other ethnic groups. However, virtually every school has at least one teacher who develops every student's reading proficiencies as well as foster the motivation to read voluntarily. Unfortunately, roughly only one of five teachers of early adolescents meets this standard (Pianta et al., 2007).

On average these researchers noted that the typical fifth-grader spent over 90 percent of class time either listening to a teacher or working alone, usually on a low-level literal worksheet task. Their description of how early adolescents spend their school days was not very different from the description I provided some 20 years earlier (Allington, 1990). I also noted the incredible curricular fragmentation that I observed as students moved from one class to another, expecting to shift their brains into another curricular area every 45 minutes or so. As I pointed out then, it seemed that middle schools were mimicking the high school plan for instruction even though curricular integration was one of the essential characteristics of the original middle school movement.

Also missing from middle school classrooms was instruction. I noted that the teacher interviews suggested that "covering the ground"—as in "We've completed chapter 3 this week"—was substituting for explanation, modeling, or summarizing of the content that the students were expected to acquire. The instruction observed was dominated by assigning students low-level tasks that often focused on locating the correct single word in a text, with that word then entered into the blank space on the worksheet. Vocabulary was not taught even though vocabulary worksheets were assigned.

It is as if students are expected to teach themselves with the teacher simply correcting the low-level work and entering a grade into the class grade book. When students experience such low quality lessons most of the day, I am unsure why anyone, including their teachers, can criticize the students for their "lack of effort." The evidence available suggests, though, that students experience such low quality instruction from 80 percent of their teachers.

Allington and Johnston (2002) provide case studies of six exemplary fourth-grade teachers drawn from a federally funded national study. The quality of the instruction offered by these teachers contrasts with the instruction offered in the typical fourth-grade classroom. Students in these exemplary classrooms read and wrote substantially more every day than students in typical classrooms. They engaged in peer conversations about their reading and writing on a daily basis and responded to far more higher-order comprehension questions than the typical fourth-grader. These exemplary teachers offered the multi-text, multi-level curriculum base that I have described in this book.

What these exemplary teachers omitted was the seemingly unending supply of low-level work that dominates most fourth-grade (and fifth-, sixth-, seventh-, and eighth-grade) classrooms. In the classrooms of exemplary teachers, long interrogation segments where students responded to low-level literal questions were absent, as were low-level worksheets. Instead, teachers expected students to converse with each other as well as develop written summaries, responses, or character analyses following their reading.

Student engagement was such that almost every student was on task. Across the year-long observation cycles, no observer noted even a single discipline event in the classrooms of these exemplary teachers while in the typical fourth-grade classroom at any given point in time almost half of the students were off task and engaged in something other than class work. We assumed that the high level of engagement in the classrooms of these exemplary teachers was related, as Raphael and colleagues (2008) suggested, to a far wider use of multiple materials and texts that students could read. Students in the exemplary teacher classrooms scored far more growth in reading achievement than students in typical classrooms, which was not surprising because the quality and quantity of the instruction was so much higher.

In the end, it is teachers who elect to assign low-level and largely meaningless academic work to their students. As I noted,

> The use of grammar dittoes, the transcription tasks displayed on the chalkboards, the round-robin oral reading of materials, the "hot seat" question and answer formats, the assignments without explanations, and the emphasis on locating rather than understanding were choices made by the teachers. When listening to some of the teacher interviews, one gets the impression that the plan is to keep students busy for 43 to 54 minutes a day, with little suggestion of any larger instructional goal. (Allington, 1990; p. 38)

Simply keeping kids busy is not the goal of education.

The situation was quite different for the 20 percent of fifth-grade students who had an effective teacher (Pianta et al., 2007). In these classrooms working in small groups, engagement in discussion, and working on tasks that required higher-order thinking was normal. The effects of these differences were observable in the achievement students registered on their annual assessments. Students with effective teachers performed at much higher levels of literacy development than students in the majority of the classrooms. The students in these classrooms didn't differ; it was the instructional environment provided by the teachers that differed.

Raphael, Pressley, and Mohan (2008) observed in sixth-grade classrooms and identified high, moderate, and low engagement classrooms. Highly engaging teachers covered much more of the curriculum and covered that material in greater depth than the less engaging teachers. In short, they offered higher quality lessons. They also offered work that was cognitively more challenging for students, assigning little low-level work. In contrast, less engaging teachers offered less challenging and more low-level work with the low engagement teachers' classrooms dominated by such work (e.g., worksheets, definitions to be copied, maps to filled in from maps in text books, endless computation activities in math class, and so on).

While classroom management was problematic only in the low engagement classrooms, the authors note that almost no theories of classroom management account for any of the 44 practices they observed in high engagement classrooms. Engaging teachers evidenced high levels of awareness of students' interest, needs, and lives outside of school compared to teachers who were less engaging. They also noted that some students were highly engaged in some classrooms but off-task in other classrooms during the same observational days.

I will now provide a description of what one exemplary middle school teacher's classroom looks and feels like.

An Exemplary Middle School English/ Language Arts Teacher

Michael is a seventh-grade language arts teacher at an urban middle school. His school does not track students by achievement levels because the research on the topic finds that low-track readers rarely are enrolled in language arts classes where the curriculum demands are similar to those for high-proficiency students (Wheelock, 1992). Because of this decision all of Michael's language arts classes have students of varying levels of reading proficiency, including students with disabilities.

Because almost half of his students read somewhere below their current grade level, Michael has created a language arts curriculum rich in reading and writing for his students. He focuses on extended reading of self-selected texts on Monday, Tuesday, Wednesday, and Thursday, and on extended composing on self-selected topics on Friday. He expects that all of his students will read 40 books each year, or one every week of school. He located this model in *The Book Whisperer* by Donalyn Miller. As we mentioned earlier, she is a sixth-grade teacher in Texas who has successfully used this goal as her basic target for every student in her language arts classes. Her book is a good introduction to the extensive reading and writing model for middle schools.

Michael's Classroom

Michael provides individualized reading lessons for his students every day. While pairs of students may be reading the same title, more often each student is reading a different book. Michael simply moves about the classroom stopping to work with every student at least once every week. These sessions are usually brief, anywhere from 1 to 3 minutes. But in these brief periods Michael checks on whether the student is having problems and, if so, provides advice.

Michael understands he teaches children who are still emerging as readers and writers. He also understands that even his students with the highest levels of proficiency in reading and writing still have much to learn as readers and writers. Thus, he has created a classroom where every student is working at a level that will foster the development of their literacy proficiencies. He also understands that early adolescence is when the majority of students, for the first time, rarely read voluntarily.

Because Michael understands the importance of literate conversation in the classroom, he engages his students in such conversations about the books they are reading. He begins his side-by-side session with students with a broad and open-ended question, even when a student is reading a book Michael is not familiar with. He has found that it is not difficult to determine whether a student comprehends the book he is reading. At other times Michael simply asks students to turn to their neighbor and discuss the book they are reading. At least once a week he holds a whole-class session to discuss what every student in the class is reading. Because it is rare that any student will be discussing a book no one else has read, these sessions are not simply one-way communication sessions.

Student self-selection of books to read is another important component of Michael's classes. He is well aware of the finding of the meta-analysis reported by John Guthrie and Nicole Humenick (2004) showed that the two most powerful factors linked to improved reading comprehension and motivation to read were ease of access to interesting books and self-selection of what to read from those books. While most books students read are selected by the students themselves, roughly once a month Michael selects books the whole class will read and discuss. His selection of these books is driven by a single question: Why read this book instead of some other book?

Michael is also aware that his students present a range of reading development and so he typically selects books that every student can handle. Occasionally he selects a book that is too difficult for some of his students to handle independently. In these cases he creates small groups of readers with differing levels of reading development. He does not create a "stupids" group, but rather a group of students with varying reading levels. At times he pairs good readers and struggling readers so they can partner-read the text. Other times during small-group time he reads the book aloud to them. In most instances he reads the first chapter or two aloud to the group and shows them how to create a list of character and setting names, often with a syllabic breakdown of those words (e.g., *a pro pri ate*) to assist students' independent pronunciations of those words.

Characteristics of Middle School Teachers Who Elicit High Student Engagement

Data derived from an observational study of middle school classrooms of high, moderate, and low engagement teachers (Raphael, Pressley, & Mohan, 2008).

Some of the 44 practices that supported student engagement:

- Possesses consistent, positive, explicit, and high expectations
- Makes personal connections to students
- Provides students with choices
- Encourages behavioral self-regulation
- Monitors whole class and individual students
- Teaches and encourages use of strategies
- Models problem solving and thinking
- Stimulates higher-level thought
- Uses opportunistic mini-lessons
- Encourages student collaboration
- Attributes student outcomes to effort
- Possesses positive classroom management

Some of the 17 practices that undermine student engagement:

- Attributes students' outcomes to ability
- Calls attention to public and salient differences between students
- Fosters competition among students
- Assigns low-level seatwork
- Lack of scaffolding
- Lack of monitoring
- Negative classroom management
- Provides threats and warnings
- Possesses negative tone

He selects some books for students because he wants all students to be exposed to a variety of genres, authors, and topics. He knows some of his students read only mysteries, or only fantasy, or only series books. It isn't that every month all students read the same book, but every month every student will read a book other students in the class are also reading. These common readings also allow Michael the opportunity to provide small-group or even whole-class lessons on important reading and writing strategies his students need to develop. But most of his instruction is offered side-by-side in the individual meetings he conducts during the daily class periods. And, most important, common readings happen at most for one week, once a month.

In order to use the common readings, his students must read the assigned books both during their class period and out of school. This has not presented any major problems since students are assigned books they can read and Michael has organized his class so most students are motivated to read the novels that they selected or the novels that he has selected for them. In addition, Michael always reads aloud the first chapter or two when he assigns a book for students to read.

When it comes to assigning grades to students, Michael's students earn mostly A and B grades. This is because every student engages in more reading than they have typically done in recent school years. His students also develop the ability to discuss what they have read and to link this to the range of texts they might soon read.

Conclusion

Michael is developing readers who understand the value of reading and who are more likely to read voluntarily than the typical student in a different middle school. His focus is on providing his students with books they can read accurately, fluently, and with understanding, and with books that will make them think. His students develop proficiencies in selecting books they want to read, stamina through engaging in long periods of reading, agency by selecting the books they will read, and self-regulation since they selected the book and now must discuss it with peers and with Michael.

We know that some of the readers of this book will become highly effective and engaging teachers of early adolescents. We also know that too many readers will adopt the typical style of teaching used in the school where they work. These teachers will likely never become either highly effective or engaging. While the school and the people who work there are important factors in what type of teacher you become, we also know that virtually all exemplary teachers made a conscious decision to work at becoming exemplary teachers (Gabriel, Day, & Allington, 2011). We also know that even though these teachers are now effective, they still are finding more room for improvement in their teaching than their typical and less effective colleagues across the hallway.

It will be up to you, the reader, to decide whether you become one of those exemplary teachers. I hope you make the decision to follow that path if only because more effective teaching is just about the only hope that struggling middle school learners have.

Developing a Plan for Enhancing the Effectiveness of the School You Work In

You may find that becoming a more effective teacher of early adolescents is easier if you convince one or more colleagues to join you while you both work to improve instructional quality. In fact, engaging everyone on the faculty in becoming a more effective teacher is one strategy proven to improve both teaching and learning (Bean & Readance, 2002). However, getting every teacher on the instructional improvement train is never easy. So few schools have any plan for improving instruction. They have plans for changing instruction by changing the scheduling of classes, by purchasing different textbooks, by adding a weekly assessment to students' schedules, by adding time in a computer lab, and so on. All these efforts *do* change instruction but rarely, if ever, *improve* instruction.

In the following section I sketch the outline of a plan that you might consider for instigating an instructional improvement plan at your school. While every school differs from every other school, the school days of early adolescents are eerily similar. Some days I wonder why there are so many schools more likely to deaden students' enthusiasm for acquiring academic knowledge than there are schools more likely to excite students about the possibilities of learning so many things they currently do not know.

Establish the Level of Challenge by Comparing Student Reading Achievement to Text Difficulty

Any effort at improving instruction for struggling readers must begin by establishing what current reading levels of students are as well as the reading demands of the curricular materials. Ideally, every teacher will know both the reading level of every student they teach and the difficulty level of every text they assign. So the first step in a schoolwide plan is gathering just this data.

Step 1: Establish Student Reading Levels   If no assessment of reading proficiency is currently given to students when they enter middle school, begin by identifying the assessment you want to put in place. This assessment needs to evaluate students' reading proficiencies, ideally both for literary reading and for reading in content areas. Most broad assessments of reading proficiency provide such assessments along with a variety of options for reporting student scores. In general, what you are hoping for here is a reliable and valid assessment of reading comprehension in early adolescents. In other words, tests such as *DIBELs, AIMsweb,* and the *Wide Range Achievement Test*—all of which focus too heavily on oral reading rate and accuracy and provide assessments of other reading sub-skills—are largely worthless here.

While the new assessments that will accompany the CCSS may be useful, I worry about recent reports from states where these tests have been administered. I am worried because the new tests are benchmarked against the new and higher standards for reading proficiency that is the reason for the CCSS. Time will tell how reliably these new tests evaluate reading proficiency and how well they rank students on that proficiency. However, given the enormous amount of funding the test developers have had, one hopes that the new tests will be better than any of the tests currently available.

The CCSS tests will be administered by a computer, and students will both read the tested material on the computer and respond to questions on the computer. Thus, many of the test-taking skills that many students have developed will be largely useless on the new assessments. There will undoubtedly be problems such as those in Indiana where the computer system crashed because it had not been built to work with the number of students who had signed up for the test. There will be system crashes such as those experienced in New York where testing had to be rescheduled in several districts so that software problems could be fixed. All written responses—and there are number of those on the CCSS assessments—will be scored by computer software. Given the problems Popham (2001) describes in using temporary workers to score written exam sections, perhaps computer software will at least judge everyone using the same standards. Nonetheless, the National Council of Teachers of English has issued a strong caution about the computer-scoring plan. Again, only time will tell how this aspect of the new CCSS assessments will work out.

Step 2: Assess the Match Between Students' Reading Proficiency and the Difficulty of the Texts They Are to Be Assigned   Instruction will no longer be planned blind when there are good assessment data on every early-adolescent's reading and writing. Finding appropriate materials for lessons depends on knowing about the reading proficiencies of the students who are entering your school. Without such data teachers and administrators can organize instructional plans but plans developed without considering the reading proficiencies of students.

A large urban school district in Michigan ordered a college-level text on ancient Egypt for use by their sixth-grade students who studied ancient Africa as part of their global studies curriculum. Unfortunately, those sixth-graders not only did not read at the college level, their average reading proficiency was early fifth-grade level, with half the students below that level. In another example a county-wide district in Florida ordered a college-level U. S. government textbook for their ninth-grade students whose average reading level was sixth grade. Suffice to say, in both school districts many students failed the courses that used these too hard texts.

I am unsure how either district decided upon using these textbooks. In both cases everyone—including the general public—knew that the students were reading below grade level because it was reported repeatedly in the news media every time state test scores were published. Given how easy it is to establish a reading difficulty range for any text, both situations make it clear that educators and/or administrators had not checked on the difficulty levels of the texts. This may be a powerful message that schools should conduct their own research into a textbook's appropriateness rather than assuming that its marketed grade level is always representative of their students' abilities and needs. After the Michigan episode, the state legislature required all textbooks distributed as samples to schools to have a sticker on the front cover indicating the reading difficulty level of the textbook, identifying which readability system had been used to establish that level.

It is easy to estimate the difficulty level of textbooks. You can go to the Lexile .com website to examine lists of books with their Lexile level listed, or you can type in sections of texts not listed to learn the Lexile range of difficulty. Identifying any text's level of reading difficulty is quick and easy, a perfect job for paraprofessionals or parent volunteers.

When qualitatively considering text difficulty, the question educators must ask themselves is this: Are my students likely to have developed much prior knowledge of this topic? Prior knowledge of any topic (or school content area) influences what sorts of texts you will be able to read. If you are a male from rural East Tennessee then it is likely you will know the word *rack* in reference to deer antlers. Of course, that same male student will likely have no knowledge of the torture device and maybe not the triangular device used to *rack* pool balls. Teachers who know their students will likely be the only ones able to make these judgments.

Along the same lines, some authors embed more information in the texts they write so as to support a reader's understanding of key terms. For instance, an author might write this sentence, "The buck had an enormous rack, or set of antlers." On the other hand, many authors will assume readers to be somewhat expert on the topic they are writing about and omit the explanatory phrase at the end of the sentence above.

Textbooks often also provide illustrations of key (but rare) terms used in the text, and many provide a glossary with definitions of the key (but unfamiliar) words they use. When considering the difficulty of any text, educators must also consider these factors alongside any estimate based on the structural qualities of a text. It isn't that estimates based primarily on sentence length and word frequency are wrong, but that at least some of the time they won't estimate the difficulty with precise accuracy.

Finally, remember that CCSS has changed the estimated text difficulty appropriate for each grade level. What used to be considered appropriate difficulty

Readability Levels Are Always Estimates

The ease in determining difficulty levels of texts should make you wonder about the accuracy of the level established. Some readability indices provide ranges of difficulty (fifth- to sixth-grade level, or Lexile level range 790–850). Other indices provide a single grade equivalent (6.4 grade level). I'll put my money on the formulas that provide ranges of difficulty, and I say this because all estimates of text difficulty rely primarily on sentence length (longer sentences are harder) and word frequency (rarer words are harder). Computers make calculating both of these factors enormously easy. However, most of the software that calculates difficulty does not distinguish, for instance, between a familiar word meaning and an unfamiliar word meaning.

Take as an example the word *rack*. Almost every student will be familiar with a spice *rack* or a magazine *rack*. But many, perhaps most, students will be unfamiliar with a *rack* as the lift that mechanics use to raise automobiles for service. Many and maybe most will not be familiar with *rack* as a set of antlers, with the medieval torture *rack* or even the triangular *rack* for setting the pool balls. The point is that each and every time *rack* appears in print it is counted and from that count a frequency is established. It does not matter that these various *racks* all mean very different things; all of the usages of *rack* establishes its frequency. Because there is only a single frequency for the word *rack*, when some of the rarer meanings of the word appear in print the procedure still assigns it the frequency of a more frequent meaning. Thus, the estimate will misjudge the difficulty of a text discussing the torture device or even a billiards game.

Another problem with readability estimates is that some readers may know all of the meanings of *rack* and others only the most common meaning (*spice rack*). Thus, what these various estimates do not consider is the familiarity the potential reader has with the general topic of the text. This is one of those qualitative factors that educators must consider.

for the eighth grade is now considered appropriate for the sixth grade. I expect it will take a few years for the new levels of difficulty to become firmly established as appropriate. In the meantime the ultimate goal is putting texts in each student's hands that they can read with understanding.

The difficulty level of some potential instructional texts, such as magazines or internet materials of any sort, are not easily established. The good news is that Jeanne Chall and her colleagues (1996) have developed a procedure for estimating text difficulty in such material. Their book, *Qualitative assessment of text difficulty: A practical guide for teachers and writers,* provides clear guidelines and exemplar texts for a more qualitative estimation of difficulty. While it will take a bit longer to use this method, even the few minutes of time required will be a small investment toward better instruction.

The point of this activity is to make every teacher smarter about the estimated difficulty level of the texts they plan to use. Students do not learn much from books they cannot read accurately, fluently, and with understanding. Every early adolescent deserves a backpack filled with books that they can read and that provide the content they are expected to learn. This is simply the first step toward more effective teaching.

The goal here is to identify how many students have desks full of texts that they cannot read. You may find there is not much of a problem to be addressed, or you may find that only about a quarter of your students can read the texts that are available. In no case would I expect to find a school for early adolescents where every student had a supply of books they could read accurately, fluently, and with understanding. I hope to see such a school one day, but I have yet to encounter that school.

Step 3: Organize Multi-Level Classroom Libraries of Texts Students Can Select to Read for the Content-Area Class   While steps 1 and 2 are shorter-term tasks, step 3 will be on ongoing process as new texts can be expected to be added every school year. The goal is creating multi-level, multi-text classroom libraries with multiple levels of text difficulty for every subject matter area and for every content teacher. When I write "classroom libraries," I mean collections of texts that cover the topics students are expected to learn. If we take American history as our example, we might decide to organize those collections of books around the historical eras that will be studied. Then we would organize sets of texts that present information about each of the selected periods.

A key aspect in the development of multi-level texts sets is what Lesesne (2010) labels "laddering." The basic idea here is that we can ease students into more complex texts by initially providing less challenging texts and then moving through a set of books from the least complex to the most complex text. As Lesesne (2010) notes, "Simply, a reading ladder is a series or set of books that are related in some way (e.g., thematically, topically, etc.) and demonstrate a slow, gradual development from simple to more complex" (p. 48).

There are multiple resources available for locating books such as the search tools on the Barnes & Nobel, Scholastic, and Lexile websites, along with those professional organization websites mentioned earlier in this chapter. The texts I've listed in the following feature box were located using the search terms "Lexile level 400-1100, Civil War"; these level numbers appear in the third column on the right.

The point of using such text sets is to both expand the volume of reading that early adolescents do and to move those adolescents into ever more

A Sample Laddered Set of Texts on the Civil War

Lisa L. Owens .*America's Civil War*. Perfection Learning.	480
Ted Lewin. *Red Legs*. HarperCollins.	540
Jason M Glaser. *John Brown's Raid on Harpers Ferry*. Capstone.	560
Matt Doeden. *Weapons of the Civil War*. Capstone.	630
Paul Fleischman & David Frampton. *Bull Run*. HarperCollins.	810
Patricia Beatty. *Turn Homeward, Hannalee*. Troll.	830
Gary Paulsen. *Soldier's Heart*. Dell Laurel Leaf.	1000
Jim Murphy. *The Boys' War*. Clarion Books.	1060

Note that I could have focused on any aspect of the Civil War era in developing the list. I also could have taken a Northern or Southern perspective in searching for books. I could also have focused on the lives of African American citizens of the day, and so on.

complex treatments of the topic of the Civil War. Providing less complex texts initially gives students the opportunity to develop basic concepts about the historical era as well as the regional geography. Reading the less complex texts works to develop both their background knowledge and the vocabulary they need for reading more complex texts with understanding. Of course, using the multiple texts found in a text set also enhances the acquisition of historical knowledge, the central mission of an American history course.

Personally, I believe that text sets such as I have described only get used when classroom teachers have been involved in their development. At present you cannot just order the text sets that you need; someone has to create each text set from scratch. If we are creating a text set for the Civil War because that is one topic found in our sixth-grade social studies curriculum, then it makes sense to create a team of sixth-grade teachers to explore texts that might be included. Depending on the state where you teach, you might even want to include only teachers who teach sixth-grade social studies. I would suggest that a reading specialist and a special education resource teacher be included each time if only because they will typically have greater expertise in text difficulty than classroom teachers and have greater expertise on the characteristics of struggling readers. School librarians are also useful team members, but if every grade level tackles this project simultaneously then the school librarian can only be a supportive consultant to each team.

I suggest that you focus first on a single grade level, say fifth or sixth grade. For instance, if fifth-grade students are the youngest students attending your middle school, then begin with grade 5. The next year focus on sixth-grade text sets and the following year focus on seventh-grade text sets. Finally you complete the curriculum transformation by creating eighth-grade text sets. If you follow this plan, by the time you get around to developing the eighth-grade text set the students will already have spent 3 years in classrooms using text sets.

Creating text sets requires that someone (or several persons, ideally) selects and then reads each selected text as well as determines the difficulty level of the text using both quantitative (Lexile or Dale-Chall) and qualitative methods. The qualitative analysis can be as simple as rating whether each book is interesting or it can be as complex as applying the analyses from the *Qualitative assessment of text difficulty* manual. In other words, we want to create topical text sets filled with books that meet several important criteria:

- Books that students will find they can read accurately and with understanding
- Books that develop content knowledge central to the topic
- Books that are interesting treatments of the topic

In many school systems you will be able to find teachers, librarians, or administrators who have already developed familiarity with the sorts of books you might select. Identifying such colleagues makes the task of creating the text sets much easier. As mentioned earlier there are also internet and print resources that will facilitate your search for books.

Purchasing these books will require a funding source. In some textbook adoption states schools can use the funds allocated for textbook purchases to purchase trade books linked to the subject matter while other states require a written plan listing the books that will have to be approved at the state level. Nonetheless you will have to trust me that funding for such purchases is accessible even if it means shifting funds away from workbook or test prep purchases or not replacing the textbooks as frequently and using the money saved to purchase the text sets of trade books. We've even seen schools where local businesses provided the funding to purchase the texts, sometimes through local educational foundations.

Step 4: Plan for Effective Professional Development for All Teachers and Administrators   Effective professional development must provide substantially more training than a one-day workshop can. The most powerful professional development efforts I have been involved with typically lasted at least a full school year along with some summer workshop and work time. We can see from preceding steps 1 and 2 that teachers need professional development to acquire the expertise to establish the difficulty level of texts and to understand that test scores provide a crude estimate of students' reading ability. I would plan to spend a full day with teachers in a workshop mode for both topics and perhaps two workshop days on text difficulty, with one focused on quantitative methods and the other focused on qualitative methods of determining the level of text difficulty.

Classroom teachers will need to develop expertise in using text sets in their lessons, and they will need guidance on how to ensure that students

Develop a Literacy Council for Your School

Anders (1998) writes convincingly about the potential of developing a Literacy Council. Members of this council advise school leadership on issues related to reading and writing across the curriculum. These are the folks who establish the type of literacy-related professional development that will be offered and whether it is for all faculty or only for interested faculty members. The council supports teams of teachers as they develop into exemplary multi-text and multi-level content teachers.

The Literacy Council should be fairly small, although it should also be reasonably representative of the various departments and grade levels of the school. In an ideal world every middle school would employ at least one certified reading specialist who would always be a member of the council, but, failing that, council members should still be interested in an inquiry-based approach to literacy problem solving.

have selected texts appropriate to their reading development. I would also suggest offering another day-long session on how to develop and support students' abilities to engage each other in discussion and in literate conversation. And another day might be set aside for professional development in supporting students' efforts during writing. And so on. In most school districts teachers already have 3 to 5 days of professional development scheduled during every school year. Those days should be used to target professional development providers who can support teachers as they become more expert in such tasks as evaluating text difficulty, interpreting student performances on reading assessments, and selecting good books for inclusion in the text sets. My experience has been that school systems are quite happy when teachers present a plan for professional development they need in order to provide more effective instruction.

The greater the involvement of teachers in identifying the areas of expertise to be developed and the scheduling of the workshops, the greater the likelihood that teachers take what they learned and positively alter their instruction. Finally, in-classroom coaching is often useful if the coaches can provide useful demonstrations and feedback on the lessons observed.

Step 5: Things Take Time (TTT)   Always remember the triple Ts rule. We are almost always better off if we slow down when teachers seem to be overwhelmed. Our work in schools suggests setting a three-year timeline at the very minimum for putting this sort of change in place. Too many school reform efforts have failed because they were implemented too quickly before teachers had become familiar with and expert in the components of a new plan. While change is always difficult, mandated, or imposed, change is even harder.

For projects such as the one sketched here, a 4- or 5-year plan is needed because it will take at least 4 years to develop text sets for grades 5 through 8. Let's say we not only develop fifth-grade text sets during the first year but also develop the fifth-grade teachers' expertise at the same time, and then follow that same plan for grades 6 through 9 over the next 3 or 4 years. By year 5 we should see a school dealing with the diversity in student academic proficiencies in ways that raise achievement levels far beyond where they are today.

We can create schools where early adolescents are engaged in powerful lessons that foster both reading and academic development. Or we can continue to have those students attend schools where low-level worksheets and literal interrogations follow the assignment of boring, hard, and poorly written textbooks. Because those early adolescents have no voice or power to improve their lot, it is educators, who are responsible for the environments that currently exist, who could create very different and far more powerful learning environments, lessons, and tasks for students. You are one of those educators. Work for the positive change that is both needed and possible.

Summary

We can create schools for early adolescents that work better in support of continued reading and academic development. Even when you find yourself working in a school that no one is interested in changing, you can still work to ensure that you become an exemplary teacher. Many readers of this book may still recall that one exemplary teacher they had back in seventh grade. In too many cases students only experience a single teacher every day that excites them and teaches them expertly. You can become one of those too few teachers.

If you are lucky you will be working in a school where you can participate in a schoolwide plan for enhancing teaching and learning. Although putting appropriate books in students' hands is just the first step of improving teaching and learning for early adolescents, it is a critical first step because without it most other efforts to improve teaching and learning will fail.

Book Study Guide for
What Really Matters for Middle School Readers

Written by

Lisa Wiedmann, former Reading Specialist
for the Rhinelander Public Schools, Rhinelander, WI.

Book Study Guidelines

Many schools now are organized in professional learning communities (PLCs) because they recognize the power of collaborative learning. Book studies often play a large role in helping PLC's reflect upon and achieve best practices. The intent of a book study is to provide a supportive context for accessing new ideas and affirming best practices already in place. Marching through the questions in a lockstep fashion could result in the mechanical processing of information; it is more beneficial to select specific questions to focus on and give them the attention they deserve.

One possibility to structure your book discussion of *What Really Matters for Middle School Readers* is to use the Reading Reaction Sheet on page 195. Following this format, make a copy for each group member. Next, select a different facilitator for each chapter. The facilitator will act as the official note taker and be responsible for moving the discussion along.

Book Study Questions for Each Chapter

chapter 1: Reading Development in Grades 5 through 9: Problems and Promise

1. In your school, are students asked to provide written responses to questions on exams often, somewhat often, or seldom? Are there certain content areas where written responses are required more than others? When developing exam questions requiring written responses, do most teachers focus on questions that require integration and interpretation of content information? Or is literal recall still the focus of most examination items?

2. Allington states that the CCSS will require many teachers to acquire new ways of teaching and believes that this will be a good thing. Do you agree or disagree? Explain your answer.

3. Allington describes the instructional climate of Monroe Middle School where the failure to meet expectations seems to be thought of as a problem of the students rather than a problem with the instructional design. When your faculty discusses students who are failing to achieve, how often does the discussion center on changing the delivery of instruction? Why is this so?

4. Use Allington's reader/text matching tool with the students in your school and discuss what you learn from the data.

5. Use Allington's tool to gather data on the organization and delivery of classroom lessons in your school and discuss what you learn from the data.

6. Do you agree with those who believe that texts need to be difficult even though there are students in your classroom who can't read them? Explain your answer.

7. What are your thoughts on why most content-area teachers aren't teaching students to read in their discipline even though the research shows they are the ones most capable of doing so?

8. After reading this chapter, does the research Allington presents support what is being practiced in your school?

9. What information in this chapter will be the most helpful to you?

chapter 2: Decoding Is Not the Problem (but That Is What Most Remediation Targets)

1. Make a list of materials/programs used with students in your school who are receiving extra help in the area of reading. Discuss your findings in light of what Allington says about the popularity of interventions with a focus on decoding skills as compared to interventions with a focus on comprehension.

2. Considering what Allington says about non-word pronunciation, what do you think is the reason so many schools continue to use this as an assessment tool?

3. Do you feel your school offers struggling readers sufficient opportunities to expand the volume of reading they engage in every day?

4. How often are students in your school who have an IEP receiving instruction in one-size-fits-all commercial materials? Why do you think this is the case?

5. True or False: Too often my school would fall into the category of providing a design of instruction that ignores the real reading problems of the struggling readers. Discuss examples that support your answer.

6. Share ways in which your interventions help students develop the ability to self-monitor and self-teach.

7. Allington describes three activities to encourage vocabulary development. Describe other activities you have found to be effective.

8. Does the research Allington presents support what is being practiced in your school? Or does the research suggest it is time for a thorough review of existing school practice?

9. What information in this chapter will be the most helpful to you?

chapter 3: "It's the Words, Man": Limited Meaning Vocabulary and How to Improve It

1. Allington states that one cause for deficits in adolescent readers is a focus on skills development rather than increasing the volume of reading. Do you believe this describes what happens in your school? Why or why not?

2. Thinking about the libraries in your classrooms/school, what is there about them that you feel supports or doesn't support the goal of increasing the volume of reading?

3. Describe the textbook selection process for your school. Do you feel the process is one that ensures the texts are at the appropriate reading level for all students?

4. If a student can't learn much from a book he or she can't read, do you think the CCSS focus on complex texts is a good thing for students? Explain your answer.

5. In your district where would you most likely see large amounts of whole-class instruction: Grades K–2, 3–5, 6–8, or 9–12? Why do you think this is so?

6. Discuss which textbooks in your school you would describe as "considerate" and which ones you would describe as "inconsiderate"?

7. Allington suggests various vocabulary development activities. Share with your group other ones you have used and found to be effective.

8. Discuss ways in which your school encourages students to read outside of class. Develop additional strategies that might be used by the teachers in your school to foster voluntary reading.

9. Share with your group your list of favorite books that you read aloud to your students.

10. How much time do students in your classroom spend in discussion? What strategies have you used to encourage meaningful discussion of texts with your students?

chapter 4: Read More, Read Better: Addressing a Major Source of Reading Difficulties

1. Discuss with your group whether you feel the bigger concern in your school is illiteracy or aliteracy.

2. Do you believe that in your classroom you set aside enough time daily/weekly for read-alouds and sustained silent reading? Explain to your group how important you feel these activities are for your content area.

3. If as Allington says teachers use textbooks as the key curriculum provider, why do you think the textbooks purchased are so often too difficult for many students to read?

4. What are your reasons for agreeing or disagreeing with Allington's comment about the lack of literacy leadership in middle schools?

5. What are your thoughts about having students participate in round-robin reading? What other alternatives do you and other teachers use when texts are difficult for students to read independently?

6. Would you describe most classrooms in your school as organized around transmission or participatory models of teaching? Explain your answer.

7. Why do you think students in affluent schools are so often assigned different types of tasks than are assigned to students in low-income schools?

8. Discuss where in your district or school budget you might find money to fund the purchase of more books. Brainstorm possible sources of funding to purchase additional books for your classroom libraries.

9. Looking at the four activities that will improve classroom instruction, which are ones do you believe your school does well and which are ones you feel could be improved?

10. Would you describe your classroom as a CCSS classroom? Would you describe your school as a CCSS school? Why or why not?

11. After reading this chapter, does the research Allington presents support what is being practiced in your school?

12. What information in this chapter will be the most helpful to you?

chapter 5: Reading with Comprehension: Understanding "Understanding"

1. Thinking about the textbooks you have seen or used, how would you answer Allington's question as to why textbooks are not interesting?

2. Do you agree or disagree with Allington's assertion that middle and high school instruction would improve if textbooks were no longer used? Explain your answer.

3. If you observed lessons in different content-area classrooms in your school, would you describe them as being more focused on assessment or more focused on instruction? Give examples to support your answer.

4. What opportunities do you offer for students in your classes to engage in higher level thinking?

5. Describe some of the tasks you use with your students to develop their academic language.

6. Describe some of the tasks you use with your students to build background knowledge.

7. Do you agree or disagree with Allington that the need for students to remember information is no longer as important as their need to know the reliability of the information? Explain your answer.

8. Have you seen significant changes in the design of instruction for middle and high school students in your district as a result of the research findings on comprehension? Why do you think this is so?

9. How often and in what ways are students in your class involved in writing activities in order to build engagement in learning?

10. After reading this chapter, does the research Allington presents support what is being practiced in your school?

11. What information in this chapter will be the most helpful to you?

chapter 6: Literate Conversation: A Powerful Method for Fostering Understanding of Complex Texts

1. At what school level do you see students having the most opportunities to engage in discussion? Why do you think this is so?

2. Explain why you think that literate discussions are not happening in most classrooms.

3. Make a list of the instructional practices you have observed in your school. Based on this information, discuss whether most reflect a pedagogy of transmission or one of interpretation.

4. Do you agree or disagree with Allington's belief that students are not prepared to critically engage the information cycle. What if anything is your school doing to address the issue?

5. Make a list of real-life examples that would support Allington's belief that schools must create citizens who are as skilled at asking questions as they are at answering questions.

6. Discuss whether or not your school has a "pedagogy of poverty" and what has been done or might be done to change it.

7. Brainstorm the ways your school district has helped to make sure all teachers have the skills necessary to lead productive classroom discussions and literate conversations? If this list is short, develop recommendations for activities your district might use.

8. Discuss the importance of extending responses rather than evaluating responses.

9. Share with your group ways you have found to successfully foster engagement in classroom discussions.

10. After reading this chapter, does the research Allington presents support what is being practiced in your school?

11. What information in this chapter will be the most helpful to you.

chapter 7: Getting the Gist of It All: Summarization after Reading

1. Discuss your thoughts about close reading in light of what is known about the role of prior knowledge in reading comprehension.

2. Make a list of the instructional tasks you have observed in classrooms. Which ones support thoughtful literacy and which support regurgitation literacy?

3. In what ways do you encourage your students to think about the big ideas rather than concentrating on the details?

4. Discuss what your school district does to improve students' proficiencies in reading expository texts.

5. Share with your group ways in which you help students develop their ability to write summaries.

6. Discuss specific examples of what the test data in your school tell you about your students and ways in which that data are used to improve instruction for struggling readers.

7. Analyze the materials used in your classrooms, commercial or otherwise, as to the amount of low-level literal questions. Discuss your findings.

8. Do you agree or disagree with Allington's comments that core reading programs are unlikely to develop adolescents' reading and writing abilities? Explain your answer.

9. After reading this chapter, does the research Allington presents support what is being practiced in your school?

10. What information in this chapter will be the most helpful to you?

chapter 8: Pulling It All Together: Effective Instruction All Day Long

1. Discuss whether or not you feel your school offers adequate support for struggling readers.

2. How does your school determine the focus of the instructional design of interventions for struggling readers?

3. What opportunities does your school provide struggling readers for extensive reading practice?

4. Allington states that schools are designing programs that ignore the research. Do you think this is true or not? Explain your answer.

5. In your school, is most of the instructional support for struggling readers provided by certified reading personnel or others? Why is this so?

6. Discuss what you believe might be the reason reading levels at the middle and high school have remained stagnant.

7. Are the students in your school who are assigned to intervention groups receiving help in grade-level materials or in materials matched to their instructional level? Discuss whether or not this is a good plan.

8. Allington argues that in high engagement classrooms, management is not a problem. Do you agree or disagree?

9. If teachers know that some students cannot read the science text, the social studies text, or the class novel, why do you think we still see teachers using the one-size-fits-all text for instruction?

10. After reading this chapter, does the research Allington presents support what is being practiced in your school?

11. What information in this chapter will be the most helpful to you?

Reading Reaction Sheet

Facilitator/Recorder (person who initiated the discussion): _____

Group reactants: _____

_____

Date of reaction/discussion: _____

Chapter title and author(s): _____

_____

Question #1: What ideas and information from this chapter could be used in classroom instruction?

Reactions:

Question #2: _____

_____

Reactions:

Question #3: _____

_____

Reactions:

Question #4: _____

_____

Reactions:

Bibliography

ACT. (2006). *Reading between the lines: What the ACT reveals about college readiness in reading.* Iowa City, Iowa: American College Testing, Inc.

Adler, M. (1940). *How to read a book: The art of getting a liberal education.* New York: Simon & Schuster.

Adlof, S. M., Perfetti, C. A., & Catts, H. W. (2010). Developmental changes in reading comprehension: Implications for assessment and instruction. In S. J. Samuels & A. E. Farstrup (Eds.), *What research says about reading instruction.* (4th ed., pp. 186–214). Newark, NE: International Reading Association.

Allen, J. (1999). *Words, words, words; Teaching vocabulary in grades 4-12.* York, ME: Stenhouse.

Alliance for Excellent Education. (2011). *A time for deeper learning: Preparing students for a changing world.* Washington, DC.

Allington, R. L. (1980). Poor readers don't get to read much in reading groups. *Language Arts, 57*(8), 872–877.

Allington, R. L. (1990). What have we done to the middle? In G. G. Duffy (Ed.), *Reading in the middle school* (2nd ed., pp. 32–40). Newark, DE: IRA.

Allington, R. L. (2002). What I've learned about effective reading instruction from a decade of studying exemplary elementary classroom teachers. *Phi Delta Kappan, 83*(10/June), 740–747.

Allington, R. L. (2002). You can't learn much from books you can't read. *Educational Leadership, 60*(3), 16–19.

Allington, R. L. (2010). Recent federal education policy in the United States. In D. Wyse, R. Andrews, & J. V. Hoffman (Eds.), *International Handbook of English, Language and Literacy Teaching* (pp. 496–07). New York: Routledge.

Allington, R. L. (2013). What really matters when working with struggling readers. *Reading Teacher, 66*(7), 4–14.

Allington, R. L., & Johnston, P. H. (Eds.). (2002). *Reading to learn: Lessons from exemplary 4th grade classrooms.* New York: Guilford.

Allington, R. L., & McGill-Franzen, M. (1989). School response to reading failure: Chapter 1 and special education students in grades 2, 4, & 8. *Elementary School Journal, 89*(5), 529–542.

Allington, R. L., & Weber, R. M. (1993). Questioning questions in teaching and learning from texts. In B. Britton, A. Woodward, & M. Binkley (Eds.), *Learning from textbooks: Theory and practice* (pp. 47–68). Hillsdale, NJ: Lawrence Erlbaum.

Allington, R. L., Boxer, N., & Broikou, K. (1987). Jeremy, remedial reading and subject area classes. *Journal of Reading, 30,* 643–645.

Allington, R. L., McGill-Franzen, A. M., Camilli, G., Williams, L., Graff, J., Zeig, J., et al. (2010). Addressing summer reading setback among economically disadvantaged elementary students. *Reading Psychology, 31*(5), 411–427.

Allison, N. (2009). *Middle school readers: Helping them read widely, helping them read well.* Portsmouth, NH: Heinemann.

Almasi, J. F., & Garas-York, K. (2009). Comprehension and peer discussion. In S. Israel & G. G. Duffy (Eds.), *Handbook of research on reading comprehension.* (pp. 470–493). Mahwah, NJ: Erlbaum.

Almasi, J. F., Palmer, B. M., Madden, A., & Hart, S. (2011). Interventions to enhance narrative comprehension. In A. McGill-Franzen & R. L. Allington (Eds.), *Handbook of reading disability research.* New York: Routledge.

Anders, P. L. (1998). The literacy council: People are the key to an effective program. *NAASP Bulletin, 82*(600), 16–23.

Anderson, L. W., Krathwohl, D. R., Airasian, P. W., Cruikshank, K. A., Mayer, R. E., Pintrich, P. R., et al. (2001). *A taxonomy for learning, teaching, and assessing: A revision of Bloom's taxonomy of educational objectives.* New York: Longman.

Anderson, R. C. (1984). Role of schema in comprehension, learning, and memory. In R. B. Ruddell, M. Ruddell, & H. Singer (Eds.), *Theoretical models and processes of reading.* (pp. 469–482). Newark: DE: International Reading Association.

Anderson, R. C. (2009). Intellectually stimulating talk. In R. a. P. Division (Ed.), *Reading Research Phoenix 2009: A collection of presentation abstracts.* (pp. 50–53). Phoenix: International Reading Association.

Anderson, R. C., & Armbruster, B. B. (1984). Content area textbooks. In R. C. Anderson, J. Osborn, & R. J. Tierney (Eds.), *Learning to read in American schools.* (pp. 193–224). Hillsdale, NJ: Lawrence Erlbaum Associates.

Anderson, R. C., Wilson, P. T., & Fielding, L. G. (1988). Growth in reading and how children spend their time outside of school. *Reading Research Quarterly, 23,* 285–303.

Applebee, A. N. (2013). Great writing comes out of great ideas. *The Atlantic,* downloaded on June 18, 2013 from http://www.theatlantic.com/national/archive/2012/09/great-writing-comes-out-of-greatideas/262653/

Applebee, A. N., Langer, J. A., & Mullis, I. V. S. (1988). *Who reads best? Factors related to reading achievement in grades 3, 7, and 11.* Princeton, NJ: Educational Testing Service.

Applebee, A. N., Langer, J. A., Nystrand, M., & Gamoran, A. (2003). Discussion-based approaches to developing understanding: Classroom instruction and student performance in middle and high school English. *American Educational Research Journal, 40*(3), 685–730.

Ash, G. E., Kuhn, M. R., & Walpole, S. (2009). Analyzing "inconsistencies" in practice: Teachers' continued use of round robin oral reading. *Reading & Writing Quarterly, 25*(1), 87–103.

Baumann, J. F., & Duffy, A. M. (1997). *Engaged reading for pleasure and learning.* Athens, GA: National Reading Research Center, University of Georgia.

Bean, T. W., & Readence, J. E. (2002). Adolescent literacy: Charting a course for successful futures as lifelong learners. *Reading Research and Instruction, 41*(3), 203–210.

Beck, I. L., McKeown, M.G., & Gromoll, E.W. (1989). Learning from social studies textbooks. *Cognition and Instruction, 6*(2), 99–158.

Betts, E. A. (1946). *Foundations of reading instruction.* New York: American Book Co.

Biancarosa, G., & Snow, C.. (2006). *Reading next—A vision for action and research in middle and high school literacy: A report to Carnegie Corporation of New York* (2nd ed.). Washington, DC: Alliance for Excellent Education.

Bloom, B. S. (1956). *Taxonomy of Educational Objectives: The Classification of Educational Goals* New York: David McKay.

Bloom, B. S. (1976). *Human characteristics and school learning.* New York: McGraw-Hill.

Bracey, G. W. (2003). *On the death of childhood and the destruction of public schools.* Portsmouth, NH: Heinemann.

Brozo, W. G. (1990). Hiding out in secondary content classrooms: Coping strategies of unsuccessful readers. *Journal of Reading, 33*(5), 324–328.

Brozo, W. G., & Hargis, C. H. (2003). Taking seriously the idea of reform: One high school's efforts to make reading more responsive to all students. *Journal of Adolescent and Adult Literacy, 47*(1), 14–23.

Brunn, P. (2010). *The lesson planning handbook.* New York: Scholastic.

Budiansky, S. (2001). The trouble with textbooks. *Prism* (February), 24–27.

Buly, M. R., & Valencia, S.W. (2002). Below the bar: Profiles of students who fail state reading assessments. *Educational Evaluation and Policy Analysis, 24*(3), 219–239.

Burke, J. (2010). *What's the big idea: Question-driven units to motivate reading, writing, and thinking.* Portsmouth, NH: Heinemann.

Carnegie Council on Advancing Adolescent Literacy (2010). *Time to act: An agenda for advancing adolescent literacy for college and career success.* New York: Carnegie Corporation of New York.

Cazden, C. B. (1986). Classroom discourse. In M. C. Wittrock (Ed.), *Handbook of research on teaching* (3rd ed., pp. 432–462). New York: Macmillan.

Cazden, C. B. (2001). *Classroom discourse: The language of teaching and learning* (2nd ed.). Portsmouth, NH: Heinemenn.

Chall, J. S. (1983). *Stages of reading development.* New York: McGraw-Hill.

Chall, J. S. (1987). *Learning to read: The great debate.* New York: McGraw-Hill.

Chall, J. S., & Conard, S.S. (1991). *Should textbooks challenge students?* New York: Teachers College Press.

Chall, J., Bissex, G., Conard, S., & Harris-Sharples, S. (1996). *Qualitative assessment of text difficulty: A practical guide for teachers and writers.* Cambridge, MA: Brookline Publishers.

Clay, M. M. (2005). *Literacy lessons designed for individuals: Part two.* Portsmouth, NH: Heinemann.

Cooney, C. B. (2002). *The ransom of Mercy carter.* New York: Laurel Leaf.

Cuban, L. (1993). *How teachers taught: Constancy and change in American classrooms, 1880–1990.* (2nd ed.). New York: Longmans.

Cuban, L. (2001). *Oversold and underused: Computers in the classroom.* Cambridge, MA: Harvard University Press.

Cunningham, A. E., & Stanovich, K. E. (1998). The impact of print exposure on word recognition. In J. Metsala & L. Ehri (Eds.), *Word recognition in beginning literacy.* (pp. 235–262). Mahwah, NJ: Lawrence Erlbaum Associates.

Cunningham, J. W. (2001). The National Reading Panel report. *Reading Research Quarterly, 30*(3), 326–335.

Cunningham, P. M. (2009). *What really matters in vocabulary: Research-based practices across the curriculum.* Boston: AllynBacon.

Cunningham, P. M. (2011). Best practices in teaching phonological awareness and phonics. In L. M. Morrow & L. B. Gambrell (Eds.), *Best practices in literacy instruction.* (4th ed., pp. 199–223). New York: Guilford.

Cunningham, P. M., & Hall, D. P. (2009). *Making words 5th grade: 50 hands-on lessons for teaching prefixes, suffixes, and roots.* Boston: Pearson Education.

Cutting, L. E., & Scarborough, H. S. (2006). Prediction of reading comprehension: Relative contributions of word recognition, language proficiency, other cognitive skills can depend on how comprehension is measured. *Scientific Studies of Reading, 10*(3), 277–299.

Daniels, H. S., & Steineke, N. (2013). *Texts and lessons for teaching literature.* Portsmouth, NH: Heinemann.

Dennis, D. V. (2013). Heterogeneity or homogeneity: What assessment data reveal about struggling adolescent readers. *Journal of Literacy Research, 45*(1), 1–21.

Dewitz, P., Jones, J., & Leahy, S. (2009). Comprehension strategy instruction in core reading programs. *Reading Research Quarterly, 44*(2), 102–126.

Duke, N. K. (2000). For the rich it's richer: Print experiences and environments offered to children in very low- and very-high-socioeconomic status first-grade classrooms. *American Educational Research Journal, 37*(2), 441–478.

Duke, N. K., Pearson, P. D., Strachan, S. L., & Billman, A. K. (2011). Essential elements of fostering and teaching reading comprehension. In S. J. Samuels & A. E. Farstrup (Eds.), *What research has to say about reading instruction.* (4th ed., pp. 51-93). Newark, DE: International Reading Association.

Duke, N. K., Pressley, M., & Hilden, K. (2004). Difficulties with reading comprehension. In C. A. Stone, E. R. Silliman, B. J. Ehren, & K. Apel (Eds.), *Handbook of Language and Literacy: Development and disorder.* (pp. 501–520). New York: Guilford.

Edmonds, M. S., Vaughn, S., Wexler, J., Reutebuch, C., Cable, A., Tackett, K. K., et al. (2009). A synthesis of reading interventions and effects on reading comprehension outcomes for older struggling readers. *Review of Educational Research, 79*(1), 262–300.

Elleman, A. M., Lindo, E. J., Morphy, P., & Compton, D. L. (2009). The impact of vocabulary instruction on passage-level comprehension of school-age children: A meta-analysis. *Journal of Research on Educational Effectiveness, 2*(1), 1–44.

Ericcson, K. A., Krampe, R. T., & Tesch-Romer, C. (1993). The role of deliberate practice in the acquisition of expert performance. *Psychological Review, 100*(3), 363–406.

Faggella-Luby, M. N., Graner, P. S., Deschler, D. D., & Drew, S. V. (2012). Building a house on sand: Why disciplinary literacy is not sufficient to replace general strategies for adolescent learners who struggle. *Topics in Language Disorders, 32*(1), 69–84.

Fielding, L. G., Wilson, P. T., & Anderson, R. C. (1986). A new focus on free reading: The role of trade books in reading instruction. In T. E. Raphael (Ed.), *The contexts of school-based literacy.* (pp. 149–160). New York: Random House.

Fisher, D., & Ivey, G. (2006). Evaluating the interventions for struggling adolescent readers. *Journal of Adolescent & Adult Literacy, 50*(3), 180–189.

Fisher, D., & Ivey, G. (2007). Farewell to a farewell to arms: Deemphasizing the whole class novel. *Phi Delta Kappan, 88*(7), 494–497.

Fleischman, H. L., Hopstock, P. J., Pelczar, M. P., & Shelley, B. E. (2010). *Highlights from PISA 2009: Performance of U.S. 15-Year-Old Students in Reading, Mathematics, and Science Literacy in an International Context.* Downloaded on May 12, 2013 from http://nces .ed.gov/pubs2011/2011004.pdf.

Flynn, L. J., Zheng, X., & Swanson, H. L. (2012). Instructing older struggling readers: A selective meta-analysis of intervention research. *Learning Disabilities Research & Practice, 27*(1), 21–32.

Gabriel, R., Allington, R. L., & Billen, M. (2009). *Leveling magazines: Considerations for selecting and using magazines in middle school classrooms and libraries.* Paper presented at the Literacy Research Association.

Gabriel, R., Allington, R. L., & Billen, M. (2012). Background knowledge and the magazine reading students choose. *Voices from the Middle, 20*(1), 52–57.

Gabriel, R., Day, J. P., & Allington, R. L. (2011). Exemplary teacher voices on the own development. *Phi Delta Kappan, 92*(8), 37–41.

Gaffney, J. S., Methven, J. M., & Bagdasarian, S. (2002). Assisting older students to read expository text in a tutorial setting: A case for a high-impact intervention. *Reading and Writing Quarterly, 18*(2), 119–150.

Gallagher, K. (2009). *Readicide: How schools are killing reading and what you can do about it.* Portland, ME: Stenhouse.

Gambrell, L. B. (1996). Creating classroom cultures that foster motivation to read. *Reading Teacher, 50*(1), 4–25.

Gamse, B. C., Jacob, R. T., Horst, M., Boulay, B., & Unlu, F. (2009). *Reading First Impact Study: Final Report (NCEE 2009-4038)* (No. (NCEE 2009-4038)). Washington, DC: National Center for Education Evaluation and Regional Assistance, Institute of Education Sciences, U.S. Department of Education.

Gelzheiser, L. M. (2005). Maximizing student progress in one-to-one programs: Contributions of texts, volunteer experience, and student characteristics. *Exceptionality, 13*(4), 229–243.

Giblin, J. C. (1997). When the plague strikes: Black death, smallpox, AIDS. New York: Harper Trophy.

Goldsmith, W. (2013). Enhancing classroom conversation for all students. *Phi Delta Kappan, 94*(7), 48–52.

Graham, S., & Hebert, M. (2011). Writing to read: A meta-analysis of the impact of writing and writing instruction on reading. *Harvard Educational Review, 81*(4), 710–744.

Guthrie, J. T., & Humenick, N. M. (2004). Motivating students to read: Evidence for classroom practices that increase motivation and achievement. In P. McCardle & V. Chhabra (Eds.), *The voice of evidence in reading research.* (pp. 329–354). Baltimore: Paul Brookes Publishing.

Haberman, M. (1995). Selecting "Star" teachers for children and youth in urban poverty. *Phi Delta Kappan, 76*(10), 777–781.

Hall, L. A. (2012). The role of reading identities and reading abilities in students' discussion about texts and comprehension strategies. *Journal of Literacy Research, 44*(3), 239–272.

Hargis, C. (2006). Setting standards: An exercise in futility? *Phi Delta Kappan, 87*(5), 393–395.

Harris, A. J., & Sipay, E. R. (1985). *How to increase reading ability.* (8th ed.). New York: Longman.

Hart, B. M., & Risley, T. R. (1995). *Meaningful differences in the everyday experiences of young children.* Baltimore: Paul Brookes.

Herber, H. (1978). *Teaching reading in content areas.* (2nd ed.). Englewood Cliffs, NJ: Prentice Hall.

Hernandez, D. J. (2011). *Double jeopardy: How third-grade reading skills and poverty influence high school graduation*: Baltimore: Annie E. Casey Foundation.

Hinchman, K. A., & Moore, D. W. (2013). Close reading: A cautionary tale. *Journal of Adolescent & Adult Literacy, 56*(6), 441-450.

Hock, M. F., Brasseur, I. F., Deshler, D. D. ,Catts, H. W., Marques, J., Mark, C. A. et al. (2009). What is the reading component skill profile of adolescent struggling readers in urban schools? *Learning Disability Quarterly, 32*(1), 21–38.

Ivey, G. (2002). Getting started: Manageable literacy practices in the content areas. *Educational Leadership, 60*(1), 20–23.

Ivey, G. (2010). Texts that matter. *Educational Leadership, 67*(6), 18–23.

Ivey, G. (2011). What not to read: A book intervention. *Voices from the Middle, 19*(2), 22–26.

Ivey, G., & Broaddus, K. (2001). Just plain reading: A survey of what makes students want to read in middle schools. *Reading Research Quarterly, 36,* 350–377.

Ivey, G., & Fisher, D. (2006). *Creating literacy-rich schools for adolescents.* Alexandria, VA: Association for Supervision and Curriculum Development.

Ivey, G., & Johnston, P. H. (2013). Engagement with young adult literature: Outcomes and processes. *Reading Research Quarterly, 48*(3), 255–275.

James-Burdumy, S., Deke, J. Lugo-Gil, J., Carey, N., Hershey, A., Gersten, R. et al. (2010). *Effectiveness of selected supplemental reading comprehension interventions: Findings from two student cohorts.* Washington, DC: National Center for Educational Evaluation and Regional Assistance, Institute of Education Sciences, USDE.

Johnston, P. (1985). Understanding reading failure: A case study approach. *Harvard Educational review, 55*(2), 153–177.

Kamil, M. L. (2004). Vocabulary and comprehension instruction. In P. McCardle & V. Chhabra (Eds.), *The voice of evidence in reading research.* (pp. 213– 234). Baltimore: Paul Brookes Publishing.

Kamil, M. L., Borman, G. D., Dole, J., Kral, C. C., Salinger, T., & Torgesen, J. (2008). *Improving adolescent literacy: Effective classroom and intervention practices: A Practice Guide. Downloaded* from http://ies.ed.gov/ncee/wwc.

Keene, E. O. (2002). From good to memorable: Characteristics of highly effective comprehension teaching. In C. C. Block, L. Gambrell, & M. Pressley (Eds.), *Improving comprehension instruction: Rethinking research, theory, and classroom practice.* (pp. 80–105). San Francisco: Jossey-Bass.

Keller, T. A., & Just, M. A. (2009). Altering cortical activity: Remediation-induced changes in the white matter of poor readers. *Neuron, 64*(5), 624–631.

Knapp, M. S. (1995). *Teaching for meaning in high-poverty classrooms.* New York: Teachers College Press.

Kohn, A. (1999). *The schools our children deserve: Moving beyond traditional classrooms and tougher standards.* Boston: Houghton Mifflin.

Krashen, S. (2011). *Free voluntary reading.* Santa Barbara, CA: Libraries Unlimited.

Kucan, L., Hapgood, S., & Palincsar, A. S. (2011). Teachers specialized knowledge for supporting student comprehension in text-based discussions. *Elementary School Journal, 112*(1), 61–82.

Kuhn, M. R. (2005). A comparative study of small group fluency instruction. *Reading Psychology, 26*(2), 127–146.

Kuhn, M. R., Schwanenflugel, P. J., & Meisinger, E. B. (2010). Aligning theory and assessment of reading fluency: Automaticity, prosody, and definitions of fluency. *Reading Research Quarterly, 45*(2), 230–251.

Kuhn, M. R., Schwanenflugel, P., Morris, R. D., Morrow, L. M., Woo, D., Meisinger, B., et al. (2006). Teaching children to become fluent and automatic readers. *Journal of Literacy Research 38*(4), 357–388.

Ladson-Billings, G. (2009). *The Dreamkeepers: Successful teachers of African-American children.* (2nd ed.). San Francisco: Jossey-Bass.

Langer, J. A. (2001). Beating the odds: Teaching middle and high school students to read and write well. *American Educational Research Journal, 38*(4), 837–880.

Langer, J. A. (2004). *Getting to excellent: How to create better schools.* New York: Teachers College Press.

Langer, J. A. (2011). *Envisioning knowledge: Building literacy in the academic disciplines.* New York: Teachers College Press.

Langer, J. A., & Applebee, A. N. (1987). *How writing shapes thinking: A study of teaching and learning.* Urbana, IL: National Council of Teachers of English.

Leach, J. M., Scarborough, H. S., & Rescorda, L. (2003). Late-emerging reading disabilities. *Journal of Educational Psychology, 95*(2), 211–223.

Lent, R. C., & Gilmore, B. (2013). *Common Core CPR: What about the adolescents who struggle . . . Or just don't care.* Thousand Oaks, CA: Corwin.

Lesesne, T. S. (2010). *Reading ladders: Leading students from where they are to where we'd like them to be.* Portsmouth, NH: Heinemann.

Lewis, M., & Samuels, S. J. (2004). Read more, read better? A meta-analysis of the literature on the relationship between exposure to reading and reading achievement. Unpublished paper, College of Education, University of Minnesota.

Loewen, J. W. (2009). *Teaching what really happened: How to avoid the tyranny of textbooks and get students excited about doing history.* New York: Teachers College Press.

Martin, N. M., & Duke, N. K. (2011). Interventions to enhance informational text comprehension. In A. McGill-Franzen & R. L. Allington (Eds.), *Handbook of Reading Disability Research.* (p. 345). New York: Routledge.

Mathson, D., Solic, K., & Allington, R. L. (2006). Hijacking fluency and instructionally informative assessment. In T. Rasinski, C. Blachowicz, & K. Lems (Eds.), *Fluency Instruction: Research-based best practice.* (pp. 106–119). New York: Guilford.

Miller, D. (2009). *The book whisperer: Awakening the inner reader in every child.* San Francisco: Jossey-Bass.

Mueller, P. N. (2001). *Lifers: Learning from at-risk adolescent readers.* Portsmouth, NH: Heinemann.

Nagy, W., Anderson, R. C., & Herman, P. (1987). Learning word meanings from context during normal reading. *American Educational Research Journal, 24,* 237–270.

National Center for Education Statistics. (2009). *The Nation's Report Card: Reading 2009* (NCES 2010–458). Institute of Education Sciences, U.S. Department of Education, Washington, DC.

National Center for Educational Statistics. (2011). *The Nation's Report Card: Reading 2011.* Washington, DC: Institute of Education Sciences, U.S. Department of Education.

National Endowment for the Arts (2007). *To read or not to read.* Downloaded from www .nea.gov/news/news07/TRNR.html.

National Reading Panel. (2000). *Teaching children to read: An evidence-based assessment of the scientific research literature on reading and its implications for reading instruction.* (http:// www.nationalreadingpanel.org).

Nystrand, M. (2006). Research on the role of classroom discourse as it effects reading comprehension. *Research in the Teaching of English, 40,* 392–412.

Nystrand, M., Wu, L. L., Gamoran, A., Zeiser, S., & Long, D. A. (2003). Questions in time: Investigating the structure and dynamics of unfolding classroom discourse. *Discourse Processes, 35*(2), 135–198.

O' Connor, R. E., Bell, K. M., Harty, K. R., Larkin, L. K., Sackor, S. M., & Zigmond, N. (2002). Teaching reading to poor readers in the intermediate grades: A comparison of text difficulty. *Journal of Educational Psychology, 94*(3), 474–485.

O'Connor, R. E., Swanson, H. L., & Geraghty, C. (2010). Improvement in reading rate under independent and difficult text levels: Influences on word and comprehension skills. *Journal of Educational Psychology, 102*(1), 1–19.

Oczkus, L. D. (2010). *Reciprocal teaching at work: Powerful strategies and lessons for improving reading comprehension.* (2nd ed.). Newark, DE: International Reading Association.

Office of the Inspector General (2007). *RMC Research Corporation's administration of the Reading First program contracts.* (No. ED-OIG/A03F0022). Washington, DC: United States Department of Education.

Okolo, C. M., Ferreti, R. P., & MacArthur, C. A. (2007). Talking about history: Discussions in a middle school inclusive classroom. *Journal of Learning Disabilities, 40*(2), 154–165.

Palincsar, A. S. (1986). The role of dialogue in providing scaffolded instruction. *Educational Psychologist, 21,* 73–98.

Palincsar, A. S. (2007). Reciprocal teaching 1982 to 2006: The role of research, theory, and representation in the transformation of instructional research. In D. W. Rowe, R. T. Jimenez, D. L. Compton, Y. Kim, K. M. Leander, & V. J. Risko (Eds.), *56th Yearbook of the National Reading Conference.* Oak Creek, WI: National Reading Conference.

Palincsar, A. S., & Brown, A. (1984). Reciprocal teaching and comprehension-fostering and comprehension-monitoring activities. *Cognition and Instruction, 1*(1), 117–175.

Pearson, P. D. (2009). The roots of reading comprehension instruction. In S. E. Israel & G. G. Duffy (Eds.), *Handbook of research on reading comprehension*. New York: Routledge.

Pearson, P. D., & Hiebert, E. H. (2013). Understanding the Common Core State Standards. In L. M. Morrow, T. Shanahan, & K. Wixson (Eds.), *Common Core Standards for English Language Arts*. New York: Guilford.

Pianta, R. C., Belsky, J., Houts, R., Morrison, F., et al. (2007). Opportunities to learn in America's elementary classrooms. *Science, 315*(5820), 1795–1796.

Pinnell, G. S., Pikulski, J. J., Wixson, K., Campbell, J. R., Gough, P. B., & Beatty, A. S. (1995). *Listening to children read aloud*. (Research report No. ED 378550). Washington, DC: National Center for Educational Statistics.

Pitcher, S. M., Martinez, G., Dicembre, E. A., Fewster, D., & McCormick, M. K. (2010). The literacy needs of adolescents: In their own words. *Journal of Adolescent & Adult Literacy, 53*(8), 636–645.

Popham, W. J. (2001). *The truth about testing: An educator's call to action*. Alexandria, VA: ASCD.

Pressley, M. (2006). *Reading instruction that works: The case for balanced teaching*. (3rd ed.). New York: Guilford.

Pressley, M., & Afflerbach, P. (1995). *Verbal protocols of reading: The nature of constructively responsive reading*. Hillsdale, NJ: Lawrence Erlbaum Associates.

Pressley, M., Hilden, K., & Shankland, R. (2006). *An evaluation of end-of-grade 3 Dynamic Indicators of Basic Early Literacy Skills (DIBELS): Speed reading without comprehension, predicting little*. East Lansing, MI: Literacy Achievement Research Center, Michigan State University.

Pressley, M., Wharton-McDonald, R., Allington, R. L., Block, C. C., Morrow, L., Tracey, D., et al. (2001). A study of effective first-grade literacy instruction. *Scientific Studies in Reading, 5*(1), 35–58.

Pressley, M., Wharton-McDonald, R., Mistretta-Hampston, J., & Echevarria, M. (1998). Literacy instruction in 10 fourth- and fifth-grade classrooms in upstate New York. *Scientific Studies of Reading, 2*(2), 159–194.

Pressley, M., Yokoi, L., Rankin, J., Wharton-McDonald, R., & Mistretta, J. (1997). A survey of the instructional practices of Grade 5 teachers nominated as effective in promoting literacy. *Scientific Studies of Reading, 1*(2), 145–160.

Raphael, L. M., Pressley, M., & Mohan, L. (2008). Engaging instruction in middle school classrooms: An observational study of nine teachers. *Elementary School Journal, 109*(1), 61–81.

Reed, D., & Vaughn, S. (2010). Reading interventions for older students. In T. G. A. S. Vaughn (Ed.), *The promise of response to intervention: Evaluating current science and practice*. (pp. 143–186). New York: Guilford.

Resnick, L. B. (2010). Nested learning systems for the thinking curriculum. *Educational Researcher, 39*(3), 183–197.

Roderick, M., & Camburn, E. (1999). Risk and recovery from course failure in the early years of high school. *American Educational Research Journal, 36*(2), 303–343.

Rosenshine, B. V., & Stevens, R. (1984). Classroom instruction in reading. In P. D. Pearson, R. Barr, M. Kamil, & P. Mosenthal (Eds.), *Handbook of Reading Research*. (pp. 745–798). New York: Longman.

Rosenshine, B., & Meister, C. (1994). Reciprocal teaching: A review of the research. *Review of Educational research, 64*(4), 479–530.

Roswell, F. G., & Natchez, G. (1977). *Reading disability: A human learning approach.* (3rd ed.). New York: Basic Books.

Roth, J., Brooks-Dunn, J., Linver, M., & Hofferth, S. (2002). What happened during the school day? Time diaries from a national sample of elementary school teachers. *Teachers College Record, 105* (3), 317–343.

Scammacca, N., Roberts, G., Vaughn, S., Edmonds, M., Wexler, J., Reutebuch, C. K., & Torgeson, (2007). *Interventions for adolescent struggling readers: A meta-analysis with implications for practice.* Portsmouth, NH: RMC Research Corporation, Center on Instruction.

Schmoker, M. (2011). *Focus: Elevating the essentials to radically improve student learning.* Alexandria, VA: ASCD.

Shanahan, C. (2009). Disciplinary comprehension. In S. Israel & G. G. Duffy (Eds.), *Handbook of research on reading comprehension.* (pp. 240–260). New York: Routledge.

Shanahan, T. (2010) *Federal Institute for Education Sciences Practice Guide Representing Best Evidence Advice for Improving Educational Effectiveness.* Washington, DC: National Center for Education Evaluation and Regional Assistance, Institute of Education Sciences.

Shanahan, T., Callison, K., Carriere, C., Duke, N. K., Pearson, P. D., Schatschneider, C., & Torgesen, J. (2010). *Improving reading comprehension in kindergarten through 3rd grade: A practice guide* (NCEE 2010-4038). Washington, DC: National Center for Education Evaluation and Regional Assistance, Institute of Education Sciences,

Showers, B., Joyce, B., Scanlon, M., & Schnaubelt, C. (1998). A second chance to learn to read. *Educational Leadership, 72*(March), 27–30.

Slavin, R. E., Lake, C., Davis, S., & Madden, N. A. (2009). *Effective programs for struggling readers: A best-evidence synthesis.* Baltimore: Johns Hopkins University, Center for Data-Driven Reform in Education.

Stahl, S. A. (1999). *Vocabulary development: From reading research to practice.* Newton Upper Falls, MA: Brookline.

Stanovich, K. E. (2000). *Progress in understanding reading: Scientific foundations and new frontiers.* New York: Guilford.

Stanovich, K. E., West, R. F., Cunningham, A. E., Cipielewski, J., & Siddiqui, S. (1996). The role of inadequate print exposure as a determinant of reading comprehension problems. In C. Cornoldi & J. Oakhill (Eds.), *Reading comprehension difficulties: Processes and intervention.* (pp. 15–32). Mahwah, NJ: Lawrence Erlbaum Associates.

Sweet, A. P., & Snow, C. E. (Eds.). (2003). *Rethinking reading comprehension.* New York: Guilford.

Taylor, B. M., Pearson, P. D., Clark, K., & Walpole, S. (2000). Effective schools and accomplished teachers: Lessons about primary grade reading instruction in low income schools. *Elementary School Journal, 101,* 121–165.

Taylor, B. M., Pearson, P. D., Peterson, D. S., & Rodriguez, M. C. (2005). The CIERA School Change Framework: An evidence-based approach to professional development and school reading improvement. *Reading Research Quarterly, 40*(1), 40–9.

Taylor, B. M., Pearson, P. D., Peterson, D. S., & Rodriguez, M. C. (2003). Reading growth in high-poverty classrooms: The influences of teacher practices that encourage cognitive engagement in literacy learning. *Elementary School Journal, 104*(1), 4–28.

Terenzini, P. T., Springer, L., Pascarella, E. T., and Nora, A. (1995). Influences affecting the development of students' critical thinking skills. *Research in Higher Education, 36*(1), 23–39.

Torgesen, J., Schirm, A., Castner, L., Vartivarian, S., Mansfield, W., Myers, D., et al. (2007). *National Assessment of Title I, Final Report: Volume II: Closing the Reading Gap, Findings from a Randomized Trial of Four Reading Interventions for Striving Readers.* (NCEE 2008–4013). Washington, DC National Center for Education Evaluation and Regional Assistance, Institute of Education Sciences, U.S. Department of Education.

Torgeson, J. K., & Hudson, R. F. (2006). Reading fluency: Critical issues for struggling readers. In S. J. Samuels & A. E. Farstrup (Eds.), *What research has to say about fluency instruction.* (pp. 130–158). Newark, DE: International Reading Association.

Townsend, D., Filippini, A., Collins, P., & Biancarosa, G. (2012). Evidence for the importance of academic word knowledge for academic achievement of diverse middle school students. *Elementary School Journal, 112*(3), 497–518.

Trotter, A. (2007). Federal study finds no edge for students using technology-based reading and math products. *Education Week.* Accessed at www.edweek.org/ew/articles/2007/04/04/32software_web.h26.html?qs=federal+study.

Valencia, S. W., Place, N.A., Martin, S.D., & Grossman, P.L. (2006). Curriculum materials for elementary reading: Shackles and scaffolds for beginning teachers. *Elementary School Journal, 107*(1): 94–120.

Valli, L., Croninger, R. G., Chambliss, M. J., Graeber, A. O., & Buese, D. (2008). *Test driven: High-stakes accountability in elementary schools.* New York: Teachers College Press.

Vaughn, S., & Linan-Thompson, S. (2003). What is special about special education for students with learning disabilities? *Journal of Special Education, 37*(3), 140–147.

Wade, S. E., & Moje, E. B. (2000). The role of text in classroom learning. In M. Kamil, P. Mosenthal, P. D. Pearson & R. Barr (Eds.), *Handbook of reading research, vol. III.* Mahwah, NJ: Erlbaum.

Walmsley, S. A. (1979). The criterion referenced measurement of an early reading behavior. *Reading Research Quarterly, 14*(4), 574–604.

Wanzek, J., Vaughn, S., Scamacca, N. K., Metz, K., Murray, C. S., Roberts, G., & Danielson, L. (2013). Extensive reading interventions for students with reading difficulties after grade 3. *Review of Educational Research, 83*(2), 163–195.

Wheelock, A. (1992). *Crossing tracks: How untracking can save America's schools.* New York: New Press.

Wigfield, A., & Guthrie, J. T. (1997). Relations of children's motivations for reading to the amount and breadth of their reading. *Journal of Educational Psychology, 89,* 420–432.

Wilhelm, J. D. (1997). *"You gotta be the book": Teaching engaged and reflective reading with adolescents.* New York: Teachers College Press.

Wiske, M. S. (1998). *Teaching for understanding: Linking research with practice.* San Francisco: Jossey-Bass.

Wolk, S. (2010). What should students read? *Phi Delta Kappan, 91*(7), 9–16.

Worthy, J., Broaddus, K., & Ivey, G. (2001). *Pathways to independence: Reading, writing, and learning in grades 3-8.* New York: Guilford.

Worthy, J., Moorman, M., & Turner, M. (1999). What Johnny likes to read is hard to find in school. *Reading Research Quarterly, 34*(1), 12–27.

Ysseldyke, J. E., Thurlow, M. L., Mecklenburg, C., & Graden, J. (1984). Opportunity to learn for regular and special education students during reading instruction. *Remedial and Special Education, 5*(1), 29–37.

Zambo, D., & Brozo, W. G. (2009). *Bright beginnings for boys.* Newark, DE: International Reading Association.

Zigmond, N., Vallecorsa, A., & Leinhardt, G. (1980). Reading instruction for students with learning disabilities. *Topics in Language Disorders, 1,* 89–98.

Index

Curriculum (*continued*)
    reading instruction in, 6–8
    rethinking, 12
    textbooks as, 78–79

D

Daniels, Smokey, 136
Decoding. *See also* Pronunciation
    ability, measuring, 28
    commercial reading intervention and, 34, 160–161
    cross-checking, 28
    definition of, 25
    fluency and, 43
    Glass Analysis, 39–40
    improving, 31–34
    instruction, 29–30
    listening and, 28
    methods for, 26
    problems, 29–30
    reading comprehension and, 29–30, 32, 34, 161–162
    reading development and, 26
    reading experiences and, 27
    reading intervention and, 32
    reading proficiency and, 31
    research on, 29
    self-teaching and, 35
    of struggling readers, 29–30, 40, 45
    vocabulary and, 27–28, 33
Development. *See* Reading development
Dewey, John, 81
Dictionary usage, 59
Disciplinary literacy, 114
Disciplinary reading, 113, 146, 165
Disciplinary thinking, 108–109
Discipline events, 118
Discussions, 185. *See also* Literate conversations
    explanation of thinking in, 135
    finding the experts for, 136
    fostering engagement in, 132–133
    hand-raising in, 135
    high-quality, 123
    interrogation and, 120–121
    IRE, 120–121
    one-word answers to questions in, 134–136
    peer-led, 83, 88, 137
    randomized system for calling on students in, 135
    reading comprehension and, 128

with struggling readers, 66
student-centered, 130–131, 175
teacher-led, 120, 134–135
vocabulary development and, 66
Drawing, 106
Drop boxes, 167
Drop out rates, 116, 169–174

E
Early adolescents. *See also* Struggling readers; Students
CCSS and, 163–165
learning success of, 10–11
reading enticement of, 68–69
reading instruction in, 6–8
reading levels of, 46, 75
summarization and, 144–146
Earth science, 110
Edgy texts, 168
Education
Dewey on, 81
goal of modern, 123
participation-based education *vs.* transmission-based, 124–128
policy, 160, 171
special, 13, 14, 67–68
of teachers, 165
Educational effectiveness, 123
Education technology. *See* Technology
Eighth-grade, 2–4, 5–6, 102
Electronic worksheets, 68
ELL. *See* English Language Learner
Engagement, 132–133, 141–142, 173–176. *See also* Reading engagement
English, 56–57, 179
class, 77
language, difficulty of, 27
English Language Learner (ELL), 127
Evaluation, 2–3, 109
Experts, 136
Expository texts
reading competence and, 146–148
summarization and, 144–146
Extensive reading, 63–72, 161, 174

F
Facebook, 126
Facts, 124–125, 139
Federal Institute for Education Sciences Practice Guide, 123
Federal programs, for reading development, 160

generation, 127
misinformation, 98
reliability of, 107, 124
Informational books, 93
Initiate-Reply-Evaluate (IRE), 120–121, 129–130
Instruction. *See also* Education; Reading instruction; Teaching
achievement and plan of, 22–23, 117
assessment and, 101–103
decoding, 29–30
materials, 64, 77, 117
resources, multiple levels of, 57–58
response of struggling readers, 17–22
routines, 131, 150
vocabulary, 59
Instructional texts. *See* Textbooks
Integration, 2–3
Intellectual behavior, 107
Internet, 125–126
Interpretation, 2–3
Interrogation, 120–121, 128, 134
Interruptions, 42–43
Intervention. *See* Reading intervention
In-text aids, 40–41
Intonation pattern, 43, 44
IRE. *See* Initiate-Reply-Evaluate

J
Journalism, 125

K
K-3, reading proficiency, 5–6
King, Stephen, 64
Kohn, Alfie, 81

L
Laddering, 182–183
Langer, Judith A., 152
Language
arts, 174–177
difficulty of English, 27
of students, 22
LD. *See* Learning disabled
Learning. *See also* Education; Instruction; Reading development
authentic, 139
CCSS emphasis of, 140
cooperative, 132–133

low-income families and, 128
metacognition and, 122–123
monitoring and, 122
power of, 121–122
reading engagement and, 119–120
teacher assistance for, 129
time of, 135
tools for developing, 133
Location, 2–3
Low-income families
literate conversations and, 128
reading proficiency in, 4, 5–6
vocabulary and, 50–51
writing and, 84
Low-level academic work, 173

M

Magazines, 51–52
Managed choice, 57
Mann, Charles C., 124
Mathematics, 98
Memorization, understanding and, 125
Metacognition, literate conversations and, 122–123
Michael Webster School, 166
Miller, Donalyn, 85, 174
Minority students, 127
Misinformation, 98
Misreading, 9, 19, 35–36
Monitoring
accuracy, 122
literate conversations and, 122
self, 36–37, 114, 122–123, 168
struggling readers, 163
Monroe Middle School (fictional), 18–22
Motivation, student, 10–12, 69–72, 80, 88, 96, 169
    See also Engagement
Movies, 70, 107
Mueller, Pamela N., 82
Multi-level classroom libraries, 85, 182–184
Multi-level curriculum (multi-sourced), 11, 47, 77, 118, 172
books in, 85
instructional resources, 57–58
reading intervention and, 16–17
for struggling readers, 16–17
texts, 182–184
Multiple-choice tests, 2, 142, 155
Music, 67

N

O

P

close reading and, 141
drawing and, 106
filling in gaps in, 104
learning and, 141
schema theory, 104–106
text difficulty and, 180
understanding and, 141
vocabulary and, 183
writing and, 105
Problem solving, 101, 155
Professional development, 184–185
Professional learning communities (PLCs), 187
Proficiency. *See* Reading proficiency
Pronunciation, 25–26. *See also* Decoding
basal readers, 50
difficulty of, 27, 55
in-text aids, 40–41
of new words, 38–39
of non-words, 28–29
struggling readers, 33–36
word structure and, 37–38
Publishers, textbook, 54, 99

Q

Qualitative analysis of text difficulty (QATD), 52, 181–184
Qualitative assessment of text difficulty: A practical guide for teachers and writers (Chall),
181–182
Questions. *See also* Discussions; Literate conversations
and answer exchanges, 120–121
follow-up, 122, 130
higher-order, 121–122, 153–156, 173
low-level recall, 131, 139–140, 142, 153–154, 156
one-word answers for, 134–136
open-ended, 130–131
understanding and, 140
Quick writing, 105, 112, 130, 152–153

R

Race/ethnic group
ACTs and, 171
reading development and, 4–5
The Ransom of Mercy Carter (Cooney), 19
Readability, 58, 97, 181. *See also* Text difficulty
Reader-text match tool, 18–21
Readicide, 70
Readicide (Gallagher), 94

Reading instruction (*continued*)
    struggling readers, 12–17
    technology and, 8
Reading intervention. *See also* Commercial reading intervention
    all-day-long, 16–17, 89
    computerized, 163
    decoding and, 32
    intensive, 37
    at Monroe Middle School (fictional), 21–22
    multi-level curriculum and, 16–17
    personalization of, 30–31
    phonics and, 87
    programs, 14–15
    reading comprehension and, 33
    for struggling readers, 13–16, 22, 160
    student needs and, 161
    technology-based, 15
    traditional design of, 16
Reading levels
    on ACTs, 116
    differences in, 103
    of early adolescents, 46, 75
    establishing student, 178–179
    grade and, 46
    groups, 175
    range of, 46
    text difficulty and, 53–56, 72, 89, 96, 179–182
Reading proficiency
    assessment of, 178–179
    CCSS and, 165
    class time spent on, 6
    decoding and, 31
    difficulty and, 9–10
    drop out rates and, 169–170
    before Eighth-grade, 5–6
    factors of, 4
    gender and, 4, 78
    grades 5-9, 1–23
    improving, 63–64
    independent levels of, 55
    K–3, 5–6
    in low-income families, 4, 5–6
    NAEP levels of, 3
    race/ethnic group and, 4–5
    reading instruction and, 7
    struggling readers, 6, 8

technology and, 67–68

testing, 178–179

textbooks and, 9

text difficulty and, 179–182

"Reading Rebound," 166

"Reading Recovery," 167

Reading Research Quarterly, 86

"Reading Buddy," 167

Recall

lessons and textbook, 101–102

low-level questions, 131, 139–140, 142, 153–154, 156

thoughtfulness *vs.*, 126–128

Reciprocal teaching, 132–133

Remembering, 107, 109

Repeated reading, independent reading and, 44

Required courses, 110

Rewritten sentences, text difficulty and, 97

Rote learning, 124

Round-robin oral reading (RRR), 82, 100–101

S

Schema Theory, 104–106

Schools

accountability of, 23

books and, 76

day, 6, 7, 44, 85, 87

developing effectiveness of, 178–186

example of programs for struggling readers in, 164–174

hatred of, 166

high, 164

literacy councils for, 185

reading environment out of, 63–72

reading lessons of today in, 89–90

urban, 6

Scientific reading instruction, 22

Scripts, 104–106

Self-monitoring, 36–37, 114, 122, 168

Self-selected books, 51, 68, 80, 87–90, 167–168, 174–175

Self-teaching, decoding and, 35

Semantic feature analysis (SFA), 61–62

Semantic gradients, 62–63

Semantic webs, 59–60, 63

SFA. *See* Semantic feature analysis

Sight vocabulary, 31

Silent reading, 167

Simpson's Paradox, 5, 127

failure, 118
grading, 177
hand raising, 135
individual needs of, 11
into literate conversations, easing, 128–138
language of, 22
motivation of, 10–12, 69–72, 80, 88, 96, 169
partnering for summarization, 150
partnering of, 132–136
poor, 128
randomized system for calling on, 135
reading achievement and success of, 79–80
reading aloud to, 64–66, 85
reading intervention and needs of, 161
reading levels, establishing, 178–179
reciprocal teaching roles of, 132–133
teacher responsibility for, 89
teacher's personal assessment of, 155
text difficulty and behavior of, 81–83, 162
text difficulty and success of, 89
TPS, 133–136
through writing, learning about, 112
Sub-vocalization, 82
Suffixes, 38
Summarization, 139–140
close reading and, 140–143
composing, 151–156
early adolescents and, 144–146
examples, 149
of expository texts, 144–146
higher-order questions and, 153–156
lessons, 152
of longer texts, 151
proficiency, 157
as quick writing, 152–153
reading comprehension and, 157
story maps and, 145
strategies, 146, 148–151
student partnering for, 150
teaching, 142
thinking and, 142–143, 148–156
understanding and, 143–148
Summer school, 51
Sustained Silent Reading, 87
Syllables, 37–40, 73
Syntax, 54, 79

T

Teachers
assistance for literate conversations, 129
blessing books, 84
certification of, 165
commercial reading intervention and, 33–34
content-area, 114
discussion led by, 120, 134
education of, 165
effective, 117, 154
engagement and, 173–176
exemplary, 10–12, 56–57, 172–177
indoctrination of, 16–17
merit pay for, 117
personal assessment of students, 155
professional development for, 184–185
quality of, 10–11, 116–117
reading development and quality of, 10
responsibility for students, 89
of struggling readers, 163–164
successful, 88–89
textbook problems and exemplary, 56–57
textbooks and expertise of, 83
text selection guidelines for, 71
Teaching
decoding and self, 35
effective, 117, 154
methods, 16–17, 22–23, 57–58, 88–89
reading comprehension strategies, 113–115
reciprocal, 132–133
self-selected books and effective, 89–90
summarization, 142
Technology
learning to read and, 67–68
reading instruction and, 8
reading intervention, 15
reading proficiency and, 67–68
smart phones, 107, 124
truth and, 107
Testing. *See also* American College Testing; Assessment
CCSS, 179
group achievement, 154–155
multiple-choice, 2, 142, 155
non-word, 28
reading achievement, 166

To Read or Not to Read, 76
TPS. *See* Think-pair-share
Transmission-based education, 83, 124–128
TTT. *See* Things Take Time
Tutoring, 147–148, 166

U

Understanding. *See also* Reading comprehension
   memorization and, 125
   prior knowledge and, 141
   questions and, 140
   reading comprehension and, 95–96, 99–106, 108
   reading engagement and, 109–110
   remembering and, 109–110
   self-monitoring of, 114
   summarization and, 143–148
   textbooks, 113
   writing and, 152
Urban schools, 6

V

Virginia, 98
Vocabulary, 49. *See also* Words
   academic, 102–103
   annual increase of, 51
   application of, 50
   books on development of, 66
   decoding and, 27–28, 33
   deficit, 50–51
   discussion and development of, 66
   fostering growth of, 58–63, 72–73
   independent reading and, 44
   instruction, 59
   low-income families and, 50–51
   misreading and, 19
   prior knowledge and, 180
   reading comprehension and, 51
   reading experiences and, 51–53
   semantic gradients, 62–63
   sight, 31
   of struggling readers, 31
   in textbooks, 78–79
   text difficulty and, 58
   word structure, 37–41
Voluntary reading, 51, 63, 66, 76, 80, 143, 175

W

Wcpm. *See* Words correct per minute
Web resources, 106
Westlane Middle School, 169
When the Plague Strikes: Black Death, Smallpox, AIDS (Giblin), 19
Wilhelm, Jeff, 171
Wonderment, open-ended questions or, 131
Word-by-word reading, 44
Words, 37–40, 41–44, 49, 50, 73. *See also* Vocabulary
Words correct per minute (wcpm), 19
Writing, 83–84, 174. *See also* Summarization
  analytic, 152
  assignments, 112
  learning about students through, 112
  low-income families and, 84
  prior knowledge and, 105
  proficiency, 157
  quick, 105, 112, 130, 152–153
  reading and, 111–112
  research on, 112
  strategies, 90
  thinking and, 152
  understanding and, 152